WHO'S WHO IN BLACK CLEVELAND

Celebrating African-American Achievement FOURTEENTH EDITION

CELEBRATE • WHO'S WHO IN BLACK

30 years

ESTABLISHED 1989

WHO'S WHO IN BLACK CLEVELAND

Celebrating African-American Achievement FOURTEENTH EDITION

Who's Who In Black Cleveland®
is a registered trademark of
Real Times Media

Purchase additional copies online @
www.whoswhopublishing.com

Dr. Carter D. Womack
Chief Operating Officer

Ernie L. Sullivan
Executive Vice President

Rhonda Crowder
Associate Publisher

Patreice A. Massey
Director, Creative Services

Amber Tucker
Account Supervisor
RTM360°

Kimberly Fleming
Account Executive

Larry Roberson
Account Executive

Juan SiFuentes
Graphic Designer

Photographers
Eric Benson
Mychal Lilly
Rodney Brown

Felicia C. Haney
Writer

Corporate Headquarters
Who's Who In Black
1452 Randolph, 4th Fl
Detroit, MI 48226

(313)963-8100

On the Banner page:

Rev. Otis Moss, Carole Hoover, Dominic Ozanne, Michele Crawford, Mayor Frank G. Jackson, Phoebe Lee, Glen Shumate, Dr. Renee Willis, Robert P. Madison, Ramona Lowery, James D. Cowan Jr., Margaret Hewitt, Orlando Taylor, Ariane Kirkpatrick, Scott Whitley, Fatima Ware, Justin Dean, Aaliyah Brown, W. Daniel Bickerstaff, and Virginia Carter.

On the Cover:
Reverend Dr. Otis Moss Jr.

Cover designed by: Juan SiFuentes

Cover Photo Credit:
Rodney Brown

ISBN #978-1-933879-46-8 Paperback
$39.95 each-U.S. Paperback

A Real Times Media Company

TABLE OF
CONTENTS

REAL TIMES
MEDIA

Real Times Media was established out of a passion to provide the African-American community with information that enlightens, empowers and inspires. With a legacy stretching back over 100 years, we possess an unparalleled depth of knowledge and assets that are multi generational, relevant and trustworthy.

A true multi media company focused on becoming the leading source of news, entertainment and lifestyle information from the African-American perspective, Real Times Media provides comprehensive print content that helps our communities continue to thrive and grow while chronicling the events and individuals who are making history today.

We accomplish this through our various enterprises and interests which include:

- The most extensive African-American newspaper collective in the nation, including of the Chicago Defender, the Michigan Chronicle, The New Pittsburgh Courier and the Atlanta Daily World

- Who's Who Publishing Company, the creator of the largest portfolio of publications showcasing African-American professionals

- A full-service marketing and communications company providing strategy, production and management for ad campaigns, TV/Radio production, interactive, public relations, and event marketing and promotions

- RTM Digital Studios, which is focused on the creation, distribution and licensing of original content for book publishing and film/documentary projects using its extensive archive of historical photographs and other artifacts of the African-American experience throughout the past century

- A series of live events across the country that pay honor to unsung community, business, and religious leaders

Real Times Media is poised to realize a future as rich as the legacy which precedes it. With an unrivaled connection to traditionally hard-to-reach, affluent minority markets, we offer our clients a full range of targeted solutions for all of their multicultural marketing needs. Let us do the same for you. For more information, visit us online at www.realtimesmedia.com or call (313) 963-8100.

MESSAGE FROM THE
CHIEF EXECUTIVE OFFICER

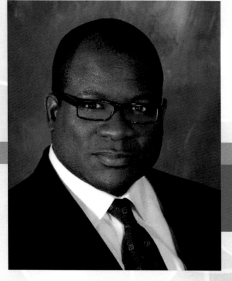

HIRAM E. JACKSON
REAL TIMES MEDIA

"We all have dreams. In order to make dreams come into reality, it takes an awful lot of determination, dedication, self-discipline and effort."
- Jesse Owens, World Record-Setting Olympic Athlete

Greetings!

It is my distinct pleasure to present the fourteenth edition of Who's Who in Black Cleveland. The Cleveland area has a reputation for its trailblazers, change agents and risk takers whose amazing stories of determination and grit inspire others to challenge the status quo. For this edition, we found amazing individuals whose commitment to service and their community have ushered in a better quality of life for the people of Cleveland. The stories you will read in this edition are astonishing.

As we present the fourteenth edition of Who's Who in Black Cleveland, I am deeply moved by the people who have taken their gifts and used them to strengthen their community, inspire the next generation and impact our nation. It is an honor to share your stories and achievements.

With the ever-changing American climate, it is imperative that we always recognize, document and applaud African American achievement and excellence. We must never lose sight of who we are. The men and women that are featured in the Who's Who in Black editions are more than role models; they inspire and give us hope. They are the fruition of the promise that hard work, commitment, and focus will manifest greatness. In other words, success is attainable! I hope that while you read these stories; you share them with the young people in your life. So that the young people of tomorrow will know that they can do and achieve anything.

Special thanks to our sponsors and advertisers, without your support this would not have been possible. Through your support, you have helped us create a piece of history, and for that, I am forever grateful.

All the best,

Hiram E. Jackson

Hiram E. Jackson

CRITERIA FOR
INCLUSION

Who's Who In Black Cleveland® is an opportunity for us to afford a measure of recognition to the men and women who have made their mark in their specific occupations, professions, or in service to others in the community.

A sincere effort was made to include those whose positions or accomplishments in their chosen fields are significant and whose contributions to community affairs, whether citywide or on the neighborhood level, have improved the quality of life for all of us.

The names of those brief biographies included in this edition were compiled from customary sources of information. Lists of a wide variety were consulted and every effort was made to reach all whose stature or civic activities merited their inclusion.

In today's mobile society, no such publication could ever claim to be complete; some who should be included could not be reached or chose not to respond, and for that we offer our apologies. Constraints of time, space and awareness are thus responsible for other omissions, and not a lack of good intentions on the part of the publisher. Our goal was to document the accomplishments of many people from various occupational disciplines.

An invitation to participate in the publication was extended at the discretion of the publisher. Biographies were invited to contribute personal and professional data, with only the information freely submitted to be included. The editors have made a sincere effort to present an accurate distillation of the data, and to catch errors whenever possible. However, the publisher cannot assume any responsibility for the accuracy of the information submitted.

There was no charge for inclusion in this publication and inclusion was not guaranteed; an annual update is planned. Comments and other concerns should be addressed to:

Who's Who Publishing Co.
1452 Randolph, Suite 400
Detroit, MI 48226
Phone: (313) 963-8100
www.whoswhopublishing.com

RHONDA CROWDER

ASSOCIATE PUBLISHER
WHO'S WHO IN BLACK CLEVELAND

One would think, the more we do this work, the easier it gets. Unfortunately, that's far from the truth. In fact, as we move deeper and deeper into the digital age, the greater the difficulty to convince people why they should invest in a print product. And, some are less sold on the idea of children embracing a book (although I see different).

However, when you consider the fact that 66 percent of the adults living in Cleveland read at level 1 or 2 and, in the Hough and Kinsman neighborhoods, the rate is 95 and 98 percent respectively, I think it's past time we figure out ways to get more books in the hands of both children and adults expeditiously. Why?

The literacy rate costs our taxpayers and business owners approximately $20 billion dollars per year. Illiteracy fuels all of the other social ills. And, most importantly, it's causing far too many of us to be left behind.

What does that have to do with the release of this 14th edition of Who's Who in Black Cleveland, a book documenting the success in African Americans in Northeast, Ohio? I strongly believe it could be one thing that helps "change the game."

How can this book change the lives adults who struggle with low literacy skills? It's simple. It may inspire them. This book - an easy reader - can provide them with realistic, attainable aspirations. They will learn the accomplishments of Rev. Otis Moss Jr. They will discover how Leroy Ozanne went from being a building inspector to establishing a construction company that is entering into its third generation. It includes stories of real people who overcame every obstacle put in front of them in attempt to improve not only themselves but our community as whole.

Or maybe being exposed to these stories early will prevent a child from becoming an adult with low literacy skills.

While at the City Club, for a discuss around the life of renowned architect Robert P. Madison and his new book, "Designing Victory: A Memoir," W. Daniel Bickerstaff II told me Madison inspired him to become an architect when came to his school to speak. A few weeks later, I learned Madison also influenced James D. Cowan Jr. after one of his teacher introduced them.

Our children, and adults, will become what they see. I can guarantee it. And, nowadays, those living in the inner city and even some inner-ring suburbs rarely to never see success as the people featured throughout these pages know it. So, if they never see it, what can we expect them to become? We must show them. Why? Because if we don't, who will?.

In closing, I want to thank everyone - from honorees to sponsors - who believe in our mission and continue to make this book possible year in and out. Salute!

Rhonda Crowder

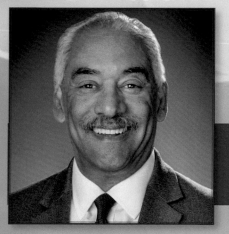

DOMINIC OZANNE

PRESIDENT
OZANNE CONSTRUCTION

Greetings friends:

I am grateful for the opportunity to join Who's Who in Black Cleveland in honoring the life of The Reverend Dr. Otis Moss, Jr. His significant accomplishments as a religious leader and close friend of Dr. Martin Luther King, Jr. have positively impacted public policy, religion, and education on a global scale. He has lectured internationally and advised several Presidents on domestic issues. We understand and appreciate the vital connection between civil rights, ethical leadership, and economic development represented by the lives of Dr. King and Reverend Moss. I am thankful for the lessons I have learned from their excellent example.

In his final book entitled Where Do We Go From Here, Chaos or Community? (1968) Dr. King outlined the plight of African Americans, providing his perspective on civil, economic, and political rights along with a plan for the future.

Dr. King taught us that we are obligated to help the less fortunate as a moral imperative and as a practical economic necessity. Throughout the book, he constantly reminds us that racism is the "hound of hell which dogs the tracks of our civilization." He notes that racism continues to exist through economic exploitation and inequality.

In Chapter V, entitled Where Are We Going, he calls for a guaranteed income as the most direct solution to poverty. He acknowledges the potential of such a program to discourage individual growth and competition. However, the greater risk to society is the creation of a group that is neither producer or consumer, incapable of caring for itself or helping others. Dr. King noted that a guaranteed income program would help the overall economy by increasing the number of consumers. He cited the famed economist John Kenneth Galbraith for the proposition that a guaranteed income program at $20 billion (1967) was

about the same as the cost of the Vietnam war. H Poor People's Campaign of 1968 called for the federa government to pass an economic bill of rights whic included commitments to a guaranteed income an full employment.

Dr. King understood that no free market economy ca survive without the opportunity for shared prosperit His vision is true today and is shared by Elon Musk, B Gates, Mark Zuckerberg, Jeff Bezos, and Warren Buffet These 5 billionaires represent more than one half of th net worth of American households. Tech billionaire like Bezos support the general concept of a universa basic income because their companies make mone by eliminating routine jobs through automation.

In closing, our nation is divided. We are engaged in fight for the soul of America. We are in a state of grac when we demonstrate the love and brotherhoo called for by Dr. King. Hate, negativity, and powe hungry selfishness reduce us to a doomed, immora nation that will destroy itself as a result of race hatre and economic inequality. African Americans ca lead this nation back to greatness by working togethe and with others to eliminate racism, poverty, an economic injustice. All Americans must embrace th moral imperative to work together to ensure equa opportunity, justice, and freedom for all. The soul o our country is at stake.

Reverend Moss, congratulations and thanks for showin us how to live a life of excellence!

Most respectfully,

Dom Ozanne

WHO'S WHO IN BLACK CLEVELAND

Celebrating African-American Achievement   FOURTEENTH EDITION

CELEBRATE · WHO'S WHO IN BLACK
30 years
· ESTABLISHED 1989 ·

transportation.

Emmanuel Transport Services gets you where you need to go in Cleveland. The company offers services, including paratransit, shuttle, taxi and rideshare options. Through the Ohio Minority Business Development Division, Emmanuel Transport Services was able to obtain bonding to allow the company to bid on contracts to expand business operations.

For more information, visit minority.ohio.gov.

Adekenule Adweso of Emmanuel Transport Services, Cleveland Heights, Ohio

Ohio | **Development Services Agency**

Ohio | **Minority Business Assistance Centers**

Mike DeWine, Governor
Jon Husted, Lt. Governor

Lydia L. Mihalik, Director

Ohio

find it here.™

ohio.org

CORPORATE SPONSORS

DIAMOND SPONSOR

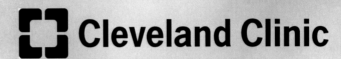

GOLD SPONSOR

SILVER SPONSORS

MEDIA PARTNERS

ADVERTISERS

AES Management/Popeyes
Baker & Hostetler
Betty Pinkney
Calfee, Halter & Griswold
Cleveland Public Library
Cleveland State University
Dominon Energy
Gaines Funeral Home
Maltza Museum of Jewish Heritage

Northeast Ohio Regional Sewer District
Ohio Development Services
Ohio Lottery
Ozanne Construction
Reverend Otis Moss III
Sherwin-Williams Company
Squire Patton Boggs
University Hospital - Cleveland

CLEVELAND
CAVALIERS

Proudly celebrates all

Who's Who in Black Cleveland 2019 Participants

All For One. One For All.

Letters of
GREETING

A LETTER FROM THE COO

WHO'S *who*
A Real Times Media Company

Greetings:

Thank you for your support as we celebrate the historic 14th Anniversary Edition of Documenting Recognizing and Celebrating African-American Achievements in Cleveland-Akron-Canton & Stark County, Ohio. This edition is also a continuation of a great story about men and women who came before us, worked hard and made sacrifices so that we would be able to pass on greater opportunities for the success to the next generation.

This edition is a special salute to African-American Living Legends and Interesting Personalities. These men and women who are included in our feature sections have changed the game and made a difference in the lives of so many in these communities and other parts of the world. Each person featured in this edition is truly leaders in their home, organizations and the community at large.

As we focus on connecting our younger people to our seasoned leaders we want you to join us in supporting our 1000 Books for 1000 Kids Campaign. We want you and your organization to donate at least one book to a girl or boy, young woman or young man. We want them to read about who in Cleveland-Akron-Canton & Stark County, Ohio that looks like them and they can grow up to be like them.

Thanks to our sponsors and advertisers for their ongoing support and faith in the team at Who's Who In Black. We truly value you for your commitment to diversity, inclusion, and the betterment for all citizens in these communities featured in this edition.

Continued blessings to you, as you continue to be blessings to others.

Always be *engaged!*

Dr. Carter D Womack

SHERROD BROWN
OHIO

COMMITTEES:
AGRICULTURE, NUTRITION,
AND FORESTRY

BANKING, HOUSING,
AND URBAN AFFAIRS

FINANCE

VETERANS' AFFAIRS

United States Senate
WASHINGTON, DC 20510 - 3505

Dear Friends:

Congratulations on the publication of the 14th edition of Who 's Who in Black Cleveland, and thank you to all those who appear in this year's edition for your lasting contributions to our community.

I'm always proud to see Cleveland's exceptional leaders, businesses, and community organizations celebrated through this annual tradition. This year's Lifetime Achievement recipient, Reverend Dr. Otis Moss Jr., and all of the 2019 honorees embody the best in our vibrant, welcoming city, and are role models to the next generation of Northeast Ohioans. Everyone celebrated in these pages has much to be proud of.

Thank you for all that you do to make our city a better place to live, work, and raise a family.

You have my best wishes for the year ahead.

Sincerely,

Sherrod Brown

Letters of
GREETING

A LETTER FROM THE SENATE

HOUSE OF REPRESENTATIVES
WASHINGTON, D. C. 20515

MARCIA L. FUDGE
11TH DISTRICT OF OHIO

Welcome to the 14th edition of Who's Who in Black Cleveland, including Akron-Canton and Stark County. As the U.S. Representative for the Eleventh Congressional District, it is a pleasure to celebrate African Americans in architecture, construction, and engineering (ACE) careers, and recognize all of this edition's honorees.

As African Americans in professions too often lacking diversity, ACE leaders and professionals have broken barriers and beat immeasurable odds. As our region, state and nation contend with aging infrastructure, we all rely on ACE leaders to restore our rails, roads, bridges and buildings.

The leaders featured in the 2019 Who's Who in Black Cleveland impact many facets of our environmental, physical and spiritual well-being. By recognizing their accomplishments, we can inspire others and help move our communities forward.

I send special congratulations to the 2019 Who's Who in Black Cleveland Lifetime Achievement Award Recipient, Rev. Otis Moss, Jr. for his civil rights, human rights. education and social justice advocacy and accomplishments, as well as his influential spiritual leadership.

I applaud the efforts of all 2019 honorees, and thank them for their contributions to the people and prosperity of Northeast Ohio.

Sincerely,

Marcia L. Fudge

Marcia L. Fudge
Member of Congress

Letters of
GREETING

A LETTER FROM THE STATE REPRESENTATIVE

Office of State Representative Stephanie Howse
House District 11

Dear Friends and Honorees,

I would like to take a moment to congratulate the outstanding African American women and men being recognized in the 14th edition of Who's Who in Black Cleveland and send a special salute to Reverend Otis Moss, Jr. for earning the Lifetime Achievement Award. Each and everyone being acknowledged in this book is a living testament of the #BlackExcellence we have within our community.

Starting my career as an engineer, I am thrilled to see a focus on African American professionals in the fields of architecture, construction and engineering. These STEM (science, technology, engineering and math) careers provide an opportunity to highlight the professionals that help bring many ideas from concept to reality. Every day we wake up in our homes, commute to our jobs on the roads and bridges, and drink clean water, we are benefitting from the handwork of the men and women in these STEM fields. African Americans comprise approximately 6% of the workforce in the industries of architecture, construction and engineering. By shining a spotlight on the men and women in these industries, we are planting the seeds for the next generation of Black girls and boys to embrace and excel in these rewarding careers.

Congratulations again to all the fine men and women being recognized in the 14th edition of Who's Who in Black Cleveland and know that you are a valued contributor to the great state of Ohio.

Yours in Service,

Stephanie Howse
Ohio State Representative

Letters of
GREETING

A LETTER FROM THE MAYOR

CITY OF CLEVELAND
Mayor Frank G. Jackson

Who's Who in Black Cleveland

Cleveland is a vibrant city that thrives on the influence of our diverse communities and their rich cultural histories. Our unique city continues to be enhanced by the contributions of African Americans who came before us as well as those who are recognized in the 14th edition of Who's Who in Black Cleveland.

As I reflect on the role of African American figures on the success of our great city, my hope is that Cleveland will continue to instill a shared sense of community for residents and visitors alike. My vision for Cleveland is to be a city where economic prosperity, sustainable neighborhoods and opportunities to thrive are accessible to all residents. As Mayor, I appreciate the many contributions of those featured here. Whether through architecture, engineering, construction or civic engagement, these leaders are part of this vision.

In the 14th edition of Who's Who in Black Cleveland, you will see entrepreneurs and corporate executives, community leaders and politicians, activists and innovators, emerging leaders and youth achievers who act as catalysts for change in their communities. Through hard work and dedication to our city, these leaders demonstrate what it truly means to be a Clevelander.

Sincerely,

Frank G. Jackson,

Mayor

RICHMOND HEIGHTS LOCAL SCHOOLS

and the

Ozanne Construction Company

Constructing a pathway to opportunities

By Rhonda Crowder

When Dr. Renee T. Willis became superintendent of the Richmond Heights Local Schools five years ago, she received a vision for delivering "educational excellence with equity for all" - one she calls "divine."

There were several things she wanted to see happen but two were most important: increasing academic performance and constructing a new 21st century facility for middle and high school students as the current one is near 100 years old. Within the first few years, she achieved her first goal.

Now, she's witnessing the second one come to fruition.

After listening to the community, passing an historic levy, securing the bond, and navigating the politics of it all, the blueprints are drafted and Ozanne Construction has been contracted to build it. On May 28, 2019, key stakeholder

including students, broke ground on the site that will house the brand new Richmond Heights Upper School.

"This school will be a 21st Century Community Learning Center," said Willis. "It will be a school by day and community center by evening."

Among the many features, The Richmond Heights branch of the Cuyahoga County Library will be located on the campus as well as 1000 square feet for the YMCA's Silver Sneakers Program for the senior citizens of the community. With retractable seating, the cafeteria will be a multi-purpose area that can convert into a mini auditorium. The community will be able to rent the space for wedding receptions and other events. Because it can be divided into three smaller courts, the gym will accommodate both the district's varsity competitive sports teams (including its state championship contending team) as well as the city's youth recreation league.

"It's all about serving the community," Willis continued.

But, the forthcoming aviation program is most exciting. "It's definitely a major focal point," said Willis, who wrote the Ohio Department of Education's "Expanding Opportunities for Each Child" grant which will create a career pathway to aviation as well as outfit the aviation classroom. The aviation classroom will

have real flight simulators, and unmanned aerial vehicles (UAV), more commonly known as drones. Instruction will be provided via distance learning from either Kent State University or the Aspen Aerospace Institute.

Additionally, the grant will fund a career pathway in manufacturing as well as a "makerspace" that will be used as the incubator to this pathway.

"The Maker's Movement is all about having students become critical thinkers, innovators, and entrepreneurs," said Willis. "We wanted our students to have exposure, access and opportunities to things that they typically have not had."

Willis is grateful for a flexible construction partner, as the current renderings for the aviation classroom consists merely of 4 new walls and some electrical outlets. They are currently meeting to make minor adjustments in light of the new technology, equipment and simulators afforded by this new grant.

"Working with Ozanne has been good because they understand the bigger vision and mission for our students," said Willis. "It's been a perfect union and collaboration. The Ozanne team, led by Fred Rodgers, Jr., has the heart for what we're trying to do in Richmond."

The school is slated to open in January 2021, a century since the

Dr. Renee T. Willis, Superintendent Richmond Heights Local Schools

Fred Rodgers, Project Manager Ozanne Construction

construction of the original building. Now, that the construction of the new Upper School is underway, Willis is shifting her focus to a capital campaign to include sponsorships and philanthropic gifts with naming rights in order to make a new football stadium a reality. "Who wants a new school in front of an old stadium?" said Willis.

"Dr. Willis and the Richmond Heights Board have done an excellent job moving their capital program forward," noted Dominic Ozanne. "The aviation program is visionary and has the potential to be a national model."

"WHEN YOU RECEIVE A VISION, YOU CAN REST ASSURED THAT THE PROVISION WILL FOLLOW," WILLIS ADDED. "WE'RE CONTINUING TO RECEIVE NOT ONLY PROVISION, BUT WE ARE BEING BLESSED WITH GREAT PARTNERS IN THE WORK SUCH AS OZANNE CONSTRUCTION.

Focus Fund
powered by JumpStart

PROVIDING VENTURE CAPITAL INVESTMENT FOR OHIO-BASED TECH STARTUPS LED BY WOMEN AND PEOPLE OF COLOR.

LEARN MORE AT **jumpstartinc.org/focusfund**

JumpStart serves entrepreneurs and small business owners across Northeast Ohio with offices in Cleveland and Canton. **Learn more at jumpstartinc.org.**

jumpstart

THE JUMPSTART ENCORE MENTORING PROGRAM*

Matching leaders (age 50+) who want to give back to their community with entrepreneurs in search of advice to grow their businesses. The program strives for 90% of its mentors to be women and people of color.

LEARN MORE AT **jumpstartinc.org/mentoring**

*This program is part of the Cleveland Foundation's Encore Cleveland initiative, designed to provide an

CORPORATE
SPOTLIGHT

Koby Altman
General Manager

Raymond Brown III
Sr. Manager, Digital Production

Koby Altman was named the 11th general manager in Cleveland Cavaliers history in July of 2017. As the GM, he manages and oversees all aspects of scouting, personnel, player acquisitions and transactions, and all team operations. He also guides the team's player appearance committee in partnership with the business side of the Cavs organization.

In the 2017-18 season, Altman's first year as GM, the Cavaliers won the Eastern Conference Finals, advancing to their fourth straight NBA Finals. In the summer of 2018, he selected Collin Sexton with the eighth overall pick in the NBA Draft and signed five-time NBA All-Star Kevin Love to a new multi-year contract extension.

Prior to being named GM, Altman was a part of the Cavaliers' basketball staff for five years and has been an integral part of a team that reached four straight NBA Finals and won an NBA Championship in 2016.

Altman, a Brooklyn, New York native, played collegiately at Middlebury College. Altman is on the National Board of Directors for the Posse Foundation, which identifies, recruits and trains individuals with extraordinary leadership potential, providing full-tuition leadership scholarships from Posse's partner colleges and universities.

Raymond S. Brown III has spent over 15 years in the field of web and graphic design, fueled by an artistic passion that continues to energize his efforts. An artist at heart, Brown has been drawing, painting and sketching characters, as well as a wide variety of subjects since the age of 8.

Since then he's found an undying love for finding the design aspect in everything, even the most unlikely of places. With no fear of taking an artistic approach to web development, where traditionally the artist and the programmer would bump heads, is not uncommon.

His career success officially began as a web designer with Cleveland.com, eventually transitioning to a leadership role before joining the Northeast Ohio Media Group as senior creative consultant before finding a place with the Cleveland Cavaliers as a frontend web developer where he also has provided illustrations for special projects like the Cavs Emoji Keyboard and various specialty night posters.

Brown is often found at his studio listening to hip hop or jazz music while painting or drawing.

Austin Carr
Director, Community & Business Development
TV Analyst Fox Sports Ohio

Sherman Q. Cartwright
Senior Manager of Operations

Austin Carr is a Cavaliers legend. The number one overall player chosen in the 1971 NBA Draft, Carr was named to the All-Rookie team and represented Cleveland in the 1974 All-Star Game. He ranks as the second in field goals made, fourth on all-time list in scoring (10,265) and was selected to the Cavaliers' All-Time Starting Five. Carr was honored when his number, 34, was retired by the team on January 3, 1981.

He was a two-time All American at Notre Dame where he averaged 34.5 points per game. He currently holds the record for the most points in an NCAA Tournament game (61). He was elected to the National Collegiate Basketball Hall of Fame class of 2007.

In June of 1991, Carr rejoined the Cavaliers as the director of community and business development. He became the fulltime TV color analyst for Cavs basketball in 1997.

Carr won the Walter Kennedy Citizenship Award in 1980 and continues his charitable activities with United Black Fund, the March of Dimes, and the Center for Prevention of Domestic Violence.

Carr is the proud parent of Jason and Ashley.

A native of Cleveland Heights, OH, Sherman Q. Cartwright attended Villa Angela -St. Joseph High School in Cleveland. He attended Cleveland State University, where he was a student manager for legendary Coach Rollie Massimino for three years and earned a BS in Sports Management. During his senior year at CSU, Cartwright interned in the operations department at the Cavaliers Operating Company. Following his internship with the Cavaliers, Cartwright joined the National Association of Collegiate Directors of Athletics (NACDA) in Westlake as an intern for one year. He then went to Northwood, University in West Palm Beach, FL from August 2005-August 2007. There he worked as an Assistant Athletic Director for compliance and athletic academic advising.

In August 2007 Cartwright returned to Cavaliers Operating Company as a Conversions Coordinator overseeing conversions and assisting in day to day operations at the Quicken Loans Arena. Cartwright currently holds the position of Sr. Manager of Operations at the Cavaliers Operating Company and Rocket Mortgage Fieldhouse.

Shelly Cayette
Vice President, Global Corporate
Partnerships

Damion Chatmon
Sr. Director, Emerging Technologies

Shelly Cayette is the vice president for global corporate partnerships for the Cleveland Cavaliers where she manages a team responsible for all of the sponsorship relationships with local and national companies involving marketing, advertising, media, promotional activation, digital, community and hospitality.

Currently Cayette sits on the Advisory Board for Achievement Centers for Children with Disabilities and the Advisory Board for the Downtown Cleveland Alliance. She also is a member of Women in Sports and Events and Black Sports Professionals.

Cayette comes from New Orleans, Louisiana where she held positions in Marketing, Sponsorship and Community Investment for the New Orleans Hornets for eight years prior to moving to Cleveland. She was responsible for team marketing initiatives, sponsorship sales and oversaw the development and execution of community outreach initiatives that addressed relevant social responsibility issues as well as strengthened the positive image of the team.

There she sat on the board of the Salvation Army, Café Hope, Knowledge First Foundation and Greater New Orleans Inc.

Cayette graduated from Tulane University A.B. Freeman School of Business in New Orleans, Louisiana.

Damion Chatmon is the senior director of emerging technology for the Cavaliers Operating Company. His role defines the Cavaliers strategic approach to the identification, evaluation and development of new technology offerings to enhance fan experience, grow revenue streams, innovate the tech stack and improve internal processes.

Chatmon is a founding member of Black Sports Professionals group, and serves as the Cleveland Chapter Development Advisor. He also holds various leadership positions within his church, fraternity, Omega Psi Phi, Inc. and with North Star Lodge No. 638 F&AM of Fairview, Ohio.

Chatmon, a Niagara Falls, NY native joined the Cavaliers after working with the Tampa Bay Lightning and the Buffalo Sabres. He is a graduate of Buffalo State College with a BA in English and a Minor in Italian after studying abroad in Siena, Italy.

He and his wife Phaedra reside in North Ridgeville with their three daughters, Bella, Nina and Mia.

Kevin Clayton
Vice President, Diversity, Inclusion, and Engagement

Ahmaad Crump
In-Arena Host/Game Presentation Coordinator

Kevin is in his first season as Vice President of Diversity, Inclusion & Engagement for the Cleveland Cavaliers. This newly formed position leads one of only four established diversity-focused team functions in professional sports. Clayton is responsible for developing and leading the D&I strategic plan for all Cavaliers properties, including Rocket Mortgage FieldHouse. Additionally, his responsibilities will include the planning and execution of activities related to community engagement across the entire Cavalier footprint.

Prior to joining the Cavaliers, Clayton was the Chief Diversity and Inclusion Officer for Bon Secours Mercy Health, the largest healthcare provider in Ohio and fourth-largest employer. In the role, Clayton also led the executive talent acquisition, language services and supplier diversity functions.

Clayton has an extensive executive background working with notable corporate icons including Proctor & Gamble, United States Tennis Association, American Cancer Society, and Russell Athletic.

Clayton is a Cleveland native and currently serves as the First Vice President on the National Board of Community Health Charities and is also a board member of the Cuyahoga County Urban League.

Ahmaad Crump is the in-arena host for the Cleveland Cavaliers, a position he started in prior to the 2005-06 season. As the in-arena host, Crump engages the crowd throughout Cavaliers games, making announcements, participating in skits and entertaining the Cleveland audience. Each game, he announces the starting lineup for both teams. For his outstanding work, he has been named as a host at NBA All-Star Games five times (2010, 2011, 2016, 2017, and 2018). In addition to hosting, he also makes community appearances on behalf of the Cavaliers.

Prior to being named in-arena host, Crump joined the Cavaliers family in 2003 as a member of the Cavaliers entertainment team, The Scream Team.

A native of Cleveland Heights, Crump graduated from Central State University and worked for Cleveland law firm Ulmer and Berne LLP before joining the Cavaliers.

Crump, 42, is married with two children and resides in Richmond Heights. He enjoys playing softball, flag football and basketball in his spare time as well as karaoke.

CORPORATE SPOTLIGHT

B.J. Evans
Director of Basketball Communications

Lydia C. Hardy
Manager, Housekeeping

B.J. Evans was named director of basketball communications for the Cavaliers in June 2013. Evans leads a team that promotes on- and off-court endeavors of its players, coaches, front office staff as well as facilitating request for local, national and international media.

Prior to joining the Cavs, Evans spent nine seasons with the Charlotte Bobcats as vice president of communications. His professional sports experience also includes two seasons with the Miami Heat and the inaugural season of NBA D-League.

Evans has also served as assistant commissioner for Media Relations at the Mid-Eastern Athletic Conference that included a NCAA Committee Representative appointment for the Women's Basketball Tournament. Additionally, his experience includes stints as Sports information director and game operations manager at N. C. A&T State Univ. and at the Univ. of Maryland-Eastern Shore. During the 1996 Centennial Olympic Games, he served as Tribune Manager at the inaugural beach volleyball venue.

A native of North Carolina, Evans earned a Public Relations degree from N.C. A&T. He and his wife, Kyle, have one daughter, Bailey, born in September 2011.

Lydia C. Hardy has been with the Cavaliers organization for twelve seasons and currently is currently the manager of housekeeping. She attended Tiffin University where she studied business. Previously, Hardy, who is a lifelong resident of Cleveland, attended Glenville High School.

In her position, Hardy is responsible for the supervision of day-to-day housekeeping operations, as well as assuring the cleanliness during events and coordinating ongoing project maintenance of the building. Throughout her career with the Cavaliers, she has been instrumental in the hiring, development and retention of hundreds of team members who have relied on her expertise and empathy as their first line of support. Hardy has always been committed to leading her team with sincere compassion and positive engagement.

Over her tenure with Quicken Loans Arena, Hardy and her team have prepared the Q for family shows, major entertainer concerts and, of course, our Cleveland Cavaliers, Monsters and Gladiators.
In her free time, Hardy enjoys her ministerial work where she reaches many people and being with her family and friends. She is a proud mother and grandmother and a true friend to many, including her co-workers.

Corey James
Sr. Manager, Community Engagement/Foundation Development

Alberta Lee
Vice President, Human Resources

Corey James is entering his 13th season with the Cavalier's organization, his first as director, community engagement and foundation development.

James' primary focus is now working to implement the organizational diversity and inclusion strategy while also developing new opportunities for the Cavaliers Charitable Foundation. He also helps plan and execute activities related to community engagement for all properties.

James started with the Cavaliers in June of 2007 as an account executive in ticket sales. He spent the last five seasons managing corporate partnership relationships, where he spent the latter working primarily with NIKE, New Era Cap, and the first ever 'Cavs Legacy Partner', Goodyear. The legacy partnership was one of the first in the NBA and is represented by the Goodyear Wingfoot on the front of the Cavs jersey.

A Louisville, KY native, James graduated from The Ohio State University, receiving an undergraduate degree from The Fisher College of Business in June of 2007. He is a member of the Associate Board of the Greater Cleveland Sports Commission, Ohio State Alumni Association, and Black Sports Professionals.

Alberta Lee begins her fifth season, as the Vice President of Human Resources for the Cavaliers. Previously Alberta served as the Chief Human Resources Administrator for Monroe Community College in Rochester, New York.

As an accomplished professional, she leads all functions of Human Resources while serving as a strategic partner. Over the years Alberta Lee has been recognized for her ability to be collaborative, creative and compassionate when dealing with people and organizational matters.

A Michigan native, Lee graduated from Saginaw Valley State University, receiving a bachelor's in business administration and a master's degree from Central Michigan University. She holds a national senior human resources professional certification.

Lee is a member of Delta Sigma Theta Sorority Inc. She credits her parents Napoleon and Nelia Lewis for instilling in her a love for God, family, community and education. Lee has served on several community boards and is looking forward to continuing her community service here in Cleveland.

She is married to Cecil B. Lee and has two sons C.J. Lee (married to Dr. Jocelyn Smith Lee) and Cameron D. Lee.

Alisha Sanford Pope
Sr. Manager, Partnership Marketing

M. Campy Russell
Television Pregame & Postgame Analyst
Director of Alumni Relations

Alisha Pope is going into her seventh season with the Cleveland Cavaliers organization. She is responsible for working with corporate partners to develop and implement integrated marketing platforms geared towards supporting the partner's continued business success and positively impacting their bottom-line. Sanford also volunteers for various organizations throughout the year including the Special Olympics.

A Maryland native, Pope joined the Cavaliers after working with NASCAR, Rally Marketing Group and Alonzo Mourning Charities. She received a Bachelor of Science in Sports Management from Barry University where she was a student-athlete. Sanford also attended May Business School at Texas A&M and received a Master of Business Administration \ specializing in Marketing.

Alisha is married with two sons and currently resides in Cleveland.

M. Campy Russell begins his 12th season providing analysis on the FOX Sports Ohio pregame and postgame show, "Cavaliers Live". He also is the Cavaliers' Director of Alumni Relations which helps connect former Cavs players in the community and at Cavaliers' home games where they visit with fans, make special presentations and are involved in charitable fundraising.

Russell played 10 years in the NBA, including seven with the Cavs (1974-75 to 1979-80 and 1984-85) where he was an NBA All-Star in 1979. He played three seasons with the New York Knicks from 1980-83, leading the league in three-point field goal percentage (.439) in 1981-82. Russell was named to the Cavaliers' All-Time Team and remains in the Cavs' all-time Top 10 in six categories. He was inducted into the Ohio Basketball Hall of Fame in 2014.

Russell is an alumnus of the University of Michigan, graduating with a bachelor's degree in sports management and communications in 2000 and is a member of the University's Hall of Honor. He is the father of four daughters, Allex, Mandisa, Oyin, Saki and one son, Michael II, and is a proud grandfather of 12.

LIVING LEGENDS

Robert P. Madison, FAIA
Architect in retirement

Photos Mychal Lilly

ROBERT P. MADISON, FAIA

Architect in retirement
Robert P. Madison, Inc.

'Victory' Designed

By Rhonda Crowder

"When I started out, I wanted to be like the Fords, Henry Ford, to build something for the next generation," said Robert P. Madison, a living legend in every sense of the word.

Madison's lived an exemplary life. He wanted to become an architect because his mother said he would be one. His father was a civil engineer by education, who did not get a chance to practice in his field because of racial discrimination.

After graduating from East Technical High School, Madison went to Howard University to study architecture and did well. But, left the university to fight in World War II, as a second lieutenant .

"This is important to note," he said. "When World War II came along, most of the white soldiers wanted the Black troops to work the menial jobs, in the kitchen and such... But, the NAACP and The Urban League said 'no.' We want them to fight and die," Madison explained.

Because of that, Madison is a proud member of the historic Buffalo Soldiers. And, when 2nd Lt. Robert P. Madison returned home from the war, looking to continue his

education, he applied for admittance in the School of Architecture at the then Western Reserve University. However, they denied Madison because of his skin color.

Madison returned to the school a few days later dressed in his full uniform, Purple Heart and all. Shamingly yet grudgingly, they admitted him. "When we came back from fighting in the War, we could demand some things. My blood is on the soil of Italy, fighting for this country," he said.

The discrimination continued. He often heard the words, "You'll never work as an architect." Madison, who sees all things as possible, proved them all wrong.

He started an architecture firm with his two brothers, Julian (an engineer) and Bernard (an architect). Back then, there were Madison, Madison and Madison. "We envisioned an architecture firm with lasting prosperity." Undoubtedly, it has.

Robert P. Madison International has been in practice 62 years, 30 years with his brother. "I've hired over 250 people. We've had offices in Gary, Indiana; Detroit, Atlanta, Washington, D.C. Philadelphia and New Jersey. At one point, we did over $4 million a year in payroll," said Madison.

Aside from designing medical offices for Black doctors (one named in his honor), institutions of higher learning and the landscape of Downtown Cleveland, the U.S. Embassy in Dakkar is probably the most significant to him.

The hardest challenge he faced in his professional pursuits is being accepted by the American Institute of Architecture (AIA) as a professional architect because he was black. "I fooled them," he said with a chuckle. He credits the support of his family for its success. "I had good parents and good a wife. My first year in business, I made $400 the whole year. That wasn't enough to live off of even back then," he said.

These days, he's enjoying retirement as he on the author circuit promoting his recently released memoir, "Designing Victory," a book he wrote with Carlo Wolff. In early May, approached his 96th birthday, he shared his story at the City Club of Cleveland.

His nephew R. Kevin Madison along with his wife Sandra are the president and executive president of Robert P. Madison International, with another partner Robert Klann. They recently designed the plans for the newly renovated Karamu House Jellife Theatre.

Leroy Ozanne
Founder
Ozanne Construction Company

Photos Courtesy of The Ozanne Family

LEROY OZANNE
Founder
Ozanne Construction Company

Built to Last

By Rhonda Crowder

"My folks weren't the richest people in the world," said Leroy Ozanne, a native of Beaumont, Texas and the oldest boy of his seven siblings.

Wanting to be a musician, he attended Alabama State University on a scholarship until drafted into the Navy.

He played in the Navy band, on the U.S.S Cowpens. "After I left for the Navy and came back to the states, the music had changed," he said. At that point, he decided he wanted to be an architect and knew the Navy would help him get a college education.

With an honorable discharge he took up a friend's invitation to move to Cleveland in 1946. Upon arrival, he enrolled into a pre-engineering course at John Carroll. He also took engineering drafting, attended both John Hunting Institute and Fenn College to further familiarize himself with the industry.

"At the time the city was growing and needed building inspectors," he said, explaining how he became one of the first African Americans in that role.

As a building inspector, Leroy began to see the lack of representation in construction and figured there were business opportunities. Plus, he met a lot of people who needed assistance with building code inspections. This position afforded him the opportunity to build relationships with contractors and architects.

He incorporated Ozanne Construction in 1956, never imagining it would grow to what we see today. It is worth noting the Ozanne/Auzenne family traces its lineage from 13th century France through New Orleans and Southwest Louisiana. The family tree is full of carpenters, plasters, and masons.

"I worked from day to day trying to feed my family," he said. He did realize early on that he didn't want to build houses. "It was very competitive, and I noticed there were very few of us in commercial construction." With the increase in automobile sales and the growing oil industry, he saw an opportunity to build gas stations. "That's how I built my company."

The Martin Luther King Plaza became his first joint venture with Turner Construction. "It was the first joint venture between a majority and minority company in the United States," he said. "We formed a relationship that still endures."

But, Ozanne credits his son, Dominic and a talented staff, for taking the company to the next level. His grandson is an Ohio State University construction management graduate with an interest in real estate development. "Now, he's a member of the group. I'm real proud of that fact."

Currently living in Scottsdale, Arizona, Ozanne finds it difficult to enjoy retirement. "I'd rather be working," he said. "But, I'm old now so I have to take it easy."

Congratulations to our Rising Stars and all those featured in the annual Who's Who in Black Cleveland.

Nathaniel McQuay, MD

Kwadwo Odaro, Jr., MD

Ogechi Muoh, MD

Khendi White-Solaru, MD

 **University Hospitals**

1-866-UH4-CARE | UHhospitals.org

LIFETIME ACHIEVEMENT

REV. DR. OTIS MOSS, JR.

Photo by Rodney Brown

REV. DR. OTIS MOSS, JR.
A Living Legend for the Gospel of Liberation
A Civil and Human Rights Giant
Pastor Emeritus, Olivet Institutional Baptist Church

By Donald James
Senior National Writer
Real Times Media
Who's Who Publishing Company

For more than six decades, the name Rev. Dr. Otis Moss, Jr. has been synonymous with spiritual integrity, civil and human rights advocacy, and the empowerment of institutions and communities locally, nationally and internationally. For thirty three years, Moss served as Senior Pastor of Olivet Institutional Baptist Church, one of Cleveland's largest and most influential houses of worship. In 2008, Moss retired and was succeeded by the Rev. Dr. Jawanza Karriem Colvin, a Morehouse alum, who Moss calls a young, dynamic and prophetic leader. "Olivet was founded in 1937 and has been a growing congregation since that time," said Moss. "It has been a church, where the gospel of liberation has been at its foundation and leadership. I was honored to have succeeded a great and dynamic pastor, the late Dr. O.M. Hoover, who was also active in the Civil Rights Movement. We both served together on the board of the Southern Christian Leadership Conference with Dr. Martin Luther King, Jr. Dr. Hoover and I later served on the founding board of Operation Push with the Rev. Jesse Jackson."

While Moss has preached thousands of powerful and uplifting sermons about the gospel of Christ for several decades, he never lost sight of what was transpiring in America and beyond, as it related to civil and human rights, and seeking ways to elevate communities and its people. In addition to standing in the pulpit Sunday after Sunday, Moss also stood on the frontlines in the fight for justice and equality for African Americans and other minorities.

Born and raised on a farm in LaGrange, Georgia, a small town 67 miles southwest of Atlanta, Moss was the fourth youngest of five children. His father was a sharecropper, but was killed in an automobile accident when Moss was 16. Young Moss' mother passed when he was four.

Despite struggling with the loss of both parents, Moss learned to value education and where it could take him. After graduating from high school, Moss attended Morehouse College, where he earned a bachelor's degree. He continued in the Morehouse School of Religion/

Interdenominational Theological Center (ITC), where he received the master of divinity degree. Moss also continued to do special studies at ITC. He later received the Doctor of Ministry Degree from United Theological Seminary in Dayton, Ohio.

Yet, it was at Morehouse where Moss built the solid foundation that would support his future endeavors in the gospel of liberation, and fuel his advocacy in the civil and human rights movements. Moss, however, didn't construct this foundation alone; he had men of truth and honor at Morehouse who served as role models and mentors to guide him.

"I'm privileged and honored to have had the opportunity to meet and listen to people like Thurgood Marshall, and especially Morehouse's president, Dr. Benjamin Elijah Mays," said Moss. "During my first year at Morehouse, I also met the King family: Dr. Martin Luther King, Sr. and later, Dr. Martin Luther King, Jr. Dr. King's brother, Rev. A.D. King, also attended Morehouse."

In 1960, when the powerful Student Movement started at colleges and universities across America to protest racism and other acts of inequality, Moss was a core-part of the leadership that organized the student sit-in movement and other advocate related events in Atlanta. They were all inspired by the movement led by Dr. Martin Luther King, Jr. Moss' senior year at Morehouse amplified his civil and social conscience even more, when the Montgomery Movement, under Dr. King took flight.

Firmly rooted in the gospel of liberation, Moss incorporated the tenets of preaching, teaching, pastoring and working in the Civil Rights

Movement, all of which he deemed interrelated and inseparable. The gospel of liberation propelled him to march with King in the Selma to Montgomery struggle, and lead and participate in many other marches, protests, and activism with King and other soldiers of the struggle. Moss' dedication and activism to the Civil Rights Movement led him to become vice president of the Atlanta Chapter of the NAACP at a young age.

Between 1954 and 1961, Moss served as pastor at Mount Olive Baptist Church in LaGrange and Providence Baptist Church in Atlanta. In 1961, Moss moved north to pastor Mount Zion Baptist Church in Cincinnati. He subsequently was appointed regional director of King Jr.'s SCLC branch, and was instrumental in establishing and facilitating Operation Breadbasket initiatives throughout Greater Cincinnati. In the early 1970s, Moss was asked to co-pastor Atlanta's Ebenezer Baptist Church with Rev. Martin Luther King, Sr.

In 1975, Moss became senior pastor of Olivet Institutional Baptist Church and was instrumental in the historic church remaining one of America's dynamic urban centers of the African American religious experience. Since its inception eighty two years ago, Olivet, under the guidance of strong senior pastors including Moss, has maintained a celebrated tradition of activism through engagement and advocacy in addressing many social causes, including civil rights, social justice, and public health.

With an adult life filled with contributions to preaching the gospel of liberation and fighting for civil rights and justice for the underserved, no one would have blamed Moss if after retiring he decided to sit back, relax and enjoy life as a side-line spectator.

Yet, for those who knew Moss, they understood being a spectator

was not an option, especially when there was much work to be done in the realms of civil, social, and human rights. In other words, full retirement was not in Moss' spiritual and humanitarian DNA.

"I've been decisively busy since retiring in 2008," said Moss. "I've continued to preach, teach, speak, lecture, mentor young people, and travel nationally and internationally."

Moss is now chair emeritus of the Morehouse Board of Trustees, where he served ten years as its chair. He's proud that he and his son, Otis Moss, III, who is also a graduate of Morehouse, are the named individuals for the Otis Moss, Jr. and Otis Moss, III Annual Oratorical Contest held each year at Morehouse. Moss, Jr. is additionally humbled that a dormitory at Morehouse has been named in his honor: The Otis Moss, Jr. Residential Suites.

Closer to home in Cleveland, a proud part of Moss' legacy is the establishment of the Otis Moss, Jr. Medical Center. Built in 1997, the center is across the street from Olivet and represents the result of a close and empowering relationship between Olivet and the University Hospitals Cleveland Medical Center.

"We established a medical and health center to provide excellent health and medical care for the community," explained Moss. "It's a facility that seeks to provide excellent medical care in a spiritual supportive environment. We do not make a distinction; everyone is treated the same."

If there's been a common thread of unwavering love, strength, devotion, partnership, and total support for Moss during most of his adult life, the common denominator has been his wife, Edwina.

"Edwina and I were married on the campus of Morehouse College in 1966," said Moss, who met his future wife when she worked for the Southern Leadership Christian Conference in Atlanta. "Dr. Martin Luther King, Jr. conducted the wedding ceremony, along with one of my major professors at Morehouse, Dr. Samuel Williams."

Otis and Edwina Moss are the proud parents of three children. Their oldest son Kevin is a manager at FirstEnergy Corp. The youngest son, Otis III, is Senior Pastor of Trinity United Church of Christ in Chicago. Their late daughter Daphne was a graduate of Spelman College and Kent State University.

While Moss remains busy in many ways, he is methodically gathering notes, his thoughts, and other archival information and documents on his life, ministry and endeavors in civil rights to perhaps pen a book in a year or two. However, Moss keeps his eyes and spirit on today's civil, human and social justice movements. He acknowledges that such movements have evolved in many ways.

"Most of the civil rights leaders of my generation are dead, except for a few," Moss said. "But our children, and our children's children now have the responsibility for carrying on The Movement. The Movement has different stages and phases, but the struggle goes on because injustice is still alive. A new generation has come forward and will decide how they will carry on the struggle for liberation, justice, equality, and transformation. It is the Will of God that we work to create a more just and peaceful world."

Reverend Otis Moss III and the Chicago, IL
Trinity United Church of Christ
Family is Proud to Salute

Reverend Otis Moss, Jr.

on being Honored as
Lifetime Achievement Honoree
Who's Who In Black
Cleveland 2019

Trinity United Church of Christ | 400 West 95th Street, Chicago, IL 60628

CAROLE F. HOOVER
TWO BRATENAHL PLACE
SUITE 7A
BRATENAHL, OHIO 44108

To my friend, The Reverend Dr. Otis Moss, Jr.,

Your global contribution to the Christian ministry is acknowledged by your peers and young aspirants. The Reverend Otis Moss III is a great example of the benefit of your ministry.

The commitment you demonstrate to the teachings of Martin Luther King, Jr. is both seen and felt throughout the United States and beyond. And, the impact is enduring.

From American presidents to heads of state in developing nations and religious leaders around the globe, many turn to you for counsel. Your record of advocacy for voter rights, civil rights, human rights and World Peace is stellar. I commend you for continuously advocating for equal opportunity for all people.

Congratulations on this high honor awarded you by *Who's Who in Black Cleveland*. You truly have earned it.

I am proud to be part of your life.

Cordially,

Carole Hoover

The Contractors Assistance Association

Vital for Cleveland and Community

The Construction Industry has never been for the faint of heart.

This remains true even though the industry is far removed from the days of strong backs, bulging muscles, and rough hands. Today, whether you are a worker in the field or a manager in the front office, the requirements for success are likely to include being tech savvy, team-oriented, and a skilled communicator.

In addition to these basis qualities and subject matter expertise, to climb the rungs to management and ownership, you also need skills in prudent risk assessment and management, problem solving, relationship management, and the fortitude to be judged on the bottom line. Naturally, since this is true for laborers, tradespeople, managers, engineers, architects, contractors and other industry professionals, it applies in spades for people of color and women.

This is why an organization of black contractors first formed in Cleveland fifty years ago. Its membership comprised several storied names in Cleveland's minority construction history, including Ware Plumbing, Dunham Brothers Construction, Seawright Construction, Burks Electric, Ozanne Construction and others. While few of those companies or their corporate descendants are around today, they paved the way for their successors, who united just over a decade ago to form the Contractors Assistance Association (CAA).

Today, there are more than a score of substantial minority contractors active in CAA with a mission to strengthen contracting, education and employment opportunities among people of color and women in construction. CAA operates as an affiliate of the Construction Employers Association [CEA], a group of the largest builders in NE Ohio. The relationship greatly enhances the diversity, inclusion and programming work of both organizations.

The construction industry is core to the well-being of our local economy. It is especially vital to Cleveland area minority communities for several reasons. Construction generally has fewer barriers to entry on almost every level. If you have the necessary skills, there is a place for you. Construction is one of the largest industries around. It is estimated that more minorities are involved in some facet of construction than in any other single local industry.

Also, demographic and other changes are creating more opportunities in construction than ever before. Industry and societal needs have converged and new horizons for construction careers are beckoning diverse contractors.

CAA and CEA have several initiatives that support its members. Among them are a Mentor-Protégé / Capacity Building Program in alignment with a business coach, access to CEA educational offerings, mentor from larger local construction management and general contractor firms to access larger and more complex projects and learn to manage them.

Dominic Ozanne, was instrumental in the redevelopment of CAA and the Construction Management Academy Program, designed to promote diversity in the construction professional workforce by exposing minorities and young women to the industry as they start to contemplate life-long career decisions. This important effort placed and nurtured several young trainees in the front office of large national contractors. CMAP eventually aligned as a core component of the ACE Mentor Cleveland program, which itself is part of a larger, successful national program.

CAA and CEA collaborate with local trade unions, government agencies, and local organizations — including Tri-C, the Urban League, El Barrio, Spanish American Committee, and National Association of Women in Construction — to enhance employment opportunities for area residents and increase diversity in the construction workforce.

In recent years CAA members work on projects their forebears could only have dreamed about. The Cleveland Museum of Art, Cleveland Clinic, University Hospitals and other sizable projects have all enjoyed unprecedented participation by minority companies.

As CAA members continue to build capacity, there is every reason to expect the number of thriving area minority contractors will continue to grow.

Here's an idea!

Automate your marketing processes using one platform.

Want to learn more?

Social Media
Email
SEO
Website
Landing Page
CRM
Analytics
Blogging
Call-to-Action

Schedule a consultation.

rhondacrowderllc.com

Say Hello to a Better Day!

GOOD MORNING 5abc
CLEVELAND
Weekdays before GMA

And stay connected to us all day!

RADIO ONE

AN URBAN ONE COMPANY

Radio One Salutes the Who's Who in Black Cleveland

BIJOU STAR
Z107.9 | Mon-Fri | 10a-3p
🐦 @iambijoustar

RO DIGGA
Z107.9 | Mon-Fri | 3p-7p
🐦 @rodigga

KNYCE
Z107.9 | Mon-Fri | 3p-7p
🐦 @djknyce

INCOGNITO
Z107.9 | Mon-Fri | 7p-12a
🐦 @datboyinc

SAM SYLK
93.1WZAK | Mon-Fri | 10a-3p
🐦 @samsylkshow

HAZ MATTHEWS
93.1WZAK | Weekends
🐦 @djhazmat

AHMAAD CRUMP
93.1WZAK | Weekends
🐦 @cavsahmaad

EDDIE HARRELL JR.
REGIONAL VICE PRESIDENT

ROHNESHA HORNE
MARKETING DIRECTOR

SAM PREWITT
DIGITAL SALES MANAGER

DENZEL BRAND
PROMOTIONS DIRECTOR

ZHipHopCleveland.com

Praise 94.5
Cleveland's Inspiration Station
praisecleveland.com

1490
NEWS TALK
CLEVELAND   The Peoples Station
NewsTalkCleveland.com

93.1 FM
WZAK
wzakcleveland.com

FOCUS
CELEBRATE
PROMINENCE
RECOGNITION

EMERGING

LEADERS

"The secret of a leader lies in the tests he has faced over the whole course of his life and the habit of action he develops in meeting those tests."

To emerge is to become apparent, important or prominent. The individuals highlighted in this section have made a commitment to lead by example through their work and service.

DEVELOPING EMERGING LEADERS

Ernie L. Sullivan
Executive Vice President
Who's Who Publishing

Today, most organizations understand that effective leadership must be sustained in order to grow, innovate and reach the desired levels of success. This is why organizations work hard to train and develop emerging leaders. They understand that leaders are not born, they are taught.

Often times in organizations top performers and strong individual contributors are identified to become the new leaders. This methodology is not necessarily effective because managing oneself is quite different than moving an entire team to success. Therefore, the first step in selecting and developing emerging leaders is to insure that this is what the individual wants to do. Asking key questions can start this conversation.

For example:

Do you realize your time will now be allocated between your technical skills and your interpersonal skills?

Are you comfortable transitioning to activities like long term planning, budgeting, hiring, management meetings, etc.?

The important point here is to have these conversations prior to promoting emerging leaders into managerial roles. There is nothing more deflating than going from a top performer to a failed leader. Organizations have some level of responsibility to avoid this where possible.

Once emerging leaders are promoted, they must be helped to develop the necessary self-leadership skills. In order to guide others the leader must have:

• Self awareness

• Strong ethics

• Self motivation

• Work life balance

• A mentor/coach

Once this self foundation is built the emerging leader can be guided in developing the necessary skills to lead others. These include:

• Effective communication

• Conflict resolution

• Hiring the right people

• Decision making

• Management courage

• Team motivation

In summary, the proper identification and development of emerging leaders is essential to the success of all organizations.

F. Allen Boseman Jr. is the co-owner/principal of the Sherman Boseman Legal Group. The law firm specializes in labor and employment, entertainment, commercial litigation, complex negotiations and, problem solving. The firm was founded by Allen Boseman and Bradley Sherman in September 2017 after long successful careers at large global firms representing Fortune 500 companies. Allen's extensive experience has cultivated sophisticated legal skills and a pragmatic approach that fuels a business focused on excellence with a personal touch. In addition, Allen has built and maintained strategic relationships that are critical to how he delivers superior service to clients. Allen is in rhythm with the political, social and business communities around him and is currently serving a six-year term as the first African American commissioner and chairman for the Cuyahoga County PRC. Allen also runs a successful promotions company, Tell A Friend Promotions, that is responsible along with others, for popular events such as Gumbo. Allen is committed to Cleveland and actively works behind the scenes to shape the city's bright future.

F. Allen Boseman Jr
Co-Owner
Principal
Sherman Boseman Legal Group

Aaliyah Brown obtained a bachelor's degree in Electronic Engineering Technology in May 2019. She is the founder of Build Sessions CLE, a nonprofit organization whose mission is to create a foundation for Cleveland students within the STEM community. Aaliyah wants to debunk the idea that leaving Cleveland is the only way to be successful in your career. Build Sessions CLE strives to tap into the STEM community within the city through partnerships with local companies so that their names can become well known in the communities surrounding them. Aaliyah is also a coding instructor with the United Black Fund of Greater Cleveland at Richmond Heights schools where she has taught coding basics as well as robotics. In addition, Aaliyah has seven years of experience in industrial automation. The recent graduate looks forward to building her career so that she may create some of the same opportunities that had been presented to her during her academic career.

Aaliyah Brown
Founder
Build Sessions CLE

Nikita Cowan
Senior Accountant
Council for Economic
Opportunities in Greater

Nikita currently serves as a Senior Accountant for one of the largest Community Action Agencies and the largest Head Start program in Ohio, the Council for Economic Opportunities in Greater Cleveland. Her 11 years of experience in the niche of nonprofit accounting has provided her with a unique skill set. Her biggest strengths are analyzing and presenting financial information in digestible ways, and communication. Throughout her career, her style of communication has bridged gaps between departments resulting in increased efficiency and trust amongst teams. Nikita got her bachelorette degree in Accountancy from the University of Akron.

Nikita does not consider herself the typical finance professional. "I am a healthy dose of pragmatism and creativity. I love crunching numbers, building budgets, etc. But I also love writing. The feel of a smooth pen gliding against fresh paper is something I've always adored."

Last year, Nikita and husband, James D. Cowan Jr., welcomed their first child, Miss Penelope J. Cowan, into the world. "I strive to provide my daughter the same foundation, confidence, and core values that my mom instilled in me."

Alana Garrett-Ferguso
Community Organizer
New Voices for Reproductive
Justice

Alana Garrett-Ferguso. is an innovative youth advocate, with over seven years of experience working with youth of all ages and five years of community work. Alana is passionate about justice, education and youth. In 2018, she successfully created a project entitled, Working Through the Illness to raise mental health awareness amongst youth and young adults. Alana uses her creativity to construct kits to help youth struggling with trauma to understand their mental health. By working as the community organizer for New Voices for Reproductive Justice, she is leading campaigns to eradicate injustices against Black women, femmes, and girls by using the Reproductive Justice framework. Alana is a member of the NAACP Next Generation program and the Northeast Ohio Young Black Democrats. She sits on the Community Problem-Oriented Policing Workgroup for the Community Police Commission board. Alana is a student at Cleveland State University and is working on a voter's education guide to help bridge a gap between illiteracy and voter engagement. Her hobbies are skating, reading, arts, yoga and cooking!

Ian Gilliam is a recent graduate of Notre Dame College where he completed his bachelor's degree in Mathematics and Software Development. During the school year, Ian occupied his time being a full-time student by taking a full course load of 19 credit hours. When not in class, he fills the rest of his time working at his school's cafe where he engages with the local community and tutors many of his friends. Ian remains active in his community as a member of the college's engineering club, The Ohio Council of Teachers of Mathematics, and the Ministerial Recruitment Institute. The youngest of four and the only male, he works tirelessly to assist his parents in managing their three rental properties and primary residence. He currently pursuing a technical internship and aspires to continue his education in the engineering field.

Ian Gilliam
Graduate
Notre Dame College

Chardonnay Graham is the owner and creative director of Touch Cleveland LLC, a marketing and public relations organization. Chardonnay began her business in 2014 and became fully independent in 2018. She is a first-generation entrepreneur in her family. Chardonnay is a cum laude graduate of Notre Dame College with a dual degree in communication and public relations. Touch Cleveland services small businesses, nonprofits and startups with strategic planning and marketing management. Touch Cleveland specifically focuses on community and business development. At Touch Cleveland, the clients are hand selected based on similar objectives to create a marketing collaborative. Chardonnay also serves as digital chair for the Greater Cleveland Association of Black Journalists. In her spare time, she enjoys networking, volunteering for the homeless, writing poetry, dancing and riding her bike.

Chardonnay Graham
Owner
Creative Director
Touch Cleveland LLC

Dr. Aaryn L. Green
Diversity Fellow
John Carroll University

Dr. Aaryn L. Green is from East Cleveland, Ohio and is the current diversity fellow in the Center for Student Diversity and Inclusion at John Carroll University where she creates diversity programming and trainings, advocates for underrepresented students, and advises student organizations. She is a three-time alum of the University of Cincinnati (Bachelor's 2009, Master's 2012, Ph.D. 2018). She mentors Shaw High School students assisting and traveling with the marching band, aiding in college preparation, and raising funds for scholarships. Her photo can be found on the Village Keeper Wall at the University of Cincinnati where her legacy includes reinstating The Black Graduate and Professional Student Association, being selected as a Charles H. Taft Center research fellow, an honorary member of The Lambda Society Black Women's Honorary, and a 2017 University of Cincinnati Black Girls Rock recipient. Dr. Green has presented her research nationally and internationally and has taught upwards of 10 college courses in sociology. She is a member of Mt. Zion Congregational Church, UCC.

Dr. Ashley J. Jackson
Chiropractic Physician
A Chiropractic Healing

Dr. Ashley J. Jackson is a board licensed chiropractic physician whose primary area of expertise is family practice and overall wellness. She is the director of A Chiropractic Healing. Service to patients is of the utmost importance to her and can be seen by the high quality of care and exceptional service provided. After graduating from John F. Kennedy High School with honors, Dr. Jackson earned her bachelor's degree and chiropractic degree from Life University in Georgia. She is the recipient of a list of academic honors and professional achievements. Dr. Jackson was recognized as a Top Doctor in 2016 & 2018. She has been featured commercially on television during the Dr. Oz Show.

Dr. Byron Jackson is a multi-gifted chiropractic physician who has been featured on television internationally and authored multiple books including, Think Large I Dare You, Lose Weight and Look Great Naturally, and 100 Health Secrets. As a chiropractic physician at A Chiropractic Healing, Dr. Jackson provides consultations, evaluations, and care to patients ranging from infants, professional athletes, and the elderly. Dr. Jackson considers it an honor to be able to add value to the lives of so many at A Chiropractic Healing. He is a native Clevelander and the recipient of a long list of accomplishments including being recognized as a Top Doctor in 2016, 2017, and 2018. He has also been featured commercially on television during the Dr. Oz Show.

Dr. Byron Jackson
Chiropractic Physician
A Chiropractic Healing

Carlin D.T. Jackson is the principal consultant of Theo. Wyes David, Ltd., delivering strategy, systems architecture, commercialization, and corporate finance services to numerous clients across the country. He is the co-founder and chief technology officer of a stealth, venture capital-backed eCommerce tech-startup. In his role as a think[box] founder at Case Western Reserve University (CWRU), he mentors students, community members, and entrepreneurs. Carlin has previously held management and engineering roles at Explorys, the Federal Reserve Bank of Cleveland, North Shore Energy, and multiple research and development projects at CWRU. Carlin received a Master of Science in Finance from the Weatherhead School of Management at CWRU (Corporate Finance track with focuses in both Entrepreneurial and Health Finance). As a Louis Stokes Scholar at CWRU, he received a Bachelor's in Computer Science with minors in Finance, Management, and Mathematics. He is a board member of the Case Alumni Association. Above all, Carlin values his faith in God, parents Cedric Sr. and Linda, siblings, extended family, and friends.

Carlin D.T. Jackson
Principal Consultant
Theo. Wyes David, Ltd.

In May of 2017, Antoinne McKinney published, The Inspiration that Lies Within: Success Management and Planning, a self-help book that he uses to deliver mentoring and success coaching strategies to individuals and professionals. Antoinne has become a respected community leader and entrepreneur with both nonprofit and for-profit entities. In the past 15 years, he established the nonprofit, Young A.D.U.L.T.S. Inc. and the for-profit company, McKinney Development Enterprises. McKinney Development Enterprises owns service brands such as Simcha Media, which offers media and technology services, and A.C.E.S. International, which offers consulting and success coaching services to families and other businesses. He is also a software developer on the PINACLE Configuration Management Team at PNC Bank and holds a Bachelor of Arts degree in Urban Studies from Cleveland State University. Antoinne is an established author, entrepreneur, and widely experienced professional. Most of all, he values being a husband to his beautiful wife, Antoinette, and a father to his adorable children, Mariah and Aden.

Antoinne McKinney
Managing Partner
McKinney Development Enterprises

Malinda "Mindy" Moore is a Cleveland-based freelance writer, content creator and brand curator. Her work has been featured in Blavity, Estelle Magazine, Rolling Out, and Caged Bird Magazine. Malinda serves as an Executive Assistant for Element 13 LLC (Elmnt13) — Cleveland's go to firm for all things marketing, brand management, event planning and coordination. She has worked with an array of exclusive clientele, aiding in Elmnt13's goal of bringing visions to life. Malinda holds a Bachelor of Arts in Mass Communication and Media Studies with an emphasis in Public Relations from Mississippi Valley State University. Her passion for the media in addition to her love for the community is a driving factor in her career. Having a heart for service, Malinda is the founder of "The Golden Rule, Period.," a campaign to collect feminine hygiene products for homeless and impoverished women in the Northeast Ohio area. She is a member of Gamma Sigma Sigma National Service Sorority, NAACP and The Association for Women in Communications.

Mindy Moore
Freelance Writer
Brand Curator
Executive Assistant
Element 13 LLC

Colette Ngana, Colette Ngana is a doctoral student in sociology at Case Western Reserve University (CWRU). Colette holds a bachelor's degree in History, Philosophy, and Sociology of Science from Michigan State University as well as a master's degree in Bioethics from CWRU. Her current research is on medical sociology, social inequality, and social vulnerability specializing in the social-structural factors that lead to preventable injuries in marginalized and minoritized populations. She hopes this work strengthens her community. Colette is passionate about reproductive justice and is a member of the board of directors at Preterm. Outside of her academic and work responsibilities, Colette spends time making pottery in her home studio. She is grateful for the unwavering support of her friends and family especially her husband, David, and the love of her two cats, Gus and Ravage.

Colette Ngana
Doctoral Student
Case Western Reserve University

Courtney Ottrix is the communications director for Global Cleveland, a nonprofit that strives to strengthen the local economy by welcoming people from around the world. In this position, she presents Global Cleveland to community groups and at public events. She writes and edits a monthly newsletter, directs media relations, and manages all social media platforms. Courtney is also the creator of Courtney Covers Cleveland, a blog that grew out of her frustration with people complaining about nothing to do in Cleveland. She began posting stories of interesting people, events and places in the city and acquired the nickname "Cleveland Courtney." Born and raised in Cleveland, she graduated from Shaker Heights High School and earned a bachelor's degree at Duquesne University. Courtney is a freelance production assistant for ESPN and ABC. She has traveled widely for USA Soccer, Monday Night Football, the NBA and other sporting events. She resides on Cleveland's east side with her husband, Bryon Ottrix Sr., and the couple's four children-- Bryon Jr., Paul, Bryce and daughter Codi Lynn.

Courtney Ottrix
Writer and Blogger
Courtney Covers Cleveland

Erin Phelps
Doctoral Student
Case Western Reserve University

Erin K. Phelps is a third year Ph.D. student in the Department of Sociology at Case Western Reserve University. Her work focuses on LGBT liberation in institutions. She is a womanist, yoga teacher, and an embodier of "The Work". Erin seeks every day to hold herself accountable to people who are within the margins and continue to foster solidarity and community. Erin is president of Q Grad: The LGBTQIA+ Graduate and Professional Student Association. Throughout her time in Cleveland, Erin has shown her peers and mentors her growth as an organizer, a lecturer of LGBT related topics, and a vessel for positive change. Erin is also a 200 hour-registered yoga teacher. She received her training from Cleveland Yoga and continues to teach power yoga for nonprofits like Ellipsis Institute for Women of Color in the Academy, Gathering Place, and National Center for Transgender Equity (NCTE). Erin strives to align her scholarship and praxis to reveal private troubles as public issues for those within the margins in Cleveland and beyond.

Christina Pope
Paraprofessional Intern
NorthEast Ohio Regional
Sewer District

Christina is a recent graduate of Cleveland State, class of 2019, receiving her Bachelor's in Mechanical Engineering. She is currently a Paraprofessional Intern at the Northeast Ohio Regional Sewer District and enjoys projects that challenge her and encourage her to think. Looking back a few years ago, she would not have expected to have accomplished as much as she has. Christina started college as a soft spoken, inverted girl. She struggled with confidence in herself and would often doubt what she could achieve. However, through the assistance of mentors in her life, and those that believed in her, she matured and learned from her experiences. She eventually got an amazing on campus job, became president of the chapter of the National Society of Black Engineers at CSU, and received an offer that she didn't think was possible when her academic career began. For her work, she was also awarded the President's Award for Excellence in Diversity. She hopes to continue her work within the community, through volunteer work and being a role model for those that need one.

Shelli Reeves is the community engagement specialist at Cleveland Museum of Art (CMA). She strategically studies who CMA engages with. Shelli strives to make art accessible and to be a convener. Shelli uses art to bring people together and talk about the current social political climate. She also manages "Studio Go", CMA's mobile art studio that delivers hands-on art experiences to neighborhoods across Northeast Ohio. Therefore, in the summer months you can find Shelli creating art with people at community festivals and events as a part of the "Studio Go," program. She graduated from Ohio Wesleyan University where she majored in International Studies and Black World Studies and minored in Black World Studies and Women and Gender Studies. She is also interested in political thought, art, and African American history. Shelli's main goal is to break down barriers created by institutionalized racism and sexism by working in the arts, and as a U.S. Congressperson in the future.

Shelli Reeves
Community Engagement
Specialist
Cleveland Museum of Art

Alishia Sparks-Gullatt is an entrepreneur, mother, wife and native of Northeast, Ohio. A Point Park University alumna, Alishia acquired her dance degree while acquiring five students and two teacher adjudicated certifications for the Italian form of ballet known as Cecchetti. Alishia is a certified member of Dance Masters of America and has enjoyed dancing, competing and choreographing for most of her life. She spent her first year in Cleveland as the ballet director for The Boys and Girls Clubs of America while also keeping up with a full makeup clientele. Alishia is a former MAC cosmetics specialist. She is gearing up for New York Fashion Week as a leading makeup artist taking a team of 20 makeup artists to display their makeup artistry skills. Her company, SparkD Enterprises, has been positioned to make an impact on Ohio, the east coast, and globally. Her mission is to bless the masses with each subsidiary she oversees with class, finesse, and a top tier level of professionalism.

Alishia Sparks-Gullatt
Chief Executive Officer
SparkD Enterprises

TyJuan Swanson-Sawyer

Intern
Then Design Architecture

TyJuan Swanson-Sawyer is an intern at Then Design Architecture (TDA). She has assisted with the formatting of documents for the design development and construction document phase submissions for North Royalton Elementary School. TyJuan has worked with the National Organization of Minority Architectural Students (NOMAS), a student organization created to follow the principles of the parent organization, NOMA. The organization fights against the effects of discrimination and prejudices in the architectural profession and creates unity amongst other minority architects. She is also affiliated with Kupita Transciones Mentorship Program, a volunteering opportunity offered through the Student Multi-Cultural Center at Kent State. The program is tasked with mentoring incoming students to increase their opportunities of success. TyJuan is also involved in the Architecture Construction and Engineering (ACE) Mentors program Cleveland chapter. TyJuan graduated from Kent State University this year with a Bachelor of Science in Architecture. She will be attending graduate school in the Fall of 2019 at Kent State to earn a dual master's degree in Architecture and Urban Design.

Ashley Taylor

Event & Brand Curator
Marketing Strategist
Element13 LLC, Spaces &
Co., and Taylor Properties &
Management Group, LLC

Ashley Taylor has built a reputation as the expert for marketing, brand management, event planning and coordination in the Northeast Ohio area. She is currently serving as founder and chief executive officer of Element13 LLC, a Cleveland-based marketing and management firm. Ashley oversees day-to-day operations, development and implementation of company tasks as well as strategizing to promote and increase brand awareness among the company's exclusive clientele. Ashley is also founder and chief executive officer of Spaces & Co., a co-working space for small businesses and working professionals that aids in the productivity and development of aspiring and current entrepreneurs. Ashley is a licensed real estate agent and serves as the founder of Taylor Properties and Management Group, LLC. She holds a Master of Business Administration from University of Phoenix and a Bachelor of Arts in Telecommunications with a minor in Marketing from Bowling Green State University. She is a member of Delta Sigma Theta Sorority, Inc.

Shalira Taylor is a member of the Order of the Eastern Star, and owner of D.M.T. Cleveland, Inc. In 2018 as regional field director for the Washington State Republican Party, Shalira ran field teams winning two thirds of the races. She is a member of the African American Advisory Committee for the Republican National Committee. Shalira is also a member of the Ohio Black Republican Association, Cuyahoga County Republican Central Committee, and Republican ward leader in Cleveland. She grew up in Cleveland Heights and graduated from Cleveland Heights High School in 1999 with a degree in dental assistant. She later attended Lorain Community College where she studied and received her certifications in real estate sales and received recognition from Phi Theta Kappa Honor Society in 2008. She then transferred to Cleveland State University and pursued a bachelor's degree in Marketing/Business Management and joined Theta Phi Alpha. As a small business owner, Shalira has personally helped to create and facilitate job opportunities for people in her community.

Shalira Taylor
Owner
D.M.T. Cleveland, Inc.

Imani Tunson is the creator of Kissdedbymani. She is a self-taught make up artist with a strong passion for all things beautiful. Imani takes pride in keeping abreast of current trends and to create unique looks beyond her client's expectations. Imani recognizes that each client is unique and understands the importance of defining each individual's beauty. She specializes in natural makeup and is able to deliver for special events such as portfolios, corporate events and photo shoots. Imani is also an up and coming professional in the field of health care. She is a graduate student at Kent State University. She will graduate in the Spring of 2021 with a master's degree in Public Health. Her professional vision includes studying abroad and analyzing existing health care policies and practices. As a state tested nursing assistant, Imani is already using her talents and skills to serve her community. Imani is a member of the Mt. Zion Church in Oakwood Village and volunteers at Hospice of the Western Reserve as well as Menorah Park.

Imani Tunson
Make Up Artist
Kissedbymani

Jayah Watters-Clark
Communications Specialist
Cleveland Hopkins International
Airport

Jayah J. Watters-Clark serves as communications specialist for Cleveland Hopkins International Airport. In this capacity she is responsible for management of all digital platforms and onsite events. She also assists with media relations and serves as a secondary spokesperson for the airport. Jayah is a graduate of Cleveland Metropolitan School District, Cleveland State University where she earned a bachelor's degree in Journalism and John Carroll University where she earned a master's degree in Communications Management. Clark is a proud member of Delta Sigma Theta Sorority, Incorporated and Public Relations Society of America. She is married with two children and enjoys photography and cycling. Jayah models her life after Philippians 4:13, "I can do all things through Christ who strengthens me."

As one of the nation's top research institutions, Case Western Reserve University has among its distinguished alumni, faculty and staff a number of Cleveland's most accomplished African American leaders. It salutes them and our student leaders for their contributions to Case

Western Reserve University and to the Greater Cleveland metropolitan community, and it congratulates those who are honored for their accomplishments in this year's *Who's Who In Black Cleveland.*

Advancing diversity through inclusive thinking, mindful learning and transformative dialogue, the university is proud to join other community partners in celebrating the achievements of those who make Cleveland one of the nation's most dynamic places to live, learn and work.

case.edu/diversity

CASE WESTERN RESERVE
UNIVERSITY   EST. 1826

ACE MENTOR PROGRAM
ARCHITECTURE · CONSTRUCTION · ENGINEER
CLEVELAND

The ACE Mentor Program of America Cleveland Awarded Nearly $1 Million and Impacted Students' Futures

Brandon Moore, lead mentor for The New Tech East ACE program, pictured alongside students and his fellow mentors on the team.

Since the organization's founding in 2008, the ACE Mentor Program of America, Cleveland has awarded nearly $950K in scholarships to Cleveland Heights and Warrensville Heights high schools. This has benefited students aspiring to further their education in college or trades careers and to support their entry into careers.

The ACE Mentor Program is an after-school career pathways mentorship program that introduces high school students to the worlds of architecture, construction and engineering (the AEC industry) through project-based learning from AEC industry professionals. Students work diligently through the school year to prepare a design and construction project in response to a request for proposal (RFP) program addressing real-world problems in our communities.

Warrensville Heights students learn about basic structural principles through hands-on learning.

Students at Ginn Academy learning about career pathways from positive professional role models in the community.

Brandon Moore pictured with the students he mentors at New Tech East after a win for their project RFP.

Currently, the program engages 175 students across 11 schools — ten of which are within the Cleveland Metropolitan School District, with one additional site at Warrensville Heights High School. It is supported by a network of more than 130 AEC industry professionals, including several companies that are African-American owned.

The program's student demographic is largely minority, with 65 percent being African-American, 17 percent Hispanic, 10 percent mixed race and 6 percent Caucasian. Through their tireless support of the ACE Mentor Program, numerous AEC professionals, including numerous African-Americans, are granting students with professional minority role models, increasing students' confidence and providing them with a realistic perception of what they can professionally achieve.

Brandon Moore, project manager of GEIS Companies and New Tech East High School lead ACE mentor, began supporting the program five years ago. He was concurrently project managing Cleveland's renowned Metropolitan at the 9 and learning from other professionals on the project about how the ACE Program is working to enrich the lives of minority youth in Cleveland.

"Back then, I think I felt [that] I needed to try to find a way to give back to the community and I found a way to do that in a really cool way," stated Brandon.

Throughout Brandon's professional path, he learned firsthand during his internship with Ozanne Construction, one of the nation's largest Black-owned construction companies, the importance of having Black leaders and mentors in communities. Their service will help Black youth self-actualize so that they can become future leaders who give back to their local communities. Since mentoring in the program, Brandon has focused on helping students understand various career pathways and scholarship opportunities to bring up the next successful generation of African-American professionals.

"I try to talk to students about things I wasn't thinking about when I was 17 years old — about career and college," says Brandon. "I focus on helping them understand there is a lot of money out there that they can benefit from if they apply for college scholarships. We also help students understand that consistency, hard work and fighting through difficult times is important...and to not let your current situation hold you back."

This year, Brandon's team at New Tech East High School astounded a panel of judges, including the Cleveland director of City Planning, Freddy L. Collier Jr., and vice president of the Cleveland Foundation, Lillian Kuri, to win this year's competition.

The ACE Program will continue to support and welcome students through mentorship and effecting positive change in predominately African-American and minority neighborhoods in Cleveland. To become involved in the ACE Mentor Program of Cleveland, visit: https://www.acementor.org/affiliates/ohio/cleveland/about-us/.

who takes the lead
when others falter?

who shines light
in darkness?

who lifts up others
while climbing to the top?

you, that's **who**.

congratulations to the leaders of
Who's Who in Black Cleveland!

Going the distance for our communities.

INTERESTING PERSONALITIES

UBIQUITOUS DESIGN, LTD

AFRICAN AMERICAN CULTURAL GARDEN
PAST PAVILION AT DUSK
MARTIN LUTHER KING, JR. BOULEVARD
CLEVELAND, OHIO   October 2011

W. Daniel Bickerstaff II, AIA, NOMA

Founder and Principal Architect
Ubiquitous Design, LTD

Photo by Eric Benson

W. Daniel Bickerstaff II, AIA, NOMA

Founder and Principal Architect
Ubiquitous Design, LTD

The unyielding and ever-present architect

By Felicia C. Haney

W. Daniel Bickerstaff's path to greatness began in 1979 as a freshman at Martin Luther King High School. Robert Madison, the man who built the school, was the guest of honor at an assembly.

Later, his French teacher sprung a pop quiz that wasn't about the language. Instead, she asked about their career goals. Bickerstaff struggled for an answer as the mundane "doctor, lawyer, teacher, nurse" responses echoed throughout the room. Not that those aren't great professions, Bickerstaff wanted to be different.

When it was his turn, he blurted out "architect," not even knowing exactly what it entailed.

The teacher made them follow up with research in the field and that's when the seed began to grow. Bickerstaff's been pursuing the goal ever since and still has the paperwork from that assignment to remind him of his humble beginnings.

"I would take things my dad had around the house, always making something out of nothing," he said. This has turned into a theme for the architect's life. In fact Bickerstaff admits, "Fifty percent of my time is spent in a world that doesn't exist." Even the name of his company means to exist everywhere at once – a name he came up with while on line for Omega Phi Psi in college. Who knew it would foreshadow the two worlds he now lives in, taking the intangible and turning it into fruition.

"My job is to sit, ponder, create and then convince someone of my idea and its value to their community."

But Bickerstaff is sought after just as often. Early on in his entrepreneurial journey, shortly after he took the leap of faith to leave benefits and a good paying position with the City of Cleveland to establish Ubiquitous full time, his former employer – Mayor Frank G. Jackson – reached out with the opportunity of a lifetime...

"When I got the letter, I thought it came to the wrong person," Bickerstaff said of the request for him to help design the African American Cultural Garden. "I was working in my basement at the time."

Not for long. his business would parallel his design of the space – leaving his past position of comfort, struggling with the stress of entrepreneurship that is "unyielding and ever present" all for the promise of a future unknown. Bickerstaff also got an opportunity to work on this project with Robert Madison before the veteran architect gracefully bowed out. But Bickerstaff was past the corridor of no return and knew how important this journey would be, not only to a kid like him from 82nd and Superior but for all to revel in the beauty of this space.

It took six months of research before ever drawing a single line to prepare a design that will, upon completion, stand up to and outshine other gardens in their grandeur.

Projects like this is only one way Bickerstaff gives back. His goal is to promote the profession, especially to the black community.

"It is important to have more entrepreneurs out there being leaders in their field," he said. "We oftentimes are concerned about helping the youth, which is great" – Bickerstaff leads high school students every year for a six-week senior project – "but we need to help African-American businesses and make sure they're represented on these projects.

Ubiquitous Design is located in Shaker Heights where Bickerstaff gets on his knees praying and thanking God every day he comes into the office.

James. D. Cowan Jr.

Associate AIA
ThenDesign Architecture

James. D. Cowan Jr.

Associate AIA
ThenDesign Architecture

The drive to design

By Felicia C. Haney

James D. Cowan Jr. has always had an interest in design. As a child, he'd thumb through his grandmother's Architectural Digest magazines admiring the art on the pages. He started off drawing cars and homes. By the time he became a student at Glenville, architecture had gotten its hooks into the high schooler. He's since added graphic design, photography, digital modeling, planning and branding as skill sets.

It began during sophomore year at Glenville when an art teacher took a chance on him.

"He went above and beyond his job. I actually wish I had his phone number today to call and thank him. I never knew how big of an influence his introduction would make on me," Cowan said of being given the opportunity to meet the legendary Robert P. Madison courtesy of that teacher.

While looking around Madison's office in awe, Cowan had an epiphany.

"He had his own firm with all these plaques on the wall," Cowan said, recalling the encounter. "There were all these buildings downtown surrounding his office. I was only about 16 at the time, but it was right then in that moment I knew... I want to be an architect. I want to affect my community. I want to have some impact, design-wise, on my neighborhood."

Cowan left with not only a clear-cut career path, but was also given a bit of advice from the veteran architect... "If you're good, you'll get it." The 16 year old wasn't sure what that meant but he never forgot those words, words that later became the driving force behind Cowan's college and professional career.

"I based everything on that," said Cowan, referencing times where he felt insecure because it seemed like others started off two levels higher than him.

"I passed up a scholarship to attend an Ohio college in order to go to Howard University," Cowan said. "My freshman year was transformative. Going to a place outside of home and getting the chance to meet the cream of the crop black people from all over the world. It was a major experience."

It came at a major expense too, which prompted Cowan to take some of the burden off his parents by taking advantage of his scholarship and transfer to Kent State University's architectural school where he graduated with a Bachelor of Science in Art. He followed it up with a Master of Architecture degree from Kent as well.

"If you're good, you'll get it" echoed in his head and got him through.

"I knew I had to be twice as good, work twice as hard, get two tutors for one class if need be. It was an uphill battle going through school for architecture."

But Cowan persevered and wants more people who look like him to enter the field as well. He's been in the field since 2009 and now works as a Project Designer/Manager at ThenDesign Architecture on projects as grandiose as the new Richmond Heights High School. These are the type of community involved efforts that made him go into architecture. His focus is "building the classroom around the student" not having a building that's just "cells and bells."

Currently on the path to becoming a licensed architect, initiating programs that increase awareness of design opportunities for historically disadvantaged communities and involvement with mentorship programs that promote equity for future generations are few ways he plans to impact this design industry.

The Conwell and Jones families

Elected Officials

Photo by Lewis Burrell

The Conwell and Jones families

Elected Officials

Building stronger communities

By Rhonda Crowder

What's better than one household with two elected officials? Two! The Conwells live in Cleveland's Ward 9, which comprises of Glenville and parts of University Circle. Yvonne is Cuyahoga County Councilwoman (District 7) and her husband Kevin is a veteran city councilman.

Across town in Ward 1, (the Lee-Harvard, Lee-Seville, Union Miles and part of Mt. Pleasant neighborhoods), Tonya Johnson Jones serves as a Cuyahoga County Court of Common Pleas - Division of Domestic Relations judge and her husband, Joseph is city councilman.

And, respectively, all are working on initiatives to strengthen our community.

Kevin's passion for writing policy has positioned Glenville as the next community slated for development. The biggest project coming to Ward 9 is The Neighborhood Transformation Initiative on E. 105th Street. This incubator will house 9 minority businesses, co-office working space, apartments, and an 100 seat amphitheatre. A Veteran's Administration Fisher House sits right across to street. Both set to open this year, with more to come.

Kevin, a drummer/xylophonist, is also working with a group dubbed Play It Forward to put musical instruments in the hands of inner city children.

For Joe, economic development is his primary concern. "Economic development is important because data shows that communities where resources are invested into them not only retain citizens, they also attracts new residents."

The new John F. Kennedy High School, a $42 million project, is currently under construction in addition to new housing for seniors as well as new home construction. "I want to stabilize and strengthen our community for both current citizens and generations to come," he said.

For Yvonne, being chairwoman for the County Council's Health and Human Services committee has given her a bird's eye view of the growing needs within our community as well as the reduction of funding to provide resources to serve those needs. With that, she's focused on making sure everyone understands the importance of completing the 2020 U.S. Census.

"We all need to complete it. Talk to our friends. It's so imperative," she said.

The U.S. Census determines congressional lines and where the federal government will distribute resources, Yvonne explained. "This has to be the dinnertime conversation, barbershop/beauty salon topic and the work environment discussions. If we want solutions and money to tackle our problems, we must stand up and be counted!"

And, last but certainly not least, Tonya is attacking substance abuse and mental health issues. In the Fall of 2018, she launched the Families First Program at Domestic Relations Court in partnership with Moore Counseling and Mediation Services. Assisting parents through these difficult situations, it is a first of its kind in the State of Ohio.

"The Families First Program represents issues which are close to my heart, mental, health, substance abuse and family," said Tonya. "This program ensures that parents receive the services they need in order to have stable, positive impact on the lives of children."

She's confident the program will provide parents with the tools necessary to co-parent effectively when divorce is inevitable. "It will also link our parents to treatment providers who can guide them to stability and sobriety, allowing them to become better parents and foster healthier children in Cuyahoga County," she continued.

The four has also worked on projects together, as well, such as hosting an expungement clinic earlier this year. "We have to work together for the good of the whole, to create a better quality of life. That's how we leverage our political capital," said Kevin. "That what counts."

Michele Crawford

Project Manager in the Capital, Construction and Facilities
Department
Cuyahoga Community College

Photo by Eric Benson

Michele Crawford

Project Manager in the Capital, Construction and Facilities Department
Cuyahoga Community College

Changing the face of architecture

By Felicia C. Haney

For nearly two years, Michele Crawford has served as Project Manager in the Capital, Construction and Facilities Department at Cuyahoga Community College. The title is not only a lot to say, but also comes with a lot to do – like coordinating and facilitating all building renovations and construction projects at the college.

It's a lot of work, but she just refers to it as "a lot of moving around." In other words, she puts the plans in motion.

Laying plans should be second nature to an architect major. But when the Regina High School grad set out for Ohio University, she had her mind set on graduating quickly – something a major like architecture does not afford you to do.

"I had an interest in math and engineering when I went to college, then second guessed myself and started taking art classes. I was trying to find the balance between the creative and the technical and ended up getting my Bachelors in interior design."

It wasn't until attending The School of the Art Institute of Chicago for graduate school that architecture became a natural progression. At the time, Crawford only knew of two black architects courtesy of family members who tried to get her connected.

"I always felt like I needed support," she said of her journey to get to this point. "I didn't know many people like me in the field at the time so I had to seek them out. Now, I feel like I know all the black architects, and there are more of them than people actually know. They're out here."

This is why mentoring is such a passion for Crawford who wants to see more African-Americans enter the industry. "The work ethic through school and through jobs is very demanding, which turns people off," she admitted. "But it can be flexible in terms of hours and workload. I make sure that I am a support system and serve as a resource for students, including my two mentees."

Interning at Robert P. Madison International served as a huge help during her college years and made a heavy impact early on in her career.

"It was great," she said of the experience. "I interned there twice actually and worked there full time when I returned from grad school."

This is the same type of influence Crawford attempts to be for others, which is why she has expanded her willingness to share her skill set with community and professional organizations as a member of the American Institute of Architects as well as the National Organization of Minority Architects. She also serves on a variety of boards that include youth arts, development and neighborhood organizations.

"Right out of college I worked for Habitat for Humanity in Charlotte," she said. This experience fed her desire for investigation of land, politics and economics in architecture and inspired her to be a contributing member of her environment.

"I have a social and civic desire to give back and help improve the quality of life for others," said Crawford.

As a result, she's pushing the effort to change the face of architecture to look more diverse. Now, eight years into the industry, her plan to become a licensed architect is simultaneously underway. Crawford is just three tests away from achieving her goal that will help "represent African-American women in architecture."

She's worked on various projects including Cleveland Heights High School – housed in the neighborhood where she grew up – and the downtown Hilton Hotel, which is her most memorable to date.

I. Kaye Gaines
CEO
Gaines Funeral Homes

Photo by Mychal Lilly

I. Kaye Gaines
CEO
Gaines Funeral Homes

The Trendsetter of Funeral Directors

By Felicia C. Haney

I. Kaye Gaines... The name reads like a woman who's ready to take an oath, willing to pledge her service and able to get the job done. As CEO of Gaines Funeral Homes, she has done all of the above. But her road to running two locations of the family business didn't even begin with a step in the funeral home's direction.

When it comes to carrying on tradition, it is oftentimes found that the younger generation is not apt to inherit the task and more concerned with blazing their own trails. Kaye was no different. She was only 15 years old when her family bought their first funeral home on Union Ave. from the Ferfolia family, right in the E. 93rd Street neighborhood where she grew up.

After graduating from John Adams High School, she had no passion for the position that ironically now serves as her ministry.

Kaye would avoid delving into the practice and in fact tried many other occupations. Thirteen years would pass before she attended Cuyahoga Community College. This is where she received her licensure as well as her calling to serve the people of Cleveland as a female funeral director; something at the time was trailblazing in itself.

For Kaye, the experience for has been transformative in an industry where only few thrive. "Marcella Boyd Cox, Patty Wills, Evelyn Davis, Cynthia Miller, my mother, myself... we paved the way for women," Kaye said. "We're kind of like the Rosa Parks of funeral service. When you have a nurturer as opposed to a man smoking a cigar in a black hat, it makes the environment feel less cold. I'd love to see more women make their way into the field."

For her, functioning as funeral director is more about service than anything.

"It's a servant's position and I love serving the families," Kaye said. "I will always consider it a ministry. You have to have a heart to serve. It takes patience, dedication and commitment."

She understands that death is a natural part of life. In fact, Gaines lost four of her own family members within four years and at one point didn't know how the Gaines family business would continue. Lucky for her, this time the next generation was ready to step up to the plate, which helps her to go above and beyond in her duties.

Kaye, along with five others on staff, is a certified grief facilitator. This training helps her to help families with the support they need. It also helps her to deprogram from a necessary but stressful profession. As a certified funeral celebrant, she continues to bring life to the dark side of the funeral business. In this function, she plans tailor-made funeral services that send fallen family members off in a way that's characteristic of how they lived their lives.

Kaye is jovial about performing this function due to her forward thinking that further serves the people. "You have to change with the times in an ever-changing world. We're a black-owned funeral home but people don't always want a traditional church service with a minister. We've been willing to provide that. In fact, we were the first black funeral home to have celebrants... Not to toot my own horn, 'cause to God be the glory, but I am the trendsetter of funeral directors." And that's how Kaye Gaines will leave her mark on the industry.

Akil Hameed
Founder and Chief Executive Officer
FASS Real Estate Services

Photo by Kameron Khan Photography

Akil Hameed

Founder and Chief Executive Officer
FASS Real Estate Services

Building Wealth through Real Estate

By Rhonda Crowder

Akil Hameed grew up in Shaker Heights and graduated from Shaker Heights High School in 1996. Watching his father and grandmother, who owned an apartment building in East Cleveland and a convenience store, sparked his interest in entrepreneurship.

But, his father-in-law, a lifelong investor, told him he should always invest in real estate, even if he's working a full-time job. With that bit of advice, Hameed and his wife began to buy property in 2004.

Wanting to put both his bachelor's in business administration and master's in marketing from Florida A&M, and his experience from working as a buyer at Neiman Marcus in Dallas to work after returning to Cleveland, he continued down the career path he'd started on.

"It wasn't until I was laid off from my job that I started to do real estate as a business," said Hameed. "I always knew I wanted to do it. I just had to take a leap of faith."

That was in 2006. At the same time, a financial advisor suggested he consider property management. Hameed listened. "FASS started as a rental referral business. We were an agency linking tenants to landlords." They also helped rehab properties.

Currently, FASS manages 300+ properties.

From there, Hameed pondered more long-term options in real estate and began the process of becoming a broker. "I used my education to leverage the time, so I didn't have to go into the classroom." It took him a year to acquire the license.

"That opened up a lot of doors from me," he continued. "I've been managing agents for over ten years now. We've developed into a full-service agency."

Hameed credits his fast-tracked success to participation in Project REAP (Real Estate Associate Program). He became involved with REAP while in the process of purchasing his first piece of commercial real estate, his current office in Shaker Heights on Lee Road. "It was a 12-week program that touched on all the aspects of commercial real estate."

Two key opportunities stemmed from that project, a mentor-relationship from David Browning, managing director of CBRE, a Fortune 500 commercial real estate services and investment firm, and becoming a court-appointed receiver. He's done receivership work for Cuyahoga, Summit, and Lake Counties. "Both of these experiences have been instrumental in my career development as a real estate professional," he said.

When asked about his biggest challenge in real estate, Hameed said, "Always being the minority business owner, trying to engage in larger projects. Breaking through the door."

He's currently working to open FASS's corporate services division, offering business consulting to entrepreneurs. "We'll provide them with a roadmap to help them take their business ideas and plans from A to Z."

Hameed was named the 2016 Ohio Realtist Association State President, nominated for the 2016 Akron Cleveland Association of Realtors (ACAR) Board of Directors, appointed coordinator for the 2015 Cleveland Project REAP Commercial Real Estate program, received the Million Dollar Producer Award from the National Association of Real Estate Brokers 2015, Ohio Realtist Association Broker of the Year Award for Top Producer 2014.

He is involved with numerous boards, a member of Alpha Phi Alpha Fraternity, and prides himself of giving back to the community. In his spare time, Hameed coaches track and field for Cuyahoga Valley Christian Academy as well as The Bedford Sprint Masters.

Hameed and his wife are parents to four children. "They are the reason I work so hard, to provide them with a better life than the one I experienced."

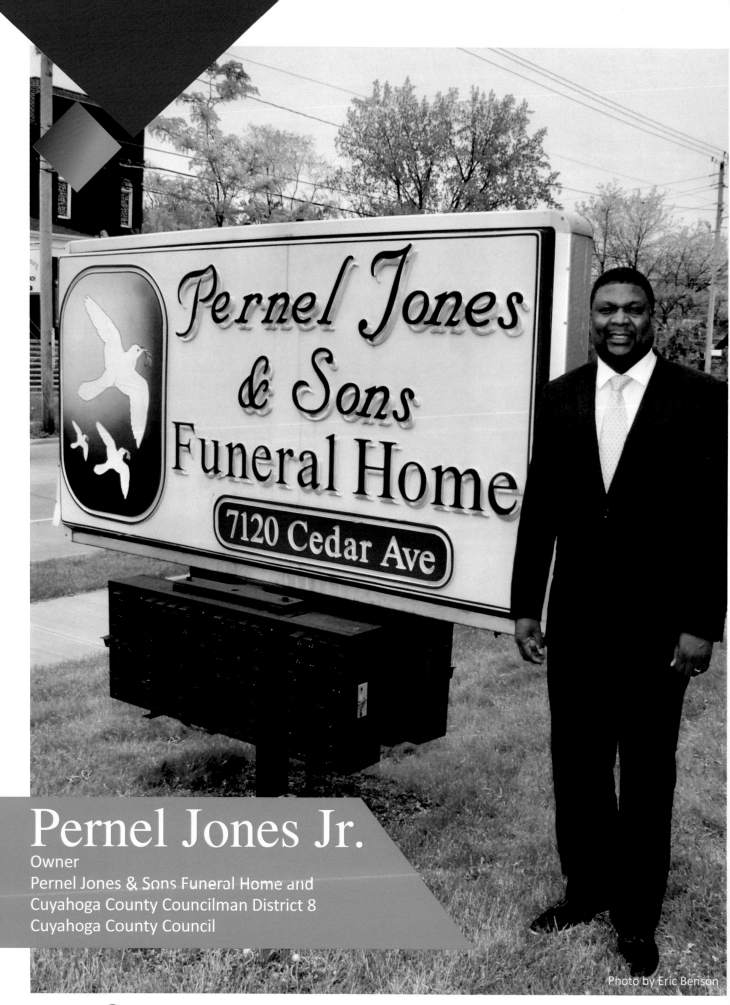

Pernel Jones Jr.

Owner
Pernel Jones & Sons Funeral Home and
Cuyahoga County Councilman District 8
Cuyahoga County Council

Photo by Eric Benson

Pernel Jones Jr.

Owner
Pernel Jones & Sons Funeral Home and
Cuyahoga County Councilman District 8
Cuyahoga County Council

Committed to the Community

By Felicia C. Haney

Pernel Jones Jr. literally grew up in the funeral home his family owned on 73rd Street and Cedar Ave. Their house was only footsteps away on the same street, a street he still lives on to this day. He has now taken the reins of the funeral home from his retired father and he and his brother now run it like their father and uncle did.

So how does a licensed funeral director end up with a career in politics?

When Jones Jr. married his wife Tammy 25 years ago, he decided to stay in the neighborhood. But something was different... Crime infested the area and banks had redlined their business. Mrs. Jones was ready to keep up with other couples who packed their bags for suburbia. Before they could secure their white picket fence, Jones Jr. received a special request...

"Frank Jackson was my city councilman at the time and he asked me to be on a Weed and Seed steering committee to rid crime and plant positivity in the community. I agreed," said Jones Jr. "We worked with a dozen resources to clean up drug activity and prostitution, and knock down houses. Because of our efforts we were able to receive federal funding. We used the money to raise police presence, put up cameras and transform our streets. I got to see government having a positive impact on the lives of residents."

As a result, the Jones' took their white picket fence deposit and invested it back into the Central neighborhood, building a brand new house on 73rd Street, even closer to the funeral home. In return, then mayor Mike White took personal interest in Pernel Jones and Sons Funeral Home helping them to receive a million dollar loan to secure the funeral home's and family's financial future.

By now, the political bug bit Jones Jr. Fresh from this victory, he decided to run for Cleveland City Council in 2005 representing Ward 5. He lost, ran again in '09 and lost again. The following year Cuyahoga County Council was created and an uneasily defeated Jones Jr. campaigned.

"I didn't know what [former County Commissioner] Peter Lawson Jones did, but I knew his name and I knew I was in campaign mode for the newly created position. In the end, I found out that county government was a way for me to give back on a bigger scale even more than city council."

Jones Jr. took office January 2011 and now serves as the Cuyahoga County Council Vice President.

He's had successes becoming the primary sponsor of a $50 million demolition fund, establishing a social entrepreneurship program that mentors the reentry population as well as a rehab program set to go into effect January 2020.

What's most important is "helping the most vulnerable people in this segment of the population... When filling out death certificates, I oftentimes notice young people never even finished high school. It hit home when I saw a friend of mine on my own table at the funeral home. He lost his life to gun violence."

Because of situations like this, Jones Jr. personally carries the torch handed to him by his mentor C.J. Prentiss in the form of the Closing The Achievement Gap program, one he now models after his other mentor Tedd Ginn Sr.'s model.

"I keep a map of 33 school systems. CTAG is my baby. I want it to grow and I want all my babies to graduate."

Phoebe Lee
Chief Executive Officer
Affinity Apparel

Phoebe Lee
Chief Executive Officer
Affinity Apparel

Fashioned for Success in Business

By Rhonda Crowder

"At 6 years old, my mother bought me a sewing machine for Christmas — not a toy one either," said Phoebe Lee as she recalled how she developed an affinity for fashion. "I was so mad at her. I wanted shoes, toys..."

Her father loved to thrift and one day took her into a store where she discovered sequins.

"I think my parents wanted to encourage me to do my own thing...got tired of buying the trendy stuff," she continued. "So, I started making my own clothes."

On top of that, Phoebe's best friend worked as a model, which also nurtured her growing interest.

By the age of 18, the Shaker Heights High School graduate found herself at the Magic Show in Las Vegas. There, she was wholesaling some of the biggest, Black brand names in fashion at the time. She's even opened a store in Atlanta and dabbled in modeling. She has also appeared on Good Morning America, the Today show, New York Live, VH1 and other networks.

Lee eventually found all of that to be a rat-race and wanted out.

She complained to her mother about the nature of her business and how she desired to do something with more consistency. Her mom — her confidant — is an entrepreneur who understands the ins and outs of the Minority Business Enterprise (MBE) certification landscape and suggested that Lee sell uniforms.

Phoebe established VDP Safety and Uniforms in January 2013 while still living in New York. Eventually, caring for her father during his illness brought Lee back to Cleveland but also allowed her to work more closely with her mother.

"That was a changing point in my life. It was the first time I had to put family before myself. Changed my world for the better," said Lee.

From there, she hasn't looked back.

"I put some retail thought into the B2B world," said Phoebe. "Uniforms are a product that can service everyone. It's a small necessity...As [there are] few females [that] are providers of safety equipment and uniforms, I became interested in how the uniforms fit women."

Her knowledge of fashion paired with solid business acumen lead to her current position as majority stakeholder and chief executive officer of Affinity Apparel, a nationwide uniform company based in Fairborn, Ohio.

"Now, I'm just making sure the orders are delivered," said Phoebe. "It's funny because, when I go back and see my professors they always say, 'We knew you would do something with fashion once you figured it out.'"

Lee earned a business administration degree from Clark Atlanta University (CAU) with a concentration in supply chain management. During her time there, CAU become a testing ground for this program so administrators heavily recruited business students and she was one of them.

Interestingly enough, loving to be different, she never wanted to wear the mandatory business attire.

"I always found a way to put a spin on it. But, I could get away with it because I got straight A's."

She honed her fashion skills and studied fashion design at Savannah College of Art and Design (SCAD) in Atlanta as well as the Fashion Institute of Technology (FIT) in New York City.

"I'm a third generation, Black woman entrepreneur and we all had to be creative," she said.

She used to bag candy for her mother's business, and her maternal grandmother — and namesake — owned a general store in Glen Allen, Mississippi.

Lee's hard work has been recognized by many, including former Ohio governor John Kasich, who, before leaving the office, appointed her to serve on the board of trustees for Cuyahoga Community College.

Ramona Lowery, MBA/MPA

Deputy Commissioner
City of Cleveland - Division of Water Pollution Control

Photo by Mychal Lilly

Ramona Lowery, MBA/MPA

Deputy Commissioner
City of Cleveland - Division of Water Pollution Control

Preparing the next generation of engineers

By Rhonda Crowder

"I just fell into it," said Ramona Lowery, when asked what sparked her interest in civil engineering. "I'm not one of those who can say I always tinkered with fixing things. It was more of teachers saying you're good at math, and suggesting I should try it. I didn't know another engineer. I didn't even know what engineering was until I researched it, spoke with the then VP of the Urban League, and got into the program [in college]."

Lowery grew up in the Moreland neighborhood of Shaker Heights, with a single mom who at times, worked three jobs. She took a drafting elective in high school in lieu of typing as her mom suggested. "Thinking back now, this unknowingly, peaked my interest in engineering."

Lowery graduated from Shaker Heights High then attended Cleveland State University, on a scholarship from the LINK Program. She obtained a Bachelor of Science degree in civil engineering in 1996.

Fresh out of college, she worked as a civil engineer - in the same department she currently oversees. She went to the Cleveland Division of Water in the hydraulics group then served as Sewer Superintendent/Project Manager for the City of Shaker Heights and later the Manager of Operation & Maintenance for the Northeast Ohio Regional Sewer District.

She also earned a dual Master's degree in business administration/public administration from the University of Phoenix in 2009 then returned to WPC in 2015. "It's been an interesting and fulfilling, twenty-plus years."

What she enjoys most about engineering? Lowery said, "It's something different everyday. I love taking something from the beginning to end, going out surveying the land then coming back and drafting the plans... and coming up with the design solves problems."

However, it's not a very diverse industry. "When I graduated, it was me and one other black female in my class." Lowery became the first black, and female, engineer to be hired at WPC some twenty-three years ago and still finds herself the only black, and female, in the room. She's even been assumed to be the secretary in various meetings.

Last year, she hired two African American male, civil engineers. "They are the first," she said. "While in this seat, I will continue making sure opportunities open up for all, including African Americans, who are often excluded." She believes the industry has made improvements but believes companies must make a conscious effort in being more diverse.

The chance to give others an opportunity, and help prepare the next generation of engineers and STEM professionals, brings her great joy. She's served as the advisor for the National Society of Black Engineers (NSBE) high school chapter since 2006. Additionally, she's been a volunteer for the City of Cleveland and the Northeast Ohio Regional Sewer District's Student Technical Enrichment Program (STEP) for middle school students for twenty years.

Ramona attends Mt. Olive Missionary Baptist Church where she serves as a Trustee. There, she's also on the the youth ministry, side by side with her husband, Kevin O. Lowery, J.D. She's chair of the Scholarship Committee for the Black Professional Association Charitable Foundation (BPACF) as well. Being first-generation college student herself, mentoring this population is dear to Lowery.

She wants to be remembered for making a positive impact on another's person life.

Lowery enjoys traveling and reading. Being a wife and mom of Kayla and Kevin, travel these days consist of turning the AAU games to a family vacation, with Miami, Florida being the most recent.

Glen Shumate

Executive Vice President
Construction Employers Association

Photo by Eric Benson

INTERESTING PERSONALITIES

Glen Shumate

Executive Vice President
Construction Employers Association

Building human capital

By Felicia C. Haney

You can't put the words "inclusion" and "building Cleveland" in the same breath without including the name "Glen Shumate".

For the past decade, Shumate has served as the Executive Vice President of the Construction Employers Association (CEA) where he oversees education, marketing, inclusion, workforce programs and public affairs. He came in as a consultant to help build a diversity program for the association and the entire industry.

"We want to see the minority workforce and minority businesses, working and thriving," Shumate says.

Shumate's path to the construction industry has been indirect but not without inherent logic. The Sandusky native attended the University of Toledo, was president of both the University College and Black Student Union, finishing with a Bachelor of Science degree in Marketing Logistics.

As he began his career, he discovered his talent for finding solutions to success by looking at problems creatively. The talent allowed him to navigate a series of positions across industries. His resume includes service in professional sports as community relations director for the Cleveland Indians, in tourism with Cedar Point and then as vice president of the Greater Cleveland Convention and Visitors Bureau (Destination Cleveland), and even into publishing as president of the Call & Post newspaper.

Shumate's work at CEA enables him to synthesize his commitment to community and public service, his passion for youth and mentorship, his out-of-the-box approach to problem-solving, and his understanding of economics and community development. Construction has become his passion. Not just in the brick-by-brick form that erects edifices, but the step-by-step process that builds people and organizations.

"The city can only be successful if there are people making it successful," said Shumate. "If we can build a workforce where people are thriving, making more than a living wage with benefits and retirement options... That's rewarding for me, helping others."

Shumate works with construction executives, property owners, labor union chiefs, educators, and public officials to maximize opportunities for black and brown workers, women, and others who have been historically excluded from the industry, ensuring the broadest possible participation in every aspect of the business.

Shumate also serves as executive director of Cleveland's ACE Mentor Program, currently operating in 12 area high schools to enlighten 200 students to the principles of architecture, construction and engineering. ACE Cleveland has awarded nearly $950,000 in scholarships in the past 10 years.

Shumate's secret sauce to success is simple: Education. Exposure. Experience. He employs it as his personal and professional mantra. It can best be seen in the work he is constantly doing with young people, whether they are students, apprentices, or aspiring scholars and entrepreneurs. If you noticed a woman or person of color as well as minority and disadvantaged business working on Opportunity Corridor, the Cleveland Flats East Bank Project, or the Inner Belt Bridge, chances are their path to that point was smoothed and supported by Shumate. "It's serving, developing, helping," he says when asked why his work is so important.

"I believe that you should enjoy what you do, like the people you work with and be paid reasonably well," he said. "You can be paid well and hate what you do or love what you do and not be paid enough money. For me, it's looking at how do I balance that? I'm fortunate that I have been in positions to be able to see the growth in building Cleveland and see growth in individuals and businesses knowing that I'm contributing to that success."

Adrienne C. Trimble
President & CEO
The National Minority Supplier Development
Council, Inc.

Adrienne C. Trimble

President & CEO
The National Minority Supplier Development
Council, Inc.

Adrienne Trimble is the newly appointed President and CEO of the National Minority Supplier Development Council (NMSDC). She is honored to be taking on the leadership role with NMSDC and looks forward to ensuring the organization and stakeholders remain positioned for sustainable growth and success.

Adrienne Trimble was General Manager, Diversity & Inclusion at Toyota Motor North America, responsible for leading and executing diversity & inclusion strategies and initiatives across Toyota's North American operations.

Adrienne Trimble's appointment marks a unique, significant milestone in NMSDC's long and close relationship with Toyota. Ms. Trimble led Toyota's Supplier Diversity initiative from 2005 – 2012. In this role, she directed the company's processes for developing productive supplier relationships with diverse businesses across the country. Toyota received numerous accolades under Ms. Trimble's direction, including Corporation of the Year by the National Minority Supplier Development Council (NMSDC) in 2011 as well as Corporation of the Year honors from the organization's affiliates in Arkansas (2012), Michigan (2009 and 2010), South Central Ohio (2010 and 2011), Southwest Texas (2007-11) and Tri-State KY/IN/WV (2007-11).

Her board and committee leadership positions have included NMSDC and several of its regional Councils, as well as Executive Committee roles for the Billion Dollar Roundtable. She was named Advocate of the Year by the Southwest Minority Supplier Development Council in 2012. In recognition of her efforts to advance economic development for diverse suppliers, Rev. Jesse

Jackson, Founder, and CEO of Rainbow PUSH presented Ms. Trimble with their Corporate Leader Award and Women in Leadership Award in 2011. Ms. Trimble has previous Human Resources leadership experience in financial services, healthcare and media industries.

A graduate of Wilberforce University, Ms. Trimble earned her Bachelors of Science degree in Organization Management. She was appointed to the Board of Trustees for her alma mater in 2014.

Ms. Trimble and her husband, Jamiel, reside in McKinney, Texas.

About NMSDC

The NMSDC advances business opportunities for certified minority business enterprises (MBEs) and connects them to corporate members. One of the country's leading corporate membership organizations, NMSDC was chartered in 1972 to provide increased procurement and business opportunities for minority businesses of all sizes. The NMSDC network includes a National Office in New York and 23 affiliate regional councils across the country. The network also includes five international partner organizations located in the United Kingdom, Canada, Australia, China and South Africa.

To meet the growing need for supplier diversity, NMSDC matches its more than 12,000 certified minority-owned businesses to our network of more than 1,750 corporate members who wish to purchase their products, services and solutions. NMSDC, a unique and specialized player in the field of minority business enterprise, is proud of its unwavering commitment to advance Asian, Black, Hispanic and Native American suppliers in a globalized corporate supply chain. For more information, visit www.NMSDC.org.

Cleveland Clinic

A LEADER IN REDUCING HEALTH DISPARITIES

Cleveland Clinic is dedicated to working to eradicate the health disparities that disproportionately afflict people of color.

Consider: African American men are twice as likely to die from prostate, colorectal, lung, pancreatic and breast cancer as well as diabetes, hypertension, heart disease, stroke, kidney disease, HIV, Hepatitis C, and liver disease. Similarly, Hispanic men are more likely to die from diabetes and diabetes-related kidney failure.

Health disparities exist from lack of access to quality health care, deficiencies in health literacy, hereditary and genetic predisposition, lack of diversity in the health care workforce, and other social determinants of health including poverty, hunger, and food deserts.

To improve health outcomes in communities of color, Cleveland Clinic has established clinical, research, and educational programs, including the Cleveland Clinic Minority Men's Health Fair and Minority Men's Health Center led by Charles Modlin, MD and Gordon Iheme, MD.

Empowering men to be proactive about their health

The Minority Men's Health Center provides screenings, primary care and referrals at three Cleveland locations. The seedlings for the center began in the late 1990s, when Dr. Modlin began visiting community centers and churches, talking to men about the importance of screenings to detect health problems before symptoms occurred. "Some men just weren't educated about preventive care. Others avoided it because of generational distrust of the healthcare system," Dr. Modlin says. He realized that minority men needed a "friendly portal of entry" to access preventive care.

In 2003, Dr. Modlin founded the Cleveland Clinic Minority Men's Health Fair during which Cleveland Clinic specialists and caregivers began volunteering to provide free screenings and services. Since then, more than 35,000 men have received health screenings.

Serving an underserved population

The Minority Men's Health Fair gave rise to the Minority Men's Health Center and has led to other health equity focused initiatives at the Cleveland Clinic, such as:

> Dr. Margaret McKenzie champions leadership programing at South Pointe Hospital;
> Dr. Linda Bradley developed Universal Sisters, a program to address disparities in women of color;
> Dr. Gwendolyn Lynch leads the the Neurological Institute's Minority Stroke Clinic
> Andre Lessears, Dr. Todd Breaux, Dr. Leonor Osorio, Janice Gonzales, Tiffany Guttierez lead CCHS Regional Minority Men's Health Fair and Hispanic Health Equity Initiatives
> Additional programs under development in the Heart & Vascular, Digestive Disease & Surgery, Dermatology, Orthopedics & Rheumatology and Respiratory Institutes

Throughout Who's Who in Black Cleveland, you'll find biographies of the dedicated Cleveland Clinic providers who are leading these and other initiatives to serve communities of color and motivate consumers to be proactive about health. Programs such as the Minority Men's Health Fair help send the lifesaving message: "Preventive healthcare starts with you," Dr. Modlin says.

Save the Date: Minority Men's Health Fair, Thursday, April 23rd, 2020

Charles Modlin, MD

CLEVELAND CLINIC MINORITY MEN'S HEALTH FAIR

BY THE NUMBERS

2,000
Attendees at our recent 4 simultaneously occurring Minority Men's Health Fairs, which are open to all regardless of race or ethnicity or any demographic.

12,000
Health screenings they collectively received

1,000
Number of screenings — for chronic kidney disease, hepatitis C, prostate cancer, oral cancer and other conditions — reporting abnormalities.

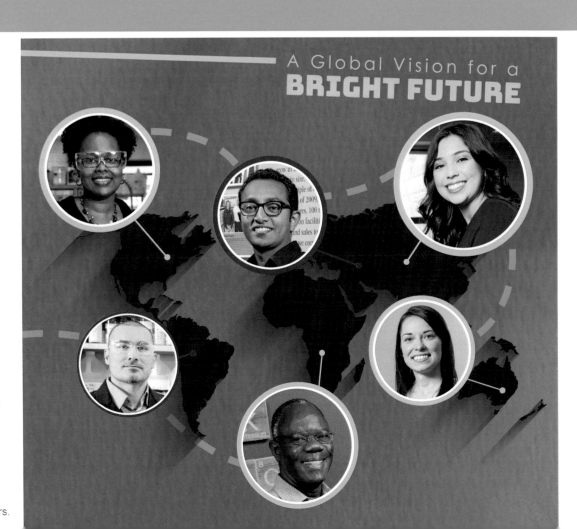

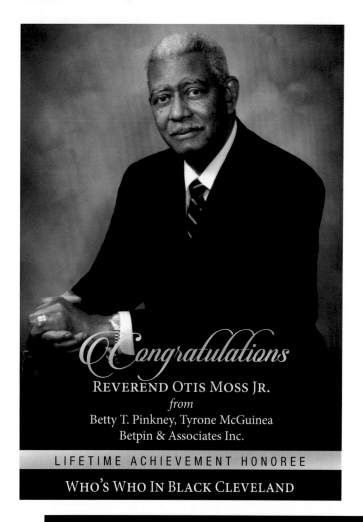

Congratulations

REVEREND OTIS MOSS JR.
from
Betty T. Pinkney, Tyrone McGuinea
Betpin & Associates Inc.

LIFETIME ACHIEVEMENT HONOREE

WHO'S WHO IN BLACK CLEVELAND

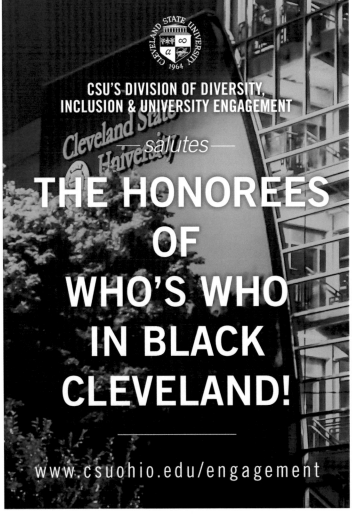

MOST INFLUENTIAL

Measuring influence is a challenging feat, but this section features the dynamic people who are moving and shaking Cleveland. Though their titles and responsibilities vary, these individuals are transforming the city into greatness.

Fletcher Berger
Mayor
Safety Director
City of Bedford Heights

The Hon. Kevin L. Bishop
Cleveland City Council
Ward 2

Fletcher Berger is serving in his third term as the first African-American Mayor of the City of Bedford Heights. Under his leadership, in light of diminished revenues, he reduced the city's payroll by $2 million over the last eight years, all while balancing the city's budget and maintaining a high-level of safety and services for Bedford Heights residents. He most recently oversaw the completion of a $3 million dollar, debt free, state-of-the-art 9-1-1 regional fire and police dispatch center located in the Bedford Heights Municipal Building. Prior to becoming Mayor, he served 10 years on City Council. Fletcher currently serves as a Democratic precinct committeeman and trustee for the city's Democratic Club and executive precinct member of the Cuyahoga County Democrats.

He is the President of the Southeast Communications Center's Council of Governments. Fletcher is a member of the National Black Caucus of Elected Officials and the National League of Cities. He's a U.S. Army Vietnam Veteran and a 33rd Degree Mason. He is the husband of Melva and father to Stacy.

Councilman Kevin L. Bishop represents Cleveland's Ward 2 which includes Mt. Pleasant, Union-Miles and Mill Creek Fall Neighborhoods. He was elected November 2017 to serve a four-year term.

Bishop serves on four council committees: Development Planning & Sustainability; Municipal Services & Properties; Transportation and Utilities.

Bishop grew up in Cleveland. His employment at the Buckeye Area Corp. and at Nestle, where he also served as a board member of Nestle's Credit Union, allowed him to become familiar with local government, the need and benefit of recreational opportunities, fiduciary responsibility and organizational compliance.

As a member of Cleveland City Council, he commits to working with the community and the council to ensure Ward 2 gets its fair share of resources. He intends to increase the economic development in Ward 2. Bishop understands firsthand the challenges and rewards of being an entrepreneur.

Bishop graduated from Chanel High School and while working a full-time job obtained a bachelor's degree in business administration from Cleveland State University.

Kevin is married to Kathryn and father to one son, Kevin II.

Lon'Cherie D. Billingsley
Assistant Prosecuting Attorney
Cuyahoga County Prosecutor's Office

The Hon. Annette McMillian Blackwell
Mayor
Maple Heights

Lon'Cherie' Billingsley is an Assistant Prosecuting Attorney in the Cuyahoga County Prosecutor's Office. She is a member of the Cleveland Metropolitan Bar Association, the Ohio Bar Association, The Young Scholars Alumni Society, and the National Bar Association. She is also a member of the Consumer Affairs Advisory Board for the City of Cleveland.

She earned a Juris Doctor from Cleveland-Marshall College of Law in 2012. She was also Law Clerk for Cleveland Municipal Court, Towards Employment, and the Spanish American Committee.

She earned a Bachelor of Arts in three years from The Ohio State University and is a 2002 alumnus of John F. Kennedy High School. She also studied abroad while in high school as a People to People Student Ambassador.

Currently, she is vice-president of the Norman S. Minor Bar Association and vice-president of the Max 8 Legacy Group, Inc.

Billingsley lives on the east side of Cleveland in the Lee-Tarkington area with her 9-year-old daughter. She has coached basketball for the youth basketball league at Earle B. Turner Recreation Center and attends The Word Church.

Annette McMillian Blackwell and her family moved to Cleveland in 1964 from Selma, AL. Mrs. Blackwell is a 53-year old wife, mother, and grandmother. She has lived in Maple Heights for 19 years, but grew on up on the northeast side of Cleveland in the Glenville neighborhood, where she still attends church and serves alongside her husband, Alonzo Blackwell, a Deacon, as a Deaconess.

Mrs. Blackwell is a very successful 35-year business professional who has worked at Keybank, as an Executive Assistant to the Vice Presidents of Installment Lending; University Hospitals, Administrative Coordinator to the President and Chief Medical Officer, Primary Care Physician Practices, and 16 years as a Senior Commercial Property Tax Analyst, at Deloitte & Touche and Ryan Global Tax Services.

Mrs. Blackwell and her husband are also local business owners in Maple Heights.

She completed her business education at Indiana Wesleyan University and attends Ursuline College, studying public relations. On January 6, 2016 she was sworn in as the City of Maple Heights 16th Mayor, and the first African-American female in the City's 100-year history.

Patricia J. Britt
Clerk of Council
Cleveland City Council

Karen K. Butler
Chief Operating Officer
NEON

Patricia J. Britt was appointed, unanimously, as City Clerk, Clerk of Council on January 14, 2008, by the Cleveland City Council.

As Clerk of Council, Britt is the chief administrative officer of the Cleveland City Council. Her duties include supervising the recording and retention of all official reports, communications and transcripts delivered to Council, and the certification of all legislation. Britt is also responsible for overseeing Council's staff and working with the 17 council members and their executive assistants.

From 1995 to 2008, Britt was a council member representing Ward 6. She concentrated on stabilizing the assets in the ward and bringing in new economic opportunities. During Britt's tenure a 14-acre brown field in Ward 6 was transformed into the Cuyahoga County Juvenile Court and Detention Center, a new MetroHealth Clinic was built at the Buckeye Shopping Center and Tony Brush Park in Little Italy was restored.

Britt has a master's degree in social work from Howard University, a certificate in state and local government from Harvard University's Kennedy School of Government, and is a certified master municipal clerk. Britt serves on committees for the National League of Cities.

Karen K. Butler is the Chief Operating Officer of Northeast Ohio Neighborhood Health Services, Inc. (NEON), a nonprofit healthcare organization with seven locations throughout Greater Cleveland.

Karen previously served as the Director of the Cleveland Department of Public Health and the Commissioner of Health for the City of Cleveland under the leadership of Mayor Frank G. Jackson.

Karen has received numerous honors and awards from local, state and national organizations for her tireless dedication and commitment to improving the health and well-being of those in greatest need.

Karen earned a Master of Business Administration from Case Western Reserve's Weatherhead School of Management, a master's degree in Health Care Administration from the University of Cincinnati and a bachelor's degree from Case Western Reserve University in Cleveland, Ohio. She is involved in numerous civic and professional organizations and has traveled to the White House to present before President Obama's Domestic Policy Council.

The Hon. Pinkey S. Carr
Judge
Cleveland Municipal Court
The Justice Center

The Hon. Stephana Childs-Caviness
City Council
Ward 1

Judge Pinkey S. Carr was elected to the Cleveland Municipal Court bench on November 8, 2011. She is a Cleveland native who graduated from John F. Kennedy High School and Baldwin-Wallace College, where she earned a Bachelor of Arts degree in political science in 1987, with a double minor in business administration and communications.

During her 18-year legal career, she sought justice as a prosecuting attorney for the City of Cleveland and Cuyahoga County for 13 years. While employed as an assistant prosecuting attorney for the Cuyahoga County Prosecutor's Office, Carr spent seven of her nine years working in the elite Major Trial Unit where she prosecuted murder and rape cases, including the Anthony Sowell serial murder case, which received international attention. She won a conviction in what is considered the highest-profile criminal case in Cuyahoga County's history. Carr was also deputized as a special assistant United States attorney for the federal prosecution of Anton Lewis who was found guilty of igniting one of the deadliest fires in the history of Cleveland, claiming the lives of nine victims.

Councilwoman Stephana Childs-Caviness proudly represents Ward 1 in the City of Euclid. She chairs the Community Engagement Committee and sits on the following Committees: Executive & Finance; Housing; City Planning & Commercial Development; and Public Service. Stephana is a Commissioner on the Recreation Commission.

Stephana is on the Cuyahoga County Central Committee; the Executive Committee of the Democratic Party; and is the President of the Euclid Democratic Club. Her community involvements include the N.A.A.C.P., the S.C.L.C., The Black Women's P.A.C., and the Cuyahoga Democratic Women's Caucus. She is a Deaconess at the Greater Abyssinia Baptist Church where the Rev. Dr. Caviness is the Pastor and the Rev. T. J. Caviness, Sr. is the Co-Pastor.

Stephana matriculated at Case Western Reserve University in the area of Communication. She is employed by Beech Brook as a Family Life Health Educator.

Stephana's greatest achievement are her children: Theophilus, Jr. (Denise); Stephen (Daniella), and Theana. She is an 18 yr. Breast Cancer Survivor and is presently battling Stage 4 Metastatic Breast Cancer. Stephana's strength and energy come from her FAITH, FAMILY & COMMUNITY.

Gregory F. Clifford
Chief Magistrate
Cleveland Municipal Court

The Hon. Cassandra Collier-Williams
Common Pleas Judge
Court of Common Pleas
Cuyahoga County

Gregory F. Clifford, Esq. is the Chief Magistrate of Cleveland Municipal Court. He serves as Immediate past president of the Ohio Association of Magistrates and vice president of the Cleveland-Marshall Law Alumni Association

Clifford obtained a Bachelor of Science in Education from Ohio University and a juris doctorate from Cleveland-Marshall College of Law.

As chairman emeritus for 100 Black Men of Greater Cleveland, Inc., Clifford is a dedicated mentor and role model for youth and young adults. An active member of St. Aloysius Catholic Church, Clifford has held numerous leadership positions in civic and non-profit organizations, including: Norman S. Minor Bar Association, Cuyahoga County Bar Association, Glenville Alumni Association, Catholic Charities, NAACP, East Cleveland Public Library and the Substance Abuse Initiative of Greater Cleveland.

Clifford, a thirty-third degree Prince Hall Mason, has been honored with the Distinguished Alumni Award for Civic Involvement from Cleveland State University, the Archbishop James P. Lyke African American Male Image Award from the Knights of St. Peter Claver, trustee of Achievement Award from Ohio Library Council, and the Norman S. Minor Trailblazer Award.

He is married and has two adult children.

Judge Cassandra Collier-Williams is a judge on the Cuyahoga County Court of Common Pleas. Judge Collier-Williams presides over large civil matters and felony criminal matters. She is one of four judges with a commercial law docket. She serves the people in numerous ways including as commissioner with the Lawyers' Fund for Client Protection. Judge Collier-Williams has received numerous awards including the Alumni of Distinction Award from Springfield Public Schools and being named one of Cleveland's Business Notable Women in Law by Crain's Cleveland Magazine. Judge Collier-Williams is a member of the National Conference of Negro Women, William K. Thomas American Inn of Court, National Bar Association Judicial Council, Ohio State Bar Association, Cleveland Metropolitan Bar Association, Life Member of Miami University Alumni Association, and Life Member of the Cleveland Marshall College of Law Alumni Association. She is the fourth African American female to be elected to the Cuyahoga County Court of Common Pleas, General Division. She proudly dispenses justice to all of Cuyahoga County.

Veronica Cook-Euell
Supplier Diversity/Program Manager
Kent State University
Founder
Euell Consulting Group, LLC.

Veronica Cook-Euell has over 14 years of experience in diversity and inclusion. She's received the Women of Power Award from the Akron Urban League, the Ohio Minority Supplier Development Council "Advocate of the Year Award" and the Minority Business Advocacy Award from Black Pages Ohio. Veronica also received the coveted President's Excellence Award from Dr. Lefton, president of KSU for her outstanding achievements and performance in her role as Supplier Diversity Program Manager. In 2014, Veronica also led KSU in receiving the "Best-In-Class for Supplier Diversity" by the Commission on Economic Inclusion.

Prior to coming to Kent State University, she helped build the Partnership for the Minority Business Accelerator. Veronica is also a serial entrepreneur.

Veronica received her Executive M.B.A. from Kent State University 2015, M. A. Degree in Psychology specializing in Diversity Management from Cleveland State University and a third Master's Degree from KSU in Special Education with specialization in American Sign Language to English Interpreting.

Veronica is married to Eddie and has two amazing sons, Willie and Jordan, a precious daughter-in-law, Dioswol and a new adorable granddaughter, Katlea Veronica Pearl!

Marcella Boyd Cox
Chief Marketing Officer
E. F. Boyd & Son Funeral Home and Crematory

Marcella Boyd Cox is the Chief Marketing Officer for the E. F. Boyd & Son Funeral Home and Crematory. She is the daughter of the late William and Mary Boyd and sister to William F. "Pepper" Boyd and Marina Grant.

Marcella grew up in the Glenville neighborhood and attended Baldwin Wallace College and Cleveland State University. She became a licensed funeral director in 1988 and has worked in her family business for more than 30 years.

She considers her work as a ministry helping grieving families cope with loss and the adjustment to the most traumatic experience in their lives.

As the CMO, Marcella develops public service events and marketing campaigns for the funeral home and was the first locally to forge new ground by promoting the funeral home through billboards and television ads. In 2015, Marcella orchestrated a citywide community celebration in commemoration of the 110th Anniversary of E.F. Boyd and Son Funeral Home and Crematory.

Marcella is strongly involved as a community volunteer working with her alma mater, Lutheran High School East Alumni Association as Financial Secretary and formerly Treasurer, 1st VP Greater Cleveland Chapter of Top Ladies of Distinction, member of the National Council of Negro Women, Cuyahoga County Section, where she served as Treasurer, Board Member Cleveland MOTTEP and the Warrensville YMCA.

Vicki Dansby
Co-founder
Imagine That

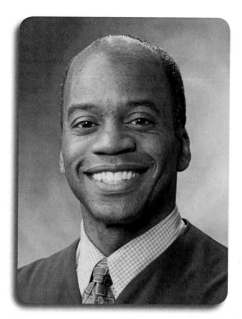

The Honorable William L. Dawson
Judge
The East Cleveland Municipal Court

Vicki Dansby, Co-Founder and EVP of Marketing, Projects & Events, of Imagine That .

Entertainment & Event Management. Prior to forming Imagine That, Vicki worked with WJW FOX 8 TV until she was recruited by the NFL Cleveland Browns Trust.

Imagine That has produced major events all over the globe. They have also consulted with and provided public relations for such celebrities as former President of South Africa the late Nelson Mandela, former Heavyweight Champion of the World the late Ken Norton, Sr., the late Bobby Womack, the late Gerald Levert and the legendary Jim Brown.

Vicki is a member of the Board of Directors of the United Black Fund of Greater Cleveland where she serves on the Grants Allocation and Development Committees and serves as the Marketing and Events chair. She's also a member of the Board of Directors of the Warrensville Heights YMCA and Leading Ladies, Inc.
She is the recipient of numerous awards.

Vicki is a graduate of the Institute of Computer Management and the University of Manheim. She and her family currently reside in Euclid, Ohio.

Judge William L. Dawson is a yoga teacher, author, motivational speaker and the administrative and presiding judge of East Cleveland Municipal Court. Prior to becoming a judge, his criminal defense practice included cases in Ohio's Municipal and State Courts, Ohio Supreme Court, United States District Court for the Northern and Southern District of Ohio and United States Court of Appeals in the Sixth Circuit. As an attorney, he handled cases ranging from traffic violations to murder. Judge Dawson has authored three books, The Legal Matrix, How the System is Controlling Your Life and its companion workbook, 99 Problems. How Your Failures, Flops & Flaws Can Lead to Your Greatness and The Cycle Breaker. Judge Dawson creates workbooks, educational manuals and programs courts, organizations and high schools. Judge Dawson created The Dawson Leadership Institute to develop and train leaders. He founded the Annie L. Dawson Foundation which provides mentoring and scholarships for college bound students. He is married to Elsie, and father to daughter, Aria, and son, William II.

Christine Fowler-Mack
Chief Portfolio Officer
Cleveland Metropolitan School District

Marcia L. Fudge
Congresswoman
Eleventh Congressional District of Ohio

Christine Fowler-Mack is the chief portfolio officer of the Cleveland Metropolitan School District. Christine serves more than 39,000 students within 106 school programs in ways that apply the best practices she has learned and taught throughout her career. The student population she serves, comprises the highest number of children of poverty in the nation, with 65% African American, 16% Hispanic, 16% Caucasian, and 3% other populations. Twenty-two percent are identified as students with disabilities. Christine was challenged to devise ways to engage the Greater Cleveland community in a shared commitment to ensuring every child in Cleveland attends a high-quality school and every neighborhood has quality school choices. Christine is the most respected and sought out national leader and innovator in the Portfolio Schools network. A graduate of the first cohort of American Association of School Administrators, she is a member of Howard University's Urban Superintendent Program and Future Chief for Change. Christine resides in Cleveland Heights with husband, Officer Quintero Mack, and two children, Kyndall Joy and Kyle Jordan.

Congresswoman Marcia L. Fudge represents the Eleventh Congressional District of Ohio, a district that encompasses 32 communities in Northeast Ohio from Cleveland to Akron. First elected in 2008, she fights for all of her constituents and maintains a steady focus on creating jobs, promoting health, investing in a quality education for all children and strengthening Social Security and Medicare. The Congresswoman currently serves on the Agriculture, and the Education and the Workforce Committees in the United States House of Representatives.

A native of Shaker Heights, Congresswoman Fudge is former mayor of Warrensville Heights and former finance director for the Cuyahoga County Prosecutor's Office. She obtained her law degree from the Cleveland-Marshall College of Law at Cleveland State University and is a graduate of The Ohio State University. She is a past national president of the Delta Sigma Theta Sorority.

As a dedicated public servant, she begins each morning with a firm promise "to do the people's work." It is this philosophy that defines Congresswoman Fudge as a Member of substance and character who always keeps her promise.

The Hon. Phyllis Cleveland
Cleveland City Council
Ward 5

The Hon. Blaine A. Griffin
Cleveland City Council
Ward 6

Councilwoman Phyllis Cleveland was sworn into office in January, 2006, representing Ward 5 which includes the neighborhoods of Central, Kinsman, Midtown, North Broadway and part of downtown.

Councilwoman Cleveland, who serves as Majority Leader, works tirelessly on ridding the city of abandoned, dilapidated properties and developing affordable housing. And she has championed several improvement projects in neighborhoods throughout her ward, including the $330 million Opportunity Corridor, connecting I-490 at East 55th Street to University Circle.

Councilwoman Cleveland is chairperson of City Council's Workforce & Community Benefits Committee; vice chair of the Finance Committee and the Development, Planning & Sustainability Committee; and a member of the Health and Human Services Committee, the Mayor's Appointments Committee and the Rules Committee.

Councilwoman Cleveland is a graduate of East Technical High School and Case Western Reserve University where she earned an undergraduate degree in English and a graduate degree in law.

Prior to serving on Council, she worked as an Assistant Cuyahoga County Prosecutor and a magistrate in the Foreclosure Department of Cuyahoga County Common Pleas Court.

Ward 6 Councilman Blaine A. Griffin represents one of Cleveland's most diverse wards, encompassing the East Side neighborhoods of Fairfax, Larchmere, Little Italy, Woodland Hills, and parts of Buckeye-Shaker, University Circle, North Broadway, Slavic Village and Union-Miles.

Griffin is chairman of council's Health & Human Services Committee and sits on four other committees – Finance, Safety, Workforce & Community Benefits and Operations.

Before to serving on the council, Griffin had been executive director of the city's Community Relation's Board.

He is a member of Mount Sinai Ministries; F.B.I. Citizen's Academy; Malone University Advisory Board; Ecclesiastes #120 Lodge of the Free and Accepted Masons; and Bezaleel Consistory #15. Griffin is a graduate of the Cleveland State University Maxine Goodman Levine College of Urban Affairs Leadership Academy and the Cleveland Leadership Center's Leadership Cleveland; Class of 2014, as well as a German Marshall Memorial Fellow.

He and his wife of 20 years, Jeanette, and their three sons live in the Larchmere neighborhood of Ward 6. Griffin graduated from Malone College in Canton, Ohio, with a Bachelor of Arts degree in communications.

The Hon. Emanuella Groves
Judge
Cleveland Municipal Court

The Hon. Anthony Hairston
Cleveland City Council
Ward 10

Judge Emanuella Groves has served on the Cleveland Municipal Court since 2001. She firmly believes that judges have the power to impact and affect change in the lives of the people who come before them. Judge Groves was instrumental in the creation of several court programs that enhance the lives of its participants.

These programs address literacy, information on rights and responsibilities when encountering the police and curfew violations. Judge Groves is the mental health docket judge. She has been honored for her service by the National Alliance of Mental Health in Cleveland. Judge Groves serves on both local and national organizations. She is a graduate of Case Western Reserve University where she was appointed as an adjunct professor. Judge Grove is a member of Olivet Institutional Baptist Church and Delta Sigma Theta Greater Cleveland Alumnae Chapter. She is married to Attorney Greg Groves and they have two children.

Ward 10 Councilman Anthony Hairston was elected to City Council in November 2017 after serving as a member of the Cuyahoga County Council since 2014. He represents an area that includes South Collinwood, St Clair-Superior, Glenville, Euclid Park and Nottingham Village neighborhoods.

Hairston serves on five council committees – Development Planning & Sustainability; Municipal Services & Properties; Health; Utilities and Rules.

He is a long-time advocate of social service programs and a champion of military veterans and worked to ensure veterans can receive free identification cards through the county's Veterans Services Commission.

Hairston, a life-long resident of the Collinwood community, is active in the Democratic Party and the Cleveland branch of the NAACP. He represented Ohio as a delegate to the 2012 Democratic National Convention in Charlotte, North Carolina.

Hairston is a graduate of Collinwood High School and received a business degree from Cleveland State University. As a college student, he received local and national awards recognizing his educational growth and achievements.

Mayor Benjamin I. Holbert III
Mayor
Woodmere Village

Michael J. Houser
Councilmember
Cuyahoga County Council

Mayor Benjamin I. Holbert III took office of Woodmere Village on January 1, 2018. His platform includes Village beautification, community aesthetics, and economic development. He is pleased to be Mayor of Woodmere during the 75th Anniversary of the Village. His servant leadership began at Kent State University where he was elected to undergraduate student government, undergraduate district representative for Omega Psi Phi Fraternity, and as president (Basileus) of Zeta Omega graduate chapter in Cleveland. He earned his Bachelor of Arts from Kent State University. He embarked on a 25-year career in broadcasting as a television reporter and anchor. He worked for WKYC TV-NBC; WOIO-CBS; WUAB-TV; WVIZ-PBS, and WJMO-1490-AM, amassing four Emmy awards. In 2012, Mayor Holbert earned a Master of Business Administration from the University of Phoenix. He was inducted into the Delta Mu Delta International Honor Society recognizing academic excellence. Mayor Holbert was inducted into The History Makers, a national educational institution committed to preserving untold personal stories of well-known and unsung African Americans. He also owns SIDES to go! BBQ in Bedford.

Councilman Michael J. Houser's public service career has spanned from the local, state and national level.

Councilman Houser, who is a champion for Voting Rights, led the creation of a Countywide Civic and Voter engagement initiative and founded the Youth Summit entitled "Your Voice Matters" that teaches students to develop personal platforms and learn the importance of community involvement, as well as how, when and where to vote. Houser also worked to protect our most vulnerable population as a leader on the County's faith-based infant mortality reduction initiative in partnership with First Year Cleveland, though his work speaking at local correctional institutes. He created an event focused on at-risk teens called "Choices and Consequences" in collaboration with Men Who Wish to Change and Cuyahoga County Office of Reentry.

A proud Cleveland public school graduate, Houser earned a Master of Public Administration degree from Cleveland State University, Levin College of Urban Affairs and graduated with honors with a Bachelor of Arts degree from Kent State University.

Karrie D. Howard
Assistant United States Attorney
United States Attorney's Office,
Northern District of Ohio (USAO)

Stephanie Howse
State Representative
District 11
Ohio House of Representatives

Karrie D. Howard is an Assistant United States Attorney with the United States Attorney's Office, Northern District of Ohio (USAO). Prior to working for the USAO, Karrie worked as an Assistant Prosecuting Attorney for the Cuyahoga County Prosecutor's Office (2013-14) and an Assistant Prosecutor for the City of Cleveland (2007-13). He was also the first Parking Violations Hearing Examiner for the City of South Euclid (2012-13). In addition to being a career prosecutor, Karrie is also an Assistant Staff Judge Advocate in the Air Force Reserves with the rank of Captain.

Karrie earned his Bachelor of Science in Business Administration from DeVry University, shortly after he completed active duty service in the United States Marine Corp. Later, he earned a Juris Doctorate from Cleveland-Marshall College of Law, and is currently in pursuit of his dual Master's Degrees in Business Administration and Human Resource Management from the University of Maryland University College.

Karrie is a member of the Masonic Lodge of William T. Boyd, #79, and the Zeta Kappa Kappa Chapter of the Omega Psi Phi Fraternity, Inc.

State Representative Stephanie Howse serves in the Ohio House of Representatives representing House District 11. As a public servant, she is dedicated to connecting residents to career and entrepreneurship opportunities to break the cycle of generational poverty, enhancing access to early childhood education and STEM (science, technology, mathematics and engineering) education and providing support for caregivers delivering long-term care.

Representative Howse currently serves as the President of the Ohio Legislative Black Caucus and is the recipient of the 2016 National Institute for Civil Discourse Award for Civility in State Governance and a MyCom Youth Voice Award Winner for Civic Leadership.

She earned a B.S. in Civil (Environmental) Engineering from Florida A&M University and a M.A. in Environmental Studies from Cleveland State University. Stephanie lives by the quote "We have to improve life, not just for those who have the most skills and those who know how to manipulate the system. But also for and with those who often have so much to give but never get the opportunity" by Dorothy Height.

Dr. David L. Hunter
Pastor
Bright Star Missionary Baptist Church

The Hon. Frank G. Jackson
Mayor
City of Cleveland

Rev. Dr. David L. Hunter is the pastor of the Bright Star Missionary Baptist Church where he has served for 41 years. He works to not only serve his parishioners but to assist the community in general. Dr. Hunter is president of The Baptist Minister's Conference of Cleveland and Vicinity, where he is pastor to other pastors in the conference. His other affiliations include; NOAH, NAACP, Alpha Phi Alpha fraternity, SCLC and The Progressive National Baptist Convention.

Dr. Hunter has worked within the community by being a teacher in the East Cleveland School System and East Cleveland Board of Education member and president for seven years.

Dr. Hunter received a Bachelor of Science degree from Alcorn State University; Master of Education degree from Cleveland State University and Doctor of Theology from Master's International School of Divinity.

A native of Mississippi; husband of Mary Hunter and proud father of two sons, Cornell and Christopher.

Mayor Frank G. Jackson is the City of Cleveland's longest-serving mayor, currently in his historic fourth term.

Mayor Jackson focuses on ensuring ALL Clevelanders are provided with excellent services and opportunities for income equity and a strong quality of life. In 2016, he successfully led the voter-approved Issue 32 to strengthen services to citizens ranging from public works to youth programs to safety to public health, sustainability and more.

He is also committed to helping businesses – large and small – to succeed. During his tenure, Jackson has also worked to strengthen the city's reputation as a world-class destination, drawing national events like the 2016 Republican National Convention to Cleveland.

Jackson earned an associate's degree from Cuyahoga Community College and a bachelor's degree, master's degree, and a law degree from Cleveland State University. He's served as Assistant City Prosecutor in the Cleveland Municipal Court Clerk's Office, Cleveland's Ward 5 on Cleveland City Council and as President of Cleveland City Council.

Jackson is a life-long resident of the Central neighborhood, a Cleveland Metropolitan School District graduate and an Army veteran.

Alex Johnson, Ph.D.
President
Cuyahoga Community College

Donald J. Jolly II
Superintendent
Warrensville Heights City School District

Since becoming president in July 2013, Dr. Alex Johnson has promoted access, equity, success and completion for the nearly 60,000 credit and non-credit students who attend Tri-C's four campuses and other locations.

Johnson currently serves locally on the boards of the United Way of Greater Cleveland,
Northeast Ohio Council on Higher Education (NOCHE), Rock and Roll Hall of Fame and Museum, Ideastream, Playhouse Square, MAGNET, Team NEO and the Greater Cleveland Partnership as well as numerous national boards.

He is the recipient of awards and honors including The Frank G. Jackson Visionary Award, The Pittsburgh Business Times CEO of the Year, and the Simon Green Atkins Distinguished Alumnus Award from Winston-Salem State University.

Previously, Johnson served as president of the Community College of Allegheny County, president of the Pennsylvania Commission for Community Colleges, and chancellor of Delgado Community College in New Orleans and president of Tri-C's Metropolitan Campus.
He also serves on Governor's Advisory Commission on Postsecondary Education.

Johnson earned a doctorate from the Pennsylvania State University, a master's degree from Lehman College and a bachelor's degree from Winston-Salem State University, and two honorary degrees.

Donald J. Jolly II was appointed a superintendent of Warrensville Heights City School District in 2015. He previously served as Academic Superintendent in Cleveland Metropolitan School District (CMSD) where he responsible for the leadership and daily management of more than 6200 scholars who attended the STEAM/Career Network of schools.

A native of Warrensville Heights, Jolly is proud graduate of Warrensville Heights High School. He received his degree in Early Childhood Education from Morris Brown College, earned a Master's degree in Curriculum and Instruction from Cleveland State University and completed the Superintendent Licensure program at Ashland University. In addition, he has been a participant in the Harvard Public Education Leadership Project and The Urban Schools Human Resource Capital Academy. Prior to serving as Academic Superintendent, Jolly served as a teacher, assistant principal, and principal.

He is a member of Omega Psi Phi Fraternity and member of 100 Black Men Association. Jolly and his wife Larita are the proud parents of three children.

The Hon. Basheer Jones
Cleveland City Council
Ward 7

The Hon. Joe Jones
Ward 1
Cleveland City Council

Ward 7 Councilman Basheer Jones was elected in November 2017, becoming the city's first Muslim council representative. He represents an area which includes the historic Hough district, as well as the St. Clair-Superior, Midtown and Asia Town neighborhoods.

Jones serves on four council committees – Development Planning & Sustainability, Health, Safety and Workforce & Community Benefits.

Jones, 33, was born in Brooklyn, N.Y., and moved to Cleveland with his family when he was a child. He graduated Cum Laude in 2006 from Morehouse College in Atlanta, Ga., earning a degree in African-American studies.

Jones has been recognized nationally for his grass-roots activism relating to issues of social justice and empowering those who are left out of the American Dream. Councilman Jones is a member of the NAACP and Alpha Phi Alpha Fraternity. He has also been a guest correspondent on CNN, MSNBC, and CSPAN.

He also authored a book, entitled, "I'll Speak for Change." And Jones is the creator of the Be the Change Leadership Series.

Councilman Joe Jones is a lifelong resident of Cleveland's Ward 1. He graduated from Aviation High School where he was active as a student leader and became involved in local politics.

Jones attended Cuyahoga Community College and Cleveland State University, studying Business Administration and Political Science. As a young man, he actively participated in Democratic Party politics, working as a grassroots organizer for U.S. Congressman Louis Stokes and volunteering for various campaigns.

At age 27, he made his first successful bid for a seat on Cleveland City Council representing the city's Ward 1 community. During his first seven years in public office, Jones helped to secure more than $100 million in new development projects in Ward 1.

Jones returned to City Council in November 2017. He is honored to, once again, have the opportunity to represent Ward 1 which includes the neighborhoods of Lee-Harvard, Lee-Seville, Mount Pleasant and Union-Miles. Jones serves on four council committees – Safety, Transportation, Workforce & Community Benefits, and Municipal Services & Properties.

Jones is married to Judge Tonya Jones, and they have two children.

The Hon. Tonya R. Jones
Judge
Court of Common Pleas,
Division of Domestic Relations

Tonya R. Jones began her term at the Court of Common Pleas, Division of Domestic Relations on January 19, 2017. She is the first African American female to serve as a judge in this Court.

Jones graduated from Cleveland State University, receiving a Bachelor of Arts Degree in Social Work. She then graduated from Cleveland Marshall College of Law. Since that time, Jones has devoted her professional career to assisting families in crisis and serving vulnerable populations. From 2000 through 2014, she maintained a full-time private law practice concentrating in Family Law.

In 2014, she was appointed as Magistrate in the Cuyahoga County Juvenile Court where she presided over delinquency, child support and child custody cases.

She is a member of the Ohio Judicial Conference's Domestic Relations Law & Policy Committee, the Cleveland Metropolitan Bar Association and the Ohio Association of Domestic Relations Judges.

She is also a member of Delta Sigma Theta Sorority, Incorporated and the National Council of Negro Women.

Judge Jones and her husband, Councilman Joe Jones, reside in the city of Cleveland with their two children.

C. Randolph Keller Sr.
Chief Prosecuting Attorney
Assistant Law Director
City of Shaker Heights
Founder & Chief Executive Officer
The Pyramid Institute

C. Randolph Keller Sr. is the chief prosecuting attorney and an assistant law director for the City of Shaker Heights. He also is founder and chief executive officer of The Pyramid Institute, which provides mentoring and supplemental education to theoretically "at risk" youngsters.

Randy grew up in Cleveland's Collinwood neighborhood and attended Cleveland public schools through eighth grade. Academic scholarships from Western Reserve Academy and A Better Chance Inc. enabled him to enroll at Western Reserve Academy, a boarding school in Hudson, Ohio. He was accepted to Vassar College in New York with a full academic scholarship, where he played college basketball and graduated cum with bachelor's degrees in economics and Africana studies. He graduated from Case Western Reserve University School of Law.

Randy is Head Boys Freshman Basketball Coach at Gilmour Academy in Gates Mills, a Life Member of Alpha Phi Alpha Fraternity and an avid golfer. He also regularly writes on his blog www.the-family-meeting.com.

He resides in Cleveland Heights with wife Margaret E. Bernstein-Keller. Their two children, C. Randolph Keller Jr. and Alexandria Louise Keller, attend Xavier University in Cincinnati.

The Hon. Anita Laster Mays
Judge
Cleveland Municipal Court

Valarie J. McCall
Chief of Communications,
Government & International Affairs
City of Cleveland

The Honorable Anita Laster Mays was elected to the Cleveland Municipal Court in November of 2003 and re-elected to another six year term in 2009. In January of 2009, she began presiding over the Greater Cleveland Drug Court. In a given week, Mays hears 200-plus criminal cases on the general docket and oversees a civil docket where cases do not exceed a $15,000 award.

In 1986 Mays received a bachelor's degree in business administration from The Ohio State University. In 1992 she received a juris doctorate degree from Cleveland-Marshall College of Law.

Mays was named a 1986 Pace Setter, became an honored member of *Who's Who Worldwide,* and in 1996 was awarded as an Outstanding Alumnus of the Cleveland Public Schools. She is a member of Sigma Gamma Rho Sorority, Inc., The Black Women's Political Action Committee and Providence Missionary Baptist Church. She serves on the Specialized Docket Committee on the Ohio Supreme Court and previously served as president of the Northern Ohio Municipal Judges Association.

Recognizing children as the future, Mays often volunteers to assist the youth with tutoring, career days and mock trials.

Valarie J. McCall, Valarie J. McCall is the city of Cleveland's Chief of Communications, Government & International Affairs. McCall serves as Mayor Frank G. Jackson's primary liaison to local and state government, federal agencies and international organizations. She also oversees the administration's appointments to boards and commissions and helps implement the mayor's policies to promote regional growth. McCall also oversees the City of Cleveland's communications strategy and media relations. McCall is the mayor's primary representative to several national organizations, including the U.S. Conference of Mayors, National League of Cities and the National Black Caucus of Local and Elected Officials. She serves on the board of several Cleveland-based organizations including the Rock & Roll Hall of Fame and Museum, Destination Cleveland, Greater Cleveland Regional Transit Authority and was the city lead for the 2016 Republican National Convention Host Committee. She is also on the board of the Northeast Ohio Area wide Coordinating Agency and was its first African American female president. Before serving in the Jackson administration, McCall was Cleveland City Council's youngest City Clerk and Clerk of Council.

Dr. Andre' K Mickel
Chairman
Department of Endodontics
Director
Post-doctorate Residency Program

Russ Mitchell
Managing Editor and Lead Anchor
WKYC TV Channel 3 (NBC)

Dr. Andre' K Mickel is chairman of the Department of Endodontics and Director of the Post-doctorate Residency Program in Endodontics at CWRU School of Dental Medicine, where in 1996 he became the first African-American and the youngest director of an endodontic residency program in the world, and then became the first Board Certified Endodontist in the history of CWRU. He has trained endodontists from five continents and more African American endodontists than any other program worldwide.

His voluminous service includes being past president/chairman of the Board of Health Legacy Cleveland, the prestigious College of Diplomates of the American Board of Endodontics, and the Ohio Association of Endodontists. An internationally respected educator and researcher, having presented hundreds of papers, abstracts and presentations, Mickel is a past recipient of his specialty's' Dr. Osetek award given to the most outstanding young Endodontic educator in the world.

A follower of Christ Jesus, who's been blessed to be a doctor, Andre' has just completed his first Inspirational book on how to achieve victory over any adversity entitled: *It is PROOF TIME, There is Hope.*

Russ Mitchell joined the WKYC team in 2012 as managing editor of the evening news and lead anchor of the 6 p.m. and 11 p.m. broadcasts. Formerly, he anchored the CBS Evening News weekend editions and The Early Show on Saturday, and served as a national correspondent for CBS.

Born in St. Louis, Missouri, Mitchell begin his professional career KMBC in Kansas City. Larger markets and bigger stations soon followed, then a move to New York as the co-anchor of the overnight CBS News broadcast, Up to the Minute. During his lengthy career with CBS, he traveled extensively and covered many of the biggest news events of the time. He was on the anchor desk with Dan Rather in September 11, 2001 and reported from Ground Zero in the days that followed.

Mitchell has received many honors including multiple Emmy Awards. Perhaps not as well-known, but equally important to Mitchell is the 2007 Missouri Honor Medal he received from his alma mater, the University of Missouri School of Journalism. He returns there every summer to help with a journalism workshop for high school students, a workshop he attended in 1977.

Dr. Sabrina J. Ellis,
Executive Pastor
Pentecostal Church Of Christ

Pastor Mario Hauser
Student Ministry Pastor
Church on the Northcoast

Dr. Sabrina J. Ellis is the executive pastor of Pentecostal Church of Christ. Her ability to develop and organize programs and ministries has been beneficial to both the congregation and community. Dr. Ellis has led her church in outreach by feeding and clothing the homeless, providing financial literacy, and mental health information and resources while developing leadership training for ministry leaders. Dr. Ellis earned a Bachelor of Arts from Notre Dame College of Cleveland and both her Master of Divinity and Doctor of Ministry from Ashland Theological Seminary. Dr. Ellis has served as chaplain for the Western Reserve Section of the National Council of Negro Women and is a member of the Cleveland Chapter of Top Ladies of Distinction. She is an author, speaker and coach, and in 2016, she was invited to serve as a host on Total Christian Television (TCT), a network with over 70 million viewers worldwide. Her husband of 37 years is Bishop J. Delano Ellis II, senior pastor of Pentecostal Church of Christ.

Pastor Mario Hauser is a husband, father, pastor, entrepreneur and leader. He serves as the student ministry pastor at all four campuses of Church on the Northcoast. Mario leads weekly gatherings, nights of worship and retreats for youth ages 12-18. His humor, use of technology and transparency creates a safe space for teens to establish positive relationships with God and each other. Mario assists with preaching on Sunday mornings and visiting the sick. He has a bachelor's degree in business, and a master's degree in ministry. His leadership experience in ministry and the corporate sector led him to create Forward Momentum, a leadership consulting company. Through Forward Momentum, Mario provides ongoing leadership training and staff development for ministries and small businesses. Mario serves as the vice president of the Cleveland Chapter of K.I.N.G., a national organization aimed at helping men become better husbands, fathers and leaders. Married to his promise Courtney, together they have three children, Faith, Taylor and Josiah.

Sergeant Vincent Montague
President
The Black Shield Police Association

Lauren C. Moore
Judge
Cleveland Municipal Court
The Justice Center

Sergeant Vincent Montague is the current president of The Black Shield Police Association. His focus is on the recruitment and development of police officers from diverse backgrounds while ensuring the needs of the membership and Cleveland Police Department are addressed fair and equitably. With over 11 years of experience in the Cleveland Division of Police, Sargeant Vincent displays his passion for policing by engaging community and city leaders, as well as fellow officers in promoting service and excellence throughout Cleveland. Sergeant Montague obtained his Bachelor of Arts degree in Political Science from Tuskegee University, and master's degree in Public Administration from Walden University. He is a member of NOBLE, National Black Police Association (NBPA), Phi Alpha Alpha Honor Society, Kappa Alpha Psi Fraternity, Inc. and Ecclesiastes Lodge #120. In his spare time, Sargeant Vincent enjoys spending time with family including his wife and two sons.

Judge Lauren C. Moore recalls, "Education was always emphasized in growing up," who graduated with honors from Shaker Heights High School and then attended Spelman College where she received a degree in English. The lure of a family and law school scholarship brought her back home to Cleveland, where she attended Case Western Reserve University to earn a juris doctorate.

After passing the bar in 1987, Moore went to work for the Legal Aid Society as both a civil attorney and public defender. Nine years later, she decided to run for judge on the Cleveland Municipal Court. Unsuccessful in her first two attempts, she was asked to serve as chief prosecutor for Cleveland and then assistant Cuyahoga County prosecutor, until she was elected to the bench in 2003 after garnering 77 percent of the popular vote. She was reelected without opposition in 2009.

Moore is very involved in the community and has participated in several mentoring and tutoring programs for young people, including the Court's Mock Trial Program.

Andrea Nelson Moore, Esq.
Assistant Director of Law
Cuyahoga County Law Department

The Hon. Michael Nelson
Judge
Cleveland Municipal Court

Andrea Nelson Moore is a graduate of Cleveland Heights High School, holds a bachelor's degree in Psychology from Baldwin Wallace College, and a law degree from Cleveland Marshall College of Law.

Andrea is currently an Assistant Director of Law with the Cuyahoga County Law Department.

Andrea was a Deputy Inspector General with the Agency of the Inspector General. She also served as a Judicial Staff Attorney for the Cuyahoga County Common Pleas Court. Additionally, Andrea was an Assistant Prosecuting Attorney with the Cuyahoga County Prosecutor's Office.

Andrea volunteers as a mentor for eighth grade students in the Cleveland Municipal School District. She also routinely volunteers with the Legal Aid Society's Expungement Clinics, serves on Eliza Bryant Auxiliary Board II, and the United Black Fund Board of Directors. Andrea recently received the distinct honor of being recognized as the Black Woman Professional of the Year from the National Association of Negro Business and Professional Women.

Andrea resides in South Euclid with her husband and teenage daughter. She is a member of New Community Bible Fellowship Church.

Judge Michael Nelson was elected judge of the Cleveland Municipal Court in 2017. Prior to that, he served as president of the Cleveland Branch NAACP and was the founding president of the 100 Black Men of Greater Cleveland. Nelson is a graduate of Central State University (CSU) where he has the distinction of being the only alumnus to have served on the board of trustees, been elected president of the CSU National Alumni Association, served as president of the Cleveland Alumni Chapter, named Alumnus of the Year and has been inducted into the school's Achievement Hall of Fame. Judge Nelson who earned his law degree from Case Western Reserve University, has received national attention for his stance regarding the horrendous conditions in the Cuyahoga County jail. Married to the former Donna Kelso, he is the father of four children; Michael Jr., Nichole, Ebony and Rayne, grandfather of five and has one great-grandchild. Judge Nelson is an avid golfer and a member of the Kappa Alpha Psi Fraternity.

The Hon. Charles L. Patton, Jr.
Judge
Cleveland Municipal Court
The Justice Center

Dr. Henry Pettiegrew II
Chief Executive Officer
East Cleveland City School District

Charles L. Patton, Jr. was elected to the Cleveland Municipal Court bench in November of 2005, fulfilling a lifelong dream to become a judge. Influenced by the civil rights struggles in the sixties, Patton, a graduate of JFK High School, enrolled at Ohio University in Athens and pursued degrees in journalism and history (Afro-American). It was then on to law school at Howard University, at which time he worked as an administrative assistant to U.S. Senator John Glenn.

In 1982 Patton came back to Cleveland to work as an assistant city prosecutor, then staff attorney for the UAW/Ford-GM Legal Office in Lorain, Ohio and in 1989, he became senior staff counsel of the Cuyahoga Metropolitan Housing Authority. The same year, Patton decided to run for a seat on the Cleveland City Council and was elected to represent the people of Ward One.

Following his years on City Council, Patton was engaged in private practice, specializing in probate, domestic relations, and civil, criminal, utility and administrative law.

Dr. Henry Pettiegrew II is chief executive officer for East Cleveland City Schools. He has served as assistant superintendent for Maple Heights City Schools where he coordinated transformational, district-wide school improvement strategies, and served as an educational administrator with specific demonstrated success in organizational systems, curriculum development, and principal professional development. He has built a reputation for delivering actionable instructional leadership and offering robust training to building the capacities of both teacher and leaders. Dr. Pettiegrew gained momentum for his career beginning as a science teacher. He gained skills in data-driven instruction, formative and summative assessment, teacher-based team development, district and building level leadership. As a catalyst to change, he masterfully lays the foundation that invites all stakeholders to ultimately build and transform schools, districts, and entire learning organizations for the better. Dr. Pettiegrew earned his Doctor of Philosophy degree in Urban Education from Cleveland State University and has provided consulting and professional development for principals, school districts and private businesses through his business, The LEAD School.

Victoria Thrasher

Minister

Abyssinia Baptist Church

Dr. Robert F. Richardson Jr.

Neurologist

University Hospitals of Cleveland

Minister Victoria Thrasher is a woman of God, and the wife of Arnold Thrasher Sr. for 37 years. She is a mother of three adult children and grandmother of four granddaughters. She is a member of the Abyssinia Baptist Church where her father the Reverend Dr. Leo Pinkard Sr., is pastor. Victoria has been in ministry her entire life. She is a dynamic motivational speaker. After the tragic death of her brother, Leo Pinkard Jr. in 2017, Victoria suffered deep grief and depression. She became a certified grief counselor and birthed Leo's Legacy named after her father and deceased brother. The group serves homeless veterans and their families to provide them with practical tools to exist and thrive in society, Victoria is employed by the United States Department of the Treasury and is a member of the Diversity and Equal Employment Opportunity Advisory Committee. She serves as a mentor instructor and counselor professional for Messiah International Ministries under Apostle Phyllis Fosh-Carter. Her favorite scripture is Romans 8:28.

Dr. Robert F. Richardson Jr., is a staff neurologist at University Hospitals of Cleveland. He is an assistant clinical professor at Case Western Reserve University, and clinical associate professor at Ohio University. He is a medical graduate of Case Western Reserve University and graduate of Stanford University. Dr. Richardson is the former director of neurology at St. Vincent Charity Medical Center, and former director of neurology at South Pointe Hospital. He led successful efforts at St. Vincent and South Pointe for their national certifications and multiple recertifications from JCAHO as primary stroke centers. Dr. Richardson speaks on stroke and multiple sclerosis in Cleveland's African American community because he believes knowledge improves access to medical care. He is the president of the board of the Kym Sellers Foundation, a foundation providing education on multiple sclerosis. He is married to Dr. Martina T. Richardson and has a son, Robert III. He was born in Memphis, Tennessee, and has lived all over the country including in England and Germany.

Davida Russell
State President
CLUW/OAPSE/AFSCME Local 4

Tony F. Sias
President
Chief Executive Officer
Karamu House, Inc.

Davida Russell is state president of the Coalition of Labor Union Women, vice president of Ohio AFL-CIO, state executive board member and president of Northeast District of the Ohio Association of Public-School Employees, executive secretary-treasurer of the North Coast Labor Federation and trustee of North Shore Labor Federation. Davida represents more than 180,000 members across Ohio. She served on President Clinton's Women's Round Table of Greater Cleveland. Davida represented public employees in Sao Paulo, Brazil, received an award from the Ambassador of Italy, commission member of County Charter Review Commission, board member of Gateway Board of Greater Cleveland, and appointed by Mayor Frank Jackson. She is vice chair of the first historic Charter Review Commission, and Ohio Commission of DD Futures Study appointed by Governor Ted Strickland. Davida is author of *The Birth of a Union: The Legacy of Noridean McDonald*. She's featured on *America's Workforce Radio 1490*. Davida earned a bachelor's degree from George Meany National Labor College. She is married to Carl and they have two daughters, Domonique and Brittany.

Tony F. Sias is President and CEO of Karamu House, America's oldest African American theatre. Under his direction since 2015, Karamu produces professional Theatre, provides Arts Education and presents Community Programs for all people while honoring the African American experience.

Before his position at Karamu, Tony served in several progressive roles for the Cleveland Metropolitan School District (CMSD) including Director of Arts Education and Artistic Director of Cleveland School of the Arts.

Tony has received the Ohio House of Representatives Tribute for Excellent Leadership in CMSD's All-City Arts Program and the Certificate of Special Congressional Recognition for Contributions in Education and Cultural Arts. Featured in The New York Times and American Theatre Magazine, Tony served as a delegate from the U.S. Department of State in Istanbul, Turkey, representing the Council of International Programs in the Youth Arts for Peace Project.

Tony is a member of the National Board of The League of Historic Theatres. He earned a Bachelor of Science degree in dramatic art from Jackson State University and a Master of Fine Arts in acting from The Ohio University.

Cordell E. Stokes
Chairman
Chief Executive Officer
CLC Stokes Consulting Group

Dr. Rachel Talton
Chief Executive Officer
Synergy Marketing & Research Inc.

As chairman and CEO for CLC Stokes Consulting Group, Cordell E. Stokes helps clients develop a comprehensive plan to achieve their goals and objectives in business development, corporate expansion and governmental relations.

Cordell E. Stokes has over fifteen plus years of professional, executive experience in non-profit and private sector management; federal and state political consultation; small, medium and large national business development and corporate expansion experience; county and federal governmental management experience and local, state and federal lobbying experience. Under the appointment of former NASA administrator Daniel S. Goldin then completed under Sean O'Keefe, Stokes served two-terms with the National Aeronautics & Space Administration (NASA) Minority Business Resource Advisory Committee (MBRAC) and co-chaired the HBCU sub-committee. He also legislatively advocated on behalf of the Big "I"-The Independent.

Insurance Agents & Brokers of America (IIABA) as well as the National African-American Insurance Association (NAAIA) through Ways and Means and Financial Services Congressional committees. Stokes also worked as government affairs director for O.T.I. Metal Finishing Military and Aerospace Corporation in Phoenix, AZ.

Dr. Rachel Talton is CEO of the award-winning firm Synergy Marketing Strategy & Research, Inc. She is also CTO (Chief Transformation Officer) of Flourish Leadership, LLC and the Flourish Conference for Women in Leadership.

Talton serves on the Board of Directors and Executive Committee of Positively Cleveland, the Board of Directors of the Cuyahoga Community College Foundation, The Akron Community Foundation, and JumpStart Inc. She is a member of the Cleveland Bridge Builders Class of 2002, as well as the Leadership Cleveland Class of 2005.

Talton has numerous recognitions. She is also a proud member of the Links, Inc., and Delta Sigma Theta Sorority, Inc.

She is the author of two books, *Your Best Life: Your Journey to Flourish in Business and in Life* and *Flourish: Having it All Without Losing Yourself.*

Talton earned her Doctorate in Management from Case Western Reserve University's Weatherhead School of Management, an MBA with a concentration in Finance from Cleveland State University, as well as a BA in Psychology.

Her personal passions include international travel, community service, and public speaking.

Dr. Janice D. Taylor Heard
Dean of Academic Affairs
Cuyahoga Community College

Felton Thomas, Jr.
Executive Director
Cleveland Public Library

Dr. Janice D. Taylor Heard has worked in higher education for 30 years. During this time, she has served in various administrative and leadership roles at Cuyahoga Community College, the University of Akron, Pennsylvania State University, University of Georgia and University of Tennessee. In 2016, served as interim president at the Western Campus. Currently Dr. Taylor Heard serves as Dean of Academic Affairs. She earned a BA in Psychology and MEd in Higher Education Administration from Kent State University. She earned her PhD in Counseling and Human Development Services from The University of Georgia. She is a graduate of the HERS Institute at Bryn Mawr College and the League of Innovation's, Executive Leadership Institute.

Dr. Taylor Heard has shared her talents with the Northeast Ohio community as a volunteer grant writer, fundraiser, board member, organizer and supporter of the arts and cultural preservation. Awards and recognitions include the Inspire Award 2016 (The McGregor Foundation), American College Personnel Association Emerging Scholar and the YWCA Women of Excellence Award. Lastly, Dr. Taylor Heard serves on the Urban League of Greater Cleveland board and is a member of Olivet Institutional Baptist Church, Alpha Kappa Alpha Sorority, Inc. and Jack and Jill of American.

Since 2009, Felton Thomas Jr. has furthered the Library's mission by launching initiatives aimed at addressing community needs in technology, education, and economic development. Under his leadership, the Library maintained its 5-star rating from the Library Journal Index of Public Library Service and was named a Top Innovator by the Urban Libraries Council.

He has been named a Mover and Shaker by the Library Journal and acting as a fellow in the Urban Library Council's Executive Leadership Institute. He served as President of the Public Library Association (PLA) in 2016 and currently serves on the PLA Board of Directors as Past President. He is also a member of the Aspen Institute Task Force on Learning and the Internet. He serves as board president of the Greater Cleveland Food Bank and as a Trustee on the boards of Sisters of Charity Foundation, University Circle Inc., United Black Fund of Greater Cleveland, and United Way of Greater Cleveland. He holds a Master of Library and Information Science from the University of Hawaii.

Thomas lives in Shaker Heights with his wife and two daughters and is an accomplished musician.

MOST INFLUENTIAL

Kim Thomas
President
Christopher Amira Studio and Academy

The Hon. Gigi Traore
Councilwoman At-Large
Village of Newburgh Heights

Kim Thomas is the owner of Christopher Amira Studio. She is co-founder of Change of Direction, a nonprofit organization that provides mentoring and emergency respite for youth in crisis. In 2018, Gov. John R. Kasich re-appointed Kim to the Ohio State Cosmetology and Barber Board serving as vice chair. Kim is a well-respected businesswoman and political consultant. Loti Phi Lambda recognized her as "Businesswoman of the Year" in 2012. She was recognized by the city of Cleveland as a "Hometown Hero" in 2017. In 2018, Mayor Frank Jackson appointed Kim to the Cleveland/Cuyahoga County Workforce Development. Kim is currently the secretary and vice chair of the Cuyahoga County Democratic Party. She is a member of the National Congress of Black Women and a member of the Black Women Political Action Committee. She serves as the membership chair and treasurer for the Cuyahoga Democratic Women's Caucus. In 2018, David Pepper, Chairman of the Ohio Democratic Party, appointed her to the State Executive Committee.

Councilwoman Gigi Traore is the first African American to serve as a council member for the Village of Newburgh Heights. She serves on the finance committee, chairs the local Business & Commerce Development committee along with the Parks & Active Transportation Masterplan committee. Councilwoman Traore implemented a Library Access Initiative in Newburgh Heights. Additionally, she serves on the boards of the Volunteer Fire Fighters Dependents Fund, Northeast Ohio City Council Association [NOCCA] and served as a U.S. delegate to China. Professionally, Councilwoman Traore is a management consultant working with political independent expenditures, nonprofits and small business entities. She respectively holds a bachelor's and master's degree from Cleveland State University and Walden University; and is a presenter as well as author. The mother of two, serves her community in capacities such as convener of The Cuyahoga Black Caucus, Junior League of Greater Cleveland, National Council of Negro Women [NCNW], mentoring five young Black professionals and as a member of Antioch Baptist Church. Her life's motto is, "Leadership Begins with Service."

The Hon. Terrence Upchurch
State Representative
Ohio House of Representatives

The Hon. Sandra Williams
State Senator
Ohio Senate District 21

Terrence Upchurch recently served as a special assistant to Cleveland City Council. From his time working in city council, Upchurch has learned and developed a keen understanding of the nuances of government which he brings to the Statehouse. Upchurch understands the importance of forming relationships in Columbus, bipartisanship, and will create a platform to fight for working class families and help municipalities meet the basic needs of its people, including essential services like police and fire rescue. In District 10 and across Ohio, Upchurch wants to reverse the impact constituents have felt of a state legislature that continues to cut community resources. He vows to be a true and trusted ally in the Statehouse for his community. From rebuilding crumbling infrastructure, to ensuring students receive a quality education, to increasing Ohio's local government fund, Upchurch believes we can once again lead the nation in innovation and sustainability. Born and raised in the greater Collinwood and Glenville communities, Upchurch is a proud graduate of St. Peter Chanel High School. He earned a bachelor's degree in Political Science from Cleveland State University.

Senator Sandra Williams proudly represents Ohio's 21st Senate district, which includes sections of the City of Cleveland, Cleveland Heights, Bratenahl, Garfield Heights, Newburgh Heights, Shaker Heights and University Heights.

As a native of the Buckeye neighborhood in Cleveland and graduate of Cleveland Public Schools, she holds a bachelor's degree from Cleveland State University in Political Science with a minor in Criminal Justice, a master's degree in Criminal Justice Administration from Tiffin University and an Executive Master's in Business Administration from Cleveland State University. Williams is also the recipient of an Honorary Doctorate Degree from Tiffin University.

In her commitment to public service, she has held a myriad of positions—as a corrections officer, probation and parole officer, mediator for the State of Ohio, legislative aide and State Representative of the 11th House District. Williams also served our country as a member of the United States Army Reserve and was honorably discharged in 1995.

As the Ranking Minority Member of the Senate Ways and Means Committee and the Senate Public Utilities committee, her legislative work focuses on energy, criminal justice reform, education, workforce development and job creation.

Calvin D. Williams
Chief of Police
City of Cleveland

Dr. Renée T. Willis
Superintendent
Richmond Heights Local Schools

Calvin D. Williams is the City of Cleveland's 40th Chief of Police. Chief Williams was appointed to the Division of Police on February 24, 1986. In 1989, he was assigned to the SWAT Unit where he served for nine years. Williams was promoted to Sergeant in July 1997 and became the SWAT Unit Supervisor, a position he held for two years. Chief Williams has also served as the supervisor of both the Vice Unit in the Fourth District and the Fugitive Unit.

In 2005, Chief Williams became the Cleveland Police Liaison to the US Marshal's Fugitive Task Force and was promoted to Commander of the Third District in March of 2006. Then in September of 2011, he was promoted to Deputy Chief of Field Operations where he was responsible for the oversight, management and efficiency of the five Neighborhood Police Districts, the Bureau of Community Policing, the Bureau of Traffic and the Office of Special Events for the Division.

For the past nine years, Chief Williams has coached youth football, leading the Sims Raiders in the Cleveland Muny League. When he has free time, the Chief golfs, a sport he took up about four years ago.

Renée T. Willis, Ph.D. is close to finishing her fourth year as the superintendent of the Richmond Heights Schools. A native Clevelander, Renée has been committed to public education in this area her entire life. She has been an educator with Cleveland Heights-University Heights, CMSD, Cleveland State and Baldwin Wallace University. Her vision for the students, families and residents of Richmond Heights has been one that will finally be actualized. The residents passed an unprecedented bond levy this past November on its first attempt, to build a 21st Century Community Learning.

She has a Ph.D. in Urban Education from CSU, a Master's in Education Administration from BW, and a Bachelor of Science in Mathematics from Spelman College. She recently graduated from the National Urban Superintendents Academy and joins the ranks of those select few that have undergone the yearlong training.

Renée is a 33-year member of Delta Sigma Theta Sorority, Inc. and was most recently the President of the Delta Foundation here in Cleveland. She is the mother of one adult daughter, Cierra Imani, who resides in Atlanta.

FOCUS
CELEBRATE
PROMINENCE
RECOGNITION

CORPORATE BRASS

The section features the cream of the crop at Cleveland's most well known corporations. To be the best, these talented executives have made the strides and sacrifices to stay on top.

Tawwana Armstrong
President
Chief Executive Officer
Big Brothers Big Sisters of Greater Cleveland

Yolanda Y. Armstrong
President and Chief Executive Officer
Friendly Inn Settlement, Inc.
and Inclusion

Tawwana Armstrong is vice president and senior global business intelligence platform owner in Technology Data & Information Management at Jones Lang LaSalle. She provides leadership for the development and delivery of an innovative, robust global "self-service" business intelligence (BI) platform at Jones Lang LaSalle; delivering strategic guidance, BI strategies, governance, architectures and technologies that help put information to use in business processes and end user experiences. Her primary responsibilities include driving an analytics organization to deliver data, analytics, and digitally engaging solutions to drive consumer, customer, operational, and financial focused insights focused on top and bottom-line business value across the organization. Tawwana also has extensive knowledge in the areas of information technology, business development and project management. Her expertise is in identifying business opportunities, conceptualizing ideas into solutions, and utilizing technology to devise cost-effective solutions. She has a Master of Business Administration with a concentration in Marketing and Entrepreneurship from Case Western Reserve University, and a Bachelor of Arts in Business from Baldwin-Wallace College.

Yolanda Y. Armstrong, MSSA, LSW is president and CEO of Friendly Inn Settlement, Inc. She oversees the daily operation of a multi-service agency. Armstrong has received various awards including Mt. Zion of Oakwood Village Hero of Faith Award, The Women of Color Foundation Star Award, Omega Psi Phi Zeta Omega Chapter Community Leader Award, Non-Profit Executive of the Year from *SMART Business Magazine*, and The Centennial Alumni Award from The Jack, Joseph, and Morton Mandel School of Applied Social Sciences at Case Western Reserve University (CWRU). Armstrong is a proud member of Delta Sigma Theta Sorority, Inc. She serves as a board member on S.H.I.N.E., Mental Health Advocacy Coalition, and is president of CKY Consulting. Armstrong has a bachelor's degree from Ohio University and a master's degree from The Jack, Joseph, and Morton Mandel School of Applied Social Sciences at CWRU. She is the mother of two daughters, Camarie and Katelyn Howell. Armstrong's favorite inspirational quote is by Michelle Obama, "When they go low, we go high."

Marquetese Betts
Supervisor
Cuyahoga County Department of Children
and Family Services

Dr. Tami Bolder
Practice Leader, NEO - Valuation & Litigation
Advisory – CBIZ, Inc.

Marquetese Betts (LISW-S), has over 20 years of experience in the field of child welfare. She is a trainer for the Ohio Child Welfare Training Program and currently works as a supervisor at Cuyahoga County Division of Children and Family Services (CCDCFS). Her training and skills include her ability to conduct forensic interviews, child and family strengths, and needs assessments. Marquetese has received multiple recognitions for her work with vulnerable populations such as CCDCFS's Director's Award and an honorable mention from the Public Children Services Association of Ohio. Marquetese has served on various committees such as CCDCFS' LGBTQ committee and co-chaired its 2014 Leadership Task Group. She currently serves on Case Western Reserve University's Alumni Board as well as Ohio's Continuous Quality Improvement (CQI) New Initiatives Subcommittee. Marquetese earned a Bachelor of Arts from Cleveland State University. Upon receiving a child welfare fellowship, she continued her education at Case Western Reserve University where she earned a Master of Science in Social Administration.

Dr. Tami Bolder leads the Northeast Ohio Valuation and Litigation practice for CBIZ, Inc. She is the local business advantage leader for the firm's women initiative. Dr. Bolder is responsible for business development and all phases of project management for Northeast Ohio clients. She oversees business valuation engagements for estate and gift tax, financing, mergers and acquisitions, divorce, and other litigation purposes. Dr. Bolder holds a Doctorate in Business Administration, Master of Business Administration from Case Western Reserve University and a bachelor's degree in Accounting/International Business from the University of Akron. She is a member of Alpha Kappa Alpha, and serves on the boards of Junior Achievement, President's Council and Cleveland Metropolitan Bar Association. Dr. Bolder is a graduate of Leadership Akron's Community Leadership Institute, Cleveland Leadership Center's Civic Leadership Institute and Bridge Builders Class of 2015. She lives in Rootstown, Ohio with her husband, Paul Bolder II, and their son, Paul Bolder III. She enjoys reading and traveling.

Lisa L. Bottoms
President
Bottom Line Consulting Group

Carl Bowers
Detective
Cleveland Division of Police

Lisa L. Bottoms is the President of Bottom Line Consulting Group. Her firm offers a variety of consulting services including strategic planning, leadership coaching and training and organizational development to governments, non-profits and small businesses. Bottoms have over 30 years of experience in building strong organizations and leaders and a passion for helping organizational and business leaders find solutions to further build their capacity and achieve their business objectives.

Lisa also serves as a speaker, panelist and moderator at national, regional and local sector conferences. She serves on numerous boards including Alpha Kappa Alpha Sorority, Incorporated, Greater Cleveland Neighborhood Centers Association, and The Links Incorporated. Awards include the YWCA Women of Professional Excellence Award and the David C. Sweets Distinguished Alumni Non-Profit Leader Award.

Lisa earned a master's degree from Cleveland State University, and bachelor's degree from Kent State University. She is married with four children and lives in Cleveland Heights.

Detective Carl Bowers #24 is currently assigned to the Bureau of Special Investigations, the Photography Unit. He has an associate degree from Cuyahoga Community College and a Bachelor of Arts in Criminology from Capital University. He is a 31-year veteran officer and proud member of the Cleveland Division of Police. Detective Bowers was recognized for saving an elderly woman's life. He received the Medal of Heroism and Rotary Club of Valor. The Cleveland Police Foundation recognized Detective Bowers for his community-based work because he was the catalyst and instrumental in implementing the Progress With Chess Program in the Cleveland Municipal School District. He received The Police Officer of The Year Award in 2019. Detective Bowers has worn many different hats over his distinguished career. He was a member of the 6th District Bike Unit, Bomb Squad Unit, and Use of Deadly Force Investigation Team. Detective Bowers is a mentor for Capital University students and the proud father of two children, Carl II and Veronica.

Marcella J. Brown, MNO
Executive Director Black Professionals
Association Charitable Foundation

Michael L. Brown
Human Resources Manager
Cuyahoga County Government

At BPACF, Ms. Brown builds an awareness of, supports and celebrates the development of Northeast Ohio's top Black Professionals and future community leaders through scholarship, leadership training and career development. She is a strategic planning and nonprofit management consultant through her private firm, BrownStone. Prior to BPACF, Ms. Brown was a development consultant for OneCommunity, a broadband technology organization. Marcella also spent several years as the Assistant Director of Development for The City Club of Cleveland, known as America's Citadel of Free Speech. She holds two Bachelor of Arts degrees in Public Affairs Journalism and Spanish, as well as a Master of Science degree in Nonprofit Organization Management. Ms. Brown has participated in several independent research studies, including expeditions to South Africa, Zimbabwe, Zambia, Egypt, and Mexico. Marcella is an engaged member of the Greater Cleveland Community, serving as the President of Lutheran Metropolitan Ministry, a member of Who's Who in Black Cleveland and the Cleveland Bar Association Certified Fee Dispute Committee.

Michael L. Brown is a human resources (HR) manager with Cuyahoga County Government and oversees the HR services for the Department of Health and Human Services (DHHS), the largest department under the county executive with 2400+ employees and the largest union. Michael is a strategic thinker, visionary and organizational consultant, who thinks outside of the box while assisting senior leadership within DHHS on operational procedures for a multigenerational staff. He spends countless hours working with line level staff, supervisors, managers, senior leaders and union representatives to create the best working environment for DHHS all with a staff of seven. Michael is the president of the Northern Ohio Chapter of the International Public Management Association for HR, and corresponding secretary for the Ohio Job and Family Services HR Association. He is a member and serves as chaplain for the Gamma Alpha Sigma Chapter of Phi Beta Sigma Fraternity, Inc. Michael lives in Streetsboro. He is married to Minnette Brown and the father of sons, D'Andre and Michael Christian and daughter, Taylor.

Cornell Hubert Calhoun III
Arts and Culture Coordinator
City of Cleveland

Tara L. Christian
Senior Client Manager
Optum United Health Group

Cornell Hubert Calhoun III is an arts and culture coordinator for Mayor Frank G. Jackson and Cleveland. He is an accomplished and widely applauded actor, producer, director and an award-winning playwright and filmmaker. His play, The Mighty Scarabs is published by the Original Works Publishing Company of Los Angeles, California. The Karamu World Premiere production was one of the top plays during the 2015-2016 theater season. His films Sterling and American Girlz were selected for the Greater Cleveland Urban Film Festivals in 2017 and 2018. His most recent film, Van's Ice Cold Lemonade has received multiple awards including being selected for the 2019 Cleveland International Film Festival. Cornell is writer and producer of the TV 20 – We Are Cleveland TV series, In the Land. He credits his success to his mentors, Cleveland theater legends, Dorothy and the late Reuben Silver.

Tara L. Christian is senior client manager for Optum Insight, a division of United Health Group. Tara has worked in the health insurance industry for 20 years. Currently, she works in Optum Payment Integrity for Fraud, Waste, Abuse and Error under Partner Services. She oversees the Medicare business and is responsible for managing the relationship between United Healthcare and Optum. Prior to joining Optum, Tara worked for Medical Mutual as a national network administrator where she was responsible for building the provider network by negotiating provider contracts within Ohio. Tara joined United Health Group in 2015 as a network contract manager and after three years was promoted to senior client manager. Tara holds a Bachelor of Arts in Business Management from Ursuline College and a Master of Business Administration in Healthcare Management from Indiana Wesleyan University. Tara is a resident of Richmond Heights and is the proud mother of Tiarra, Arthur IV and Autumn.

Traci Clark
Deputy Chief of Planning & Engineering
Cleveland Airport System

Daryl Coats
Sr. Information Technology & Business
Intelligence Manager
Northeast Ohio Regional Sewer District

Traci Clark was appointed for Cleveland Airport System in August 2007. In this capacity, she has responsibility for engineering & construction, environmental services, airport planning and real estate & noise abatement matters related to both Cleveland Hopkins International and Burke Lakefront Airports.

Clark joined the Cleveland Airport System as an Assistant Customer Service Manager in 1998 and has served in various management positions throughout her tenure. Her range of experience includes customer service, community relations, capital planning, budgeting and grant management.

Clark obtained a Bachelor's Degree in Aviation from The Ohio State University, College of Engineering and a Master's Degree in Public Administration from Cleveland State University. She is also a graduate of the Cleveland Management Academy.

In addition to being recognized by Who's Who in Black Cleveland, Clark has also been recognized as one of Kaleidoscope Magazines 40 under 40. She is a member of the Conference of Minority Transportation Officials (COMTO), Organization of Black Aerospace Professionals (OBAP), Women in Transportation (WTS) International and American Association of Airport Executives (AAAE).

Daryl Coats is a Senior Information Technology and Business Intelligence Manager for the Northeast Ohio Regional Sewer District, with more than twenty years of IT professional work experience. He is an active member of the Omega Psi Phi Fraternity. He has several years of experience in leadership, strategic planning and budgeting. He uses these skills to encourage, enrich, and maintain strong relationships with youth and parents. Mr. Coats holds a Bachelor's Degree in Computer Information Systems with a Minor in Criminal Justice from Kentucky State University and Master's Degree in Business Administration with a focus in Finance from Cleveland State University. He has completed several leadership courses from the Weatherhead School of Management at Case Western Reserve University. He is the Vice President of Youth Fitness Program 4 Life Inc., a non-profit that focuses on youth education, fitness, and health. He is the President and founding member of the Thoroughbred Investment Group LLC, an equities and real estate investment group. Mr. Coats has been married to his wife for twenty-one years and is the proud father of three lovely daughters.

Yvonne Drake
Community Marketing Representative
CareSource

Terri Bradford Eason
Director of Gift Planning
Cleveland Foundation

Yvonne Drake is a licensed health insurance agent who has worked in the Medicaid managed care industry for 19 years. For the past eight years, Yvonne has worked in the Sales and Marketing Department as a community marketing representative, representing the largest Medicaid health plan in the state of Ohio, CareSource. In her role, she is provided with the opportunity and privilege of making a difference in many people's lives by helping to improve their health and well-being. Responsible for creating marketing strategies and building brand awareness, is key for allowing consumer and member education to occur. She is known in the community as a dependable stakeholder who supports other nonprofit organizations that are contributing to making a positive impact in the lives of the underserved population. Yvonne's roots are in Brooklyn, New York but after 22 years in Cleveland Ohio, she is proud to call this amazing city home, where she resides with her husband, Julian, and two children, Marselis and Laila.

Terri Bradford Eason manages the Cleveland Foundation's Gift Planning Program. Eason joined the Foundation in October 2008 after two decades in the financial services industry holding several positions with National City (now PNC).

Eason has served as a director on several area nonprofit boards, including Cleveland Hearing & Speech Center (Former Board President), Recovery Resources, Junior Achievement, and the Women's City Club Foundation. She is Former President of Alpha Omega Chapter of Alpha Kappa Alpha Sorority, Inc., as well as Former Chairman of Alpha Omega Foundation, Inc. Currently, she serves as an At-Large Director for AKA Educational Advancement Foundation, Inc., headquartered in Chicago, Illinois. Terri is a member of the Beta Gamma Sigma National Honor Society, Cleveland Chapter of The Links, Inc., Jack & Jill of America, Inc. and Top Ladies of Distinction, Inc. She earned her MBA from Cleveland State University and a BA from Penn State University. Eason resides in South Euclid with her husband Clayton Eason, Sr. and their sons Clayton II, age 20, and Bradford, age 18.

Orlando O. Grant
Chief Executive Officer
Big Brothers Big Sisters of Lorain County

Dr. Howard Hall, Ph.D., Psy.D., BCB
Doctor and Professor
Cleveland Medical Center

Orlando O. Grant serves as the president and chief executive officer at Big Brothers Big Sisters of Lorain County. Grant presides over the premiere one to one mentoring organization where over 600 lives are touched each year. Grant facilitates a collective effort around fundraising, marketing, branding, and supportive services for Big Brothers Big Sisters.

Grant, a recent graduate of the 2017 Leadership Cleveland Class, holds a Master of Science degree from Southern New Hampshire University specializing in Non-Profit Management and, a bachelor's from the University of Akron in Business and Organizational Communication.

A lifelong resident of Northeast Ohio, Grant serves on the board of directors for St. Clair House. Orlando donates his time, talent, and treasure towards initiatives to increase efforts around children, individuals afflicted with a mental illness, and programs in the inner city.

A proud 23-year member of Iota Phi Theta Fraternity Incorporated, he also serves on the National Board of Directors and proud member of the Beta Lambda Omega Cleveland Ohio Chapter. Grant has one daughter, Brianna, and they currently reside in Euclid, Ohio.

Howard Hall, Ph.D., Psy.D. BCB, has doctorate degrees from Princeton University and Rutgers University in experimental and clinical psychology respectively. Presently, he is a professor in the department of pediatrics, psychiatry, and psychological sciences at Cleveland Medical Center. With over 30 years of practice, Dr. Hall has successfully treated children, adolescents, and adults using integrative approaches for patients with complex stress related conditions. His integrative clinics will be expanding at the new Zagara Pediatric Specialty Clinic at University Hospital's Rainbow Babies and Children's Hospital which will open this year. Dr. Hall's research includes international investigation and lecturing on nontraditional healing approaches with travels to West Africa, New Zealand, and the Middle East where his research was featured in 2005 on the National Geographic program, Is it real: Superhuman Phenomena? Dr. Hall is the recipient of numerous awards including the Sterling Registry Executives and Professionals, Pinnacle's Lifetime Achievement award and Pinnacle Registry of Outstanding Professionals. He is married to Dr. Jeanie Hall and they have two daughters, Ilea and Karelle.

Robbin Thornton Hudson
Community Programming Manager
United Black Fund of Greater Cleveland

Felicia Townsend Ivey
Business Advisor
Urban League of Greater Cleveland

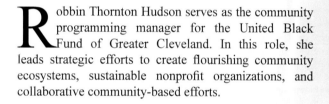

Robbin Thornton Hudson serves as the community programming manager for the United Black Fund of Greater Cleveland. In this role, she leads strategic efforts to create flourishing community ecosystems, sustainable nonprofit organizations, and collaborative community-based efforts.

Hudson has a 20-year track record of success in banking, education, and community engagement. She has worked with public entities, nonprofit organizations, foundations and corporations to build programs and services that uplift justice and opportunity. In 2017, Robbin launched Platform & Zenith, a corporate and community social responsibility firm. Prior to this, she served for eight years as director of family engagement and education initiatives at Neighborhood Leadership Institute.

Hudson serves on the board of New Bridge Center for Arts and Technology Cleveland, is an active member of Alpha Kappa Alpha Sorority, Inc., and an international leadership trainer for the Cleveland Council on World Affairs.

Hudson holds a Bachelor of Arts in Economics from Mount Holyoke College and a Master of Business Administration from the Weatherhead School of Management at Case Western Reserve University. She is the proud mother of one daughter, Torah.

Felicia Townsend Ivey, a graduate of John F. Kennedy in Cleveland, Ohio, has an associate degree in Computer Business Processing from Tri-C, and a bachelor's degree in Business Administration from Notre Dame College of Ohio. She was a computer systems business analyst and developer for 20 plus years. Having a heart for the African American community, she made a career change to financial professional and agent within the African American Unit at New York Life. In 2015, Ivey began working as a business advisor at the Urban League of Greater Cleveland. Currently, she is the business advisor in the Minority Business Assistance Center. She helps business owners build, grown, and sustain their businesses with a goal of creating jobs in the community.

Ivey is a member of Zion Chapel Missionary Baptist Church under the praetorship of Rev. George O. Stewart. She is the advisor for Zion's Guild Girls & Performing Arts Ministry at Zion, Assistant Organizer for the Hattie Jackson Guild under the Cleveland Sub-District of Women, and director of the Youth Auxiliary for the Northern Ohio Baptist District Association.

Lynnette Jackson
Relationship Manager
Key Private Bank

Michael Jeans
CEO
Growth Opportunity Partners

As a relationship manager for Key Private Bank, Lynnette Jackson delivers integrated wealth strategies and forward-thinking objective advice to her clients which include individuals, families, professionals, retirees, business owners, executives, and other high-net-worth clients. In 2016 and 2018, she was a member of the President's Club; and in 2014, she was a member of Signature Circle. Both honors signify her high-performing sales efforts. Jackson is an active member of the Northeast Ohio community and is passionate about issues facing women and girls. She is the chair of the board of trustees of her alma mater, Laurel School, the immediate past president of the Western Reserve Chapter of The Links, and a trustee of the Rainbow Babies and Children's Foundation. Jackson earned her Master of Business Administration from the Weatherhead School of Management at Case Western Reserve University and a Bachelor of Science from Hampton University. She also holds a certified wealth strategist CWS® designation. She is a graduate of Leadership Cleveland 2012 and Cleveland Bridge Builders charter class.

Michael Jeans is the founding CEO of Growth Opportunity Partners (Growth Opps), a Small Business advisory and lending company, which will become a Community Development Financial Institution. Growth Opps lends to small and mid-size businesses, providing management consulting to support their growth with a particular focus on impact in low and moderate-income areas.

Jeans is a current Board and Committee member for Our Lady of the Wayside, Cleveland Rape Crisis Center, Cleveland/Cuyahoga County Workforce Development, Growth Opportunity Partners, Center for Population Dynamics at Cleveland State University, Levin College of Urban Affairs, and the Visiting Committee for the College. Jeans shapes strategy and governance as a trustee on the Board of Directors of Westfield Bank, a $1.4B full service bank and financial institution located in Westfield, Ohio. Michael also sits on the ALCO and Board Loan Committees for the bank.

Jeans earned a bachelor's degree from Ashland University in Business Administration with a focus in Finance and a minor in Spanish. Married for over 20 years, Michael, enjoys spending time with his wife and children, in addition to travel and golf.

Tammie Sheila Jones, MS
Program Manager
Office of HIV/AIDS Services
Cleveland Department of Public Health

Darryl J. Key Sr.
Manager of Fleet Services
Northeast Ohio Regional Sewer District

Tammie S. Jones, MS is program manager for the Office of HIV/AIDS Services at the Cleveland Department of Public Health where she works tirelessly to eradicate the HIV/AIDS epidemic in her community. Jones has a passion for education and believes in sharing knowledge that allows people to access the resources needed to make informed healthy choices. Jones manages multiple grants that support HIV/AIDS and STD-related services and activities of prevention, education, awareness, testing and housing in the Greater Cleveland region. Jones being a lifelong Clevelander has over 15 years of professional experience in health education, particularly training, program development and administration. Jones provides leadership on several community health groups and has received the Award of Excellence, Award of Gratitude and has been honored by the Center for Disease Control and Prevention for her leadership in the "Take Charge, Take the Test Campaign." Jones holds a bachelor's degree in Business Administration from the University of Toledo and a master's degree in Business Management from Indiana Wesleyan University.

Darryl J. Key Sr. is manager of Fleet Services for the Northeast Ohio Regional Sewer District (NEORSD). Darryl has the responsibility of maintaining the district's 1,300 fleet assets which includes vehicles, boats, construction equipment, pumps, utility carts, small equipment, and generators. Key oversees maintenance contracts, maintains the district's fuel system, and purchases vehicles and equipment for the district. Key's proudest accomplishment at the district was a joint venture with Cleveland Metroparks in purchasing equipment to clean the sand at Edgewater and Euclid Beach. Key has been repairing and managing the repairs of vehicles and equipment for Cuyahoga County citizens for over 35 years. Key was a mechanic, technical services inspector, and manager of equipment for the Greater Cleveland Regional Transit Authority for 28 years. He left the authority and joined NEORSD in 2011. Darryl is a U.S. Navy Seabee veteran. He has been married for 30 years to his wife Angela. They have three children and three granddaughters. Key loves to travel in his spare time.

Renee Ligon
Director of Minority Business Assistance Center
Urban League of Greater Cleveland

Cecil Lipscomb
Executive Director
The United Black Fund of
Greater Cleveland, Inc.

Renee Ligon is a business development professional whose 20-year career encompasses successful collaborations with community agencies, municipalities, nonprofits, and small to large for-profit organizations. Renee's fundamental objective at the Urban League of Greater Cleveland is the cultivation of positive economic impact through the creation of tactical business alliances to grow and strengthen minority-owned businesses. Recently, Ligon was the assistant director of Diversity & Corporate Relations at Case Western Reserve University. Prior to joining Case Western Reserve University, she was vice president and relationship manager at JP Morgan Chase Bank. During her 8-year career with JP Morgan Chase, she managed the financial portfolios for commercial sector for-profit, non-profit and municipal clients. Ligon's notable and numerous boards of director appointments have included the Greater Cleveland Delta Foundation, COMPACT, UNCF of Orlando, and the Citrus Club's Women's Executive Exchange. Renee holds a Bachelor's in Communications from John Carroll University and a Master's in Human Resources Management from Nova Southeastern University.

In 2011 Cecil Lipscomb assumed the role of executive director of The United Black Fund of Greater Cleveland, Inc. (UBF). Founded in 1981, UBF, one of Cleveland's leading grant funders, is a 501(c)(3) charitable organization that provides financial (grants) and technical support to neighborhood based organizations offering a full range of health and human service programs for the residents of Cleveland's African American and lower income communities.

He serves as adjunct faculty at Ursuline College where he teaches graduate and undergraduate courses in Leadership Theory, Management, and Marketing. He is also a board member for the Center for Community Solutions.

Previously, Lipscomb was senior director of institutes at Cleveland Clinic and a director of fundraising for Case Western Reserve University's School of Engineering. Before 2004, he worked in the telecommunications sector for 10 years with two Fortune 100 companies that merged to form Verizon.

Lipscomb received his undergraduate degree from Ursuline College, his MBA from Weatherhead School of Management, and certificate of nonprofit management from Mandel Center for Nonprofit Organizations at Case Western Reserve University.

Kasey Morgan
Network Manager
MyCom Youth Development Initiative of
Greater Cleveland

Dr. Antoine D. Moss
Logistics Management Team Lead
NASA Glenn Research Center

Kasey Morgan is a Human Services Professional with a passion for youth, community and nonprofit strategic collaborations. She is an expert in community engagement, youth and parental engagement as well as strategic partnerships development. Kasey specializes in leadership training, community mobilization, nonprofit management, and creating effective programming. Her focus on communication, interpersonal management and customer satisfaction were instrumental in leading to increased funding, higher levels of student achievement and innovative engagement techniques implemented throughout the Greater Cleveland Area as well as other U.S cities.

Kasey is the Network Manager for the MyCom Youth Development Initiative of Greater Cleveland. In this role, she leads a Network of 20 neighborhoods, Lead Agencies, and a diversely staffed Intermediary Team. Previously, she served as the MyCom Program Officer for Education, Community-Based Organizations, Out of School Time Programming and Transitions. Before joining MyCom, Kasey coordinated Youth Development and Educational Opportunities for the Cleveland Metropolitan Schools. Kasey is the Managing Partner at Executive Minds Consulting and Management Group as well.

Kasey is a proud wife, mother, member of Delta Sigma Theta Sorority and University of Michigan Alumna.

Dr. Antoine D. Moss is a logistics management team lead at the NASA Glenn Research Center. At NASA Moss is responsible for leading a team that develops federal logistics programs and policies. In an effort to inspire minority students to pursue STEM careers, Moss is active in NASA's community and education outreach initiatives. Moss has also previously served as a tutor with the Federal Executive Board for its federal tutoring program.

Moss authored a book entitled Learn to Intern CEO Style: 71 Leadership Principles that Got Me And Now You Money, A Free Graduate Degree, and Respect! for college students and interns. As a previous U.S. Congressional intern, Moss tributes his book to the late-congresswoman Stephanie Tubbs-Jones. He has branded himself as a nationally recognized professional speaker and expert media resource as the Man of Inspiration.
Moss completed an undergraduate degree at Baldwin-Wallace University. He graduated from Cleveland State University (CSU) with a master's and doctorate degrees in public administration. He is the youngest and only second African-American male to complete a Doctor of Philosophy program at CSU.

Jacqueline Muhammad
Manager of Government Affairs
Northeast Ohio Regional Sewer District

Erica C. Penick
Executive Director
The President's Council

Recently named Manager of Government Affairs for the Northeast Ohio Regional Sewer District, Muhammad is responsible for directing government affairs activities. She manages the District's efforts of developing and cultivating relationships with government municipalities at all local levels from cities, county government, civic organizations and other stakeholders throughout the 62 communities in which the District serves. She is also responsible for enhancing student engagement initiatives, the Good Neighbor Ambassador Program and represents the District throughout northeast Ohio.

Previously, Muhammad was appointed to lead the Community Engagement & Legislative Affairs division of the Cleveland Airport System, where she served for eleven years responsible for all matters related to community relations/engagement, legislative affairs and social responsibility efforts.

Muhammad serves on various advisory committees, boards and volunteers on projects targeting underserved members of the community. Receiving several honors and acknowledgements for her work, she graduated magna cum laude with a bachelor's degree in Communications from Cleveland State University, is in Class 23 of Neighborhood Leadership Cleveland and graduate of Cleveland Public Schools.

Erica C. Penick is the Executive Director of The Presidents' Council, which acts as a catalyst for inclusion by supporting, developing, and advocating for current and future generations or African-American entrepreneurs and leaders through wealth creation and sustainability. This mission is carried out through The Presidents' Foundation education and technical assistance programs, The Presidents' Council Business Chamber, Northeast Ohio's primary African-American business chamber, and The Presidents' Council Action Committee.

Penick joined the organization in 2013, advanced to the role of Director of Operations in 2016 and was named Executive Director in 2018 where she has the overall strategic and operational responsibility for the organization's finances, staff, programs, development efforts, expansion and execution of its mission.

Penick holds a BS in Business Administration in Human Resources Management and received her Executive Master of Business Administration from the Cleveland State University Monte Ahuja College of Business.

Most significant, Penick loves the Lord and leads her family as God leads her. She is a member of The Cleveland Foundation Fenn Educational Fund Advisory Committee, the Ohio Diversity Council's Cleveland Advisory Board and the Eliza Bryant Village Board of Trustees.

Jamal Pittman
Manager
Business Development
American Express

Priscilla Pointer-Hicks
Public Housing Director
The City of Parma

Jamal Pittman is the manager of Business Development for the Northeast Ohio Middle Market at American Express. He is responsible for engaging CEOs, CFOs, and presidents of mid-size companies by collaborating and strengthening their relationship with American Express. Jamal endeavors to help companies earn additional revenues, embrace new technologies, and generate additional working capital. Jamal has received several recognitions such as the Platinum Award, Green Club Award, Mid-Year trip winner and other accolades. Jamal is also licensed in the state of Ohio to sell life, health, property and casualty insurance. He is a promising entrepreneur and graduate of Ohio University, earning his bachelor's degree in Management Information Systems. He loves his community and looks for ways to empower his people through history, culture, nationality and heritage. Jamal is an avid reader and enjoys studying and applying ways to make the Black dollar re-circulate.

Priscilla Pointer-Hicks came to PPHA from the Cuyahoga Metropolitan Housing Authority, the seventh-largest housing authority in the country, where she served as director of the Housing Choice Voucher program for ten years. With more than 25 years of direct experience in both the private and public sectors, as well as in the role of management consultant, Pointer-Hicks is nationally recognized as an HCVP expert who has presented to industry groups on related topics. She has served as a member of the National Conference Committee for the National Association for Housing and Redevelopment Officials (NAHRO), and formerly served as a member of the board of Towards Employment, an organization dedicated to empowering individuals to achieve and maintain self-sufficiency through employment.

Mark Ribbins
Program Director
107.3 The Wave

Shelley M. Shockley
Marketing Manager
City of Cleveland

Mark Ribbins loves guiding people toward discovery moments whether it is new music or greater spiritual horizons. A Cleveland native, he studied mass media communications at Cleveland State University which led to a career in television and radio broadcasting with several local stations; most recently, as program director and afternoon drive host for 107.3 The Wave. Mark is a consultant to jazz artists, promoters, and jazz festivals locally and nationally. He earned his Bachelor of Theology degree in Old Testament Studies from Temple Bible College and Seminary and serves as pastor of Avon Avenue Baptist Church in Cleveland's Union-Miles neighborhood. A current board member for Hospice of the Western Reserve, he has served on the Catholic Commission on Community Action and is a past board member with the Cleveland Jazz Orchestra. His greatest passion is time spent with his wife, Celeste Glasgow Ribbins, and their daughter, Julia.

Shelley M. Shockley has a passion for seeing the beauty in greater Clevelanders. She is a results-oriented professional with extensive experience in management, special event planning, marketing, public and community relations, and writing. She is a skilled and confident administrator, focused and enthusiastic team player with analytical and innovative capabilities who is adept at interacting with public and private sector., Shelley is the marketing manager at Cleveland Public Power, a division of the City of Cleveland's Public Utilities department. Shelley plays an intricate role in promoting the municipally owned electric company and developing a long-term strategic marketing plan. A native Clevelander, Shelley has enjoyed a career in writing. She was a reporter and editor for the Cleveland Call and Post newspapers for a decade and today is the managing editor for Phenomenal Woman Magazine. She is the principal creator of her firm, Shelley Shockley Communications Group. In her spare time, she enjoys relaxing with her husband, Keith Rutledge. Many people dream of worthy accomplishments, Shelley stays awake and does them!

CORPORATE BRASS

Janiece Smalls-Mitchell
Vice President/Senior Process Improvement
Consultant
PNC Financial Services

LaToya Smith
AVP and Talent Acquisition Manager
Fifth Third Bank

Janiece Smalls-Mitchell is vice president and senior process improvement consultant with PNC Financial Services. She is also an aspiring entrepreneur/owner of Miraj Naturals, a beauty and skin care line that fosters healthy skin through handmade natural and organic products. At PNC, she supports her entry level and staff level employees through active involvement and mentorship. Outside of PNC, she is active in the STE[A]M community through involvement in NSBE and SWE programs. As a budding entrepreneur, she is becoming more involved in community economic advancement and can be found at community expos and trade shows as a vendor and supporter. Janiece holds a Bachelor of Science in Industrial Engineering from Clemson University, and a master's degree in Supply Chain Management from Penn State University. In addition, she holds numerous corporate and national certifications including Lean Six Sigma – Black Belt, and Certified Project Manager. Her foundation and strength come from her family and friends. Janiece is a loving wife and proud mother of three amazing children.

LaToya Smith has been a valuable team member of Fifth Third Bank since August 1999. She is responsible for acquiring diverse talent into the bank. Additionally, she leads a team of talent acquisition consultants for Bancorp. LaToya is actively involved in the community with organizations including EL Barrio Job Readiness Program, Dress for Success and Y.O.U. LaToya is very philanthropic. She started a Giving Circle, Our Hope, Our Future. She has received professional development accolades from Kaleidoscope Magazine, Forty/Forty Club, Crain's HR Leader Finalist, Women of Color Stephanie Tubbs Jones Courage Award, CSU Link Distinguished Alumni, Girls Scout of N.E. Ohio Women of Distinction, NAACP Unsung Hero Community Award, and Cleveland Bridge Builder. She serves on United Black Fund of Greater Cleveland and Cuyahoga County Workforce. LaToya is a member of Delta Sigma Theta and Eta Phi Beta sororities. She is an intimacy coach and founder of Eros Heart, LLC. LaToya is an adjunct professor at Tri-C and Cleveland State University. She is married with two beautiful children.

Makanya L. Smith
Vice President
Public Relations Director
National Action Network

Delante Spencer Thomas
Deputy Inspector General
Cuyahoga County

Makanya L. Smith is vice president of Little Africa Food Co-op. She is responsible for performing the duties of the president in his or her absence or disability and assisting the president in his or her duties. In addition, the vice president works with the president to oversee the Little Africa Co-op development model and timeline. Makanya was a coach at Urban Community School. She is a member of the following organizations - National Action Network Greater Cleveland, Iota Phi Lambda Sorority, TBOY (Taking Back our Youth), MLSJ Consulting LLC, National Congress of Black Women Parliamentarian and Union Miles Development Corporation. She is the recipient of the John Cox Leadership award. Makanya has a bachelor's degree, master's degree, and MBA from University of Phoenix.

Delante Spencer Thomas is a licensed attorney and currently serves as deputy inspector general for Cuyahoga County. Delante investigates county officials and employees for fraud, corruption, waste, and other acts of wrongdoing. He also leads agency communications efforts by conducting countywide ethics training, designing ethics newsletters, and drafting opinions to address ethical concerns. Delante owns and operates his own private law practice and event planning firm, LMP Solutions, LLC. His practice areas include employment and housing law, small business consulting, organizational development and small civil matters. Delante is a native of East Cleveland, graduating from Shaw High School. He attended Syracuse University where he earned a bachelor's degree in Sports Management and master's degree in Public Relations. He then earned his law degree and master's degrees in Human Resources from Cleveland State University. Delante serves on the boards of the CMLaw Alumni Association, Cardinal's Nest, Towards Employment, and Norman S. Minor Bar Association. He is a member of Kappa Alpha Psi Fraternity and Greater Avery A.M.E. Church.ity and Greater Avery A.M.E. Church.

Joyce L. Walker
Vice President
Community Development
PK Management

Garth Woodson
Director of Development Finance & Inclusion
Port of Cleveland

Joyce L. Walker MSSA, is vice president of Community Development for PK Management, LLC where she is responsible for conceptualizing, developing and facilitating the implementation of projects related to her department, and manages a budget in excess of $4.7 million. Joyce holds a dual bachelor's degree in Sociology and Business Administration from Knoxville College, a master's degree in Social Administration from Case Western Reserve University and has completed post graduate studies at Harvard University and Princeton University. She is experienced in fundraising and in the field of social work focusing on families, children, elderly, as well as her current experience in the housing industry. She is a board member and advisor to the All Ways Up Foundation and the Perlman Foundation where she assisted in the distribution of over $2.5 million in scholarships to over 400 students.

Garth Woodson is director of Development Finance & Inclusion at the Cleveland-Cuyahoga County Port Authority in Cleveland. Directing the Port Authority's Development Finance Group, Garth is responsible for business development, project coordination, programs management and the implementation of its inclusion policy. The Port Authority has assisted area businesses, municipalities and developers in obtaining more than $4.5 billion of financing for projects totaling over $6.6 billion throughout Northeast Ohio since 1993. Garth has been involved in economic development, finance, business management, sales and business consulting since 1980. He has held bank sales and management positions with National City Bank, Huntington National Bank, and U.S. Bank. He has worked with Cleveland's Department of Economic Development and Cuyahoga County's Department of Development. Additionally, Garth coordinated community and economic development activities with Neighborhood Progress, Inc. for Buckeye Area Development Corporation, Larchmere Development Association and Friends of Shaker Square. Garth is a native of Cleveland/Shaker Heights, and a graduate of the University of Toledo, with a bachelor's degree in Business Administration.

FirstEnergy

Samuel Pierre-Louis
Vice President
Information Technology
FirstEnergy Service Co.

Samuel Pierre-Louis is vice president of Information Technology for FirstEnergy Service Company, a subsidiary of FirstEnergy Corp.

Pierre-Louis joined the company in May 2018 as vice president of Information Technology. He leads the delivery of FirstEnergy's cyber security, computing and telecommunications networks, enterprise applications, data center and cloud solutions, service desk, end-user device management, IT project management, customer print operations and overall IT infrastructure services.

Prior to FirstEnergy, Pierre-Louis served as vice president and chief information security officer for Providence St. Joseph Health where he led the development and execution of the organization's enterprise Cyber Security, Physical Security, Workplace Violence Prevention and Business Continuity Management services. He served in the same role at St. Joseph Health prior to the merger with Providence Health Services. He has held information technology leadership, consulting and engineering roles at organizations including MD Anderson Cancer Center, UAB Health Systems, Internet Security Systems and Siemens Energy & Automation.

Lorna Wisham
Vice President,
Corporate Affairs
& Community
Involvement
FirstEnergy Corp.

Lorna Wisham is Vice President of Corporate Affairs & Community Involvement for FirstEnergy Corp.

Wisham is responsible for community giving initiatives, employee volunteerism and executive board placements. Wisham is also President of the FirstEnergy Foundation awarding grants to qualified non-profits throughout FirstEnergy's territory. She most recently held the position of Senior Advisor, Federal Affairs for FirstEnergy, lobbying the Administration and the United States Congress.

Wisham previously worked for Downtown Cleveland Partnership and the City of Cleveland before joining FirstEnergy in 2005. She is the recipient of honors from various organizations including, SmartBusiness Magazine, the Women of Color Foundation and the Diversity Center of Northeast Ohio. Wisham is a 2005 graduate of Leadership Cleveland and currently serves on the boards of the Cuyahoga Community College Foundation and United Way of Greater Cleveland, and as a trustee for University Hospitals.

Karen A. Sealy
Senior Corporate
Counsel
FirstEnergy Service
Company

Karen A. Sealy is a Senior Corporate Counsel with FirstEnergy Service Company. She serves as a legal advisor to various business units with emphasis on corporate law, including Securities Exchange Commission (SEC) reporting and mergers and acquisition matters.

Sealy joined the company in 2011 as an attorney in the practice of federal energy regulatory law with a focus on transactions, strategy and securities authorization. She was promoted several times in the Legal Department, developing expertise in the area of mergers and acquisitions. Prior to her current role, she served as Senior Corporate Counsel in the Federal Energy Regulatory Commission (FERC) legal group with the company. Prior to joining FirstEnergy, she was an attorney with Dentons in Washington, D.C.

She earned a Bachelor of Business Administration degree in finance and investments from Bernard M. Baruch College. In addition, she received a law degree from The George Washington University Law School.

CORPORATE
SPOTLIGHT

jumpstart

jumpstart

Dr. Rachel Angel
President
Chief Executive Officer
Anexsis, a JumpStart Focus Fund
Portfolio Company

Zerrine Bailey
Emerging Talent Network Leader

Dr. Rachel Angel is the president and CEO of Anexsis. She developed PEERRO, which is an interactive software, engaging young adults seeking employment. This PEERRO platform provides immediate entry level employment opportunities, while providing a pathway to engage employers seeking qualified applicants. This innovative platform takes the guess work out of job search and application process.

Nearly six years ago, Dr. Angel, founded Ireach, non-profit, 501c3 organization to address the needs of underserved youth. Ireach, was created to address the need for our youths to re-connect, re-establish moral character, work ethics, social awareness, education, and community pride within themselves.

Dr. Angel was born in Newark, New Jersey, and at the age of five, moved to Cleveland, Ohio. She graduated from Hampton University, where she earned a Doctor of Pharmacy.

She believes there is still hope for the future of our youth, and it's our moral obligation to reach out to those who need it the most.

Zerrine Bailey is the program manager for JumpStart's newly launched Emerging Talent Network (ETN) Program. In this capacity, she helps connect 11th grade aspiring students and 12th grade emerging students from eight targeted Cleveland Metropolitan School District high schools to career placement opportunities with local companies through summer internships and full-time job opportunities.

Prior to JumpStart, she worked as the Alliance for a Healthier Generation Healthy Schools program manager for Cleveland Metropolitan School District. In this capacity, she worked with 78 schools within Cleveland Metropolitan School District to create healthier school environments. Prior to this position, Bailey was involved in workforce development through NewBridge Cleveland Center for Arts and Technology. As the director of student and partner services, she facilitated more than 30 community partnerships, resulting in the expansion of programming for youth and adult programs and helped develop and implement a vocational training program that achieved a 75% placement rate into employment.

Bailey received a Bachelor of Science in Community Health Education from Kent State University.

Shanelle Johnson
Deal Flow Associate

Gloria Ware
Director
KeyBank Center for Technology, Innovation
and Inclusive Growth

Shanelle Johnson serves as the onboarding resource for applicants seeking services from JumpStart and its network of partners. Her role involves engaging with early-stage and small business clients, identifying their service needs, providing value-added feedback, maintaining continued engagement with clients and partners to track continued progress made and making referrals within JumpStart and to our other external services partners. Her primary focus is Core City: Cleveland clients.

Prior to JumpStart, Johnson was the Minority Business Enterprise (MBE) certification director for the Ohio Minority Supplier Development Council (OMSDC), an advocate for supplier diversity. She developed strategies, objectives, and action plans for assisting certified minority-owned businesses. During her tenure, she managed the certification process, helping to streamline the process and connect MBEs with supplier diversity professionals.

Before joining OMSDC, Johnson was an assistant administrator at the City of Cleveland, where she certified diverse businesses and monitored city projects, including the Flats East Bank project, to ensure diversity and inclusion goals were being met.

Johnson received a MBA and a bachelor's degree in Finance from Cleveland State University.

At JumpStart, Inc, Gloria Ware leads the KeyBank Center for Technology, Innovation and Inclusive Growth, a component of the KeyBank Business Boost & Build program. She has a 25-year track record of success in the finance industry, providing capital, business development and strategic management advice and solutions to a diverse portfolio of startups, small businesses, nonprofits, public sector, private schools and universities. Prior to joining JumpStart, Ware served in a number of progressive banking positions, last serving as vice president of public funds for Fifth Third Bank.

Ware's community awards and recognition include the Elevated and Empowered Game Changer Aware, Notable Women in Technology, the NTA Nsoroma Business Award and induction into the Kaleidoscope Magazine 40/40 Club. She has been profiled in numerous publications for her diversity and inclusion work and small business advocacy, and currently writes a column in *Smart Business Magazine* on diversity and innovation. She is also a board member of MidTown Cleveland.

Ware is a graduate of the Venture Capital Institute, LEAD Diversity and holds a B.S. in International Business Administration from Ohio State University.

Danielle Morris
Partner
Revenue Management and Compliance

Anne Richie
Venture Partner

jumpstart

Danielle (Dani) Morris oversees revenue and compliance functions for JumpStart's venture funds and manages the organization's internal control procedures for grant award funds and reporting (~$15M annually). She has extensive nonprofit financial expertise, ranging from large ERP systems to smaller customized homegrown systems, user guide design and training, leadership and managerial functions. Her responsibilities at JumpStart include preparation and review of the annual budget, annual audited statements, ongoing budget and financial projections, monthly financial statements, and special financial reports required by funding organizations.

Prior to her time at JumpStart, Morris spent nearly 16 years at Case Western Reserve University, most recently serving as the assistant controller. Morris sits on the board of DANCECleveland. In 2014, as a board member of the Alzheimer's Association-Cleve Chp, she chaired the Walk to End Alzheimer's-Cleveland Metropark Zoo, which raised roughly $360K with more than 4,000 walkers.

Morris earned a bachelor of arts from Cleveland State University and a MBA from Case Western Reserve University.

As a venture partner, Anne Richie coaches JumpStart's clients on preparing and executing growth plans. She has an extensive background in finance and banking with the unique experience of working with distressed businesses. She is very resourceful and collaborative and approaches growth opportunities with tactical, creative and innovative strategies.

Prior to JumpStart, Richie was the chief financial officer and chief restructuring officer for a private equity-owned jet engine parts manufacturer. Prior to this position, she enjoyed a long career in banking, rising from loan officer with the Bank of Boston to senior positions with Citicorp, Wells Fargo and KeyBank where she was responsible for managing portfolios of underperforming commercial loans.

Richie holds a B.A. in Economics from Smith College and an MBA from the University of Michigan's Ross School of Business.

Christopher Smith
Senior Deal Flow Manager

Twyla Turner
Event and Marketing Traffic Manager

Christopher Smith serves as the senior onboarding resource for applicants seeking services and/or investment from JumpStart and its network of partners. His role involves engaging with early-stage and small business clients, identifying their service needs, providing value-added feedback, maintaining continued engagement with clients and partners to track continued progress made and making referrals.

Prior to JumpStart, Smith worked in economic development helping small businesses as the Small Business Development Program Coordinator for Operation HOPE. In this capacity, he spearheaded program implementation, formed strategic alliances, helped individuals develop business plans, identified business needs, provided resources within NEO's entrepreneurial ecosystem and provided credit and money management counseling.

Smith is also a social entrepreneur, small business development consultant, and graphic designer. His entrepreneurial experiences began in college competing in several business plan competitions across the nation. With experience working in all sectors he's found that stewardship, entrepreneurship, and strengthening the human capital in our inner cities to be key components of creating sustainable communities.

Smith received a Master of Public Administration from Kent State University.

Twyla Turner is an operations and event planning professional with nearly 15 years of experience in the corporate and nonprofit sectors. At JumpStart, Turner is responsible for the conceptualization and logistical planning of organizational events, while also managing the marketing department's overall budget.

Prior to JumpStart, Turner was with the YWCA Greater Cleveland, where she led and managed projects and teams to develop, cultivate and engage the community through fundraising events, social justice work and women's leadership programming.

Turner is a graduate of Bowling Green State University with a B.S. in Apparel Merchandising and Product Development. During this time, she was fortunate to study Apparel Advertising & Marketing Communication at the renowned Fashion Institute of Technology in New York City, graduating from FIT with honors. She also holds a MBA at Bowling Green State University, with an expected graduation date in 2018.

Turner is life member of Sigma Gamma Rho Sorority Inc., and resides in Cleveland with her husband, Percy and their three children.

Lamont Mackley
Partner
Core City Service and Outreach

jumpstart

Tiwanna Scott Williams, BSN, RN
Owner
PearlFlower Catering
Graduate
JumpStart's Core City: Cleveland
Impact Program

Lamont Mackley assists entrepreneurs as they work through their seed funding pursuits to stimulate initial growth and adequately prepare them for follow-on funding. He brings extensive executive and management experience to the JumpStart team. Most recently, Mackley taught business and professional studies courses at Chancellor University and the Jack Welch Management Institute. He also founded Another Level Resources, an executive coaching and development firm specializing in facilitating solutions to problems for business executives.

Mackley spent 25 years in the commercial and community development banking industry and served as president and chief executive officer at three community banks in various locations within the United States. Mackley's ability to create environments of high achievement led to his selection as leader of two entrepreneurial businesses; one in the transportation industry and the other in the distribution industry. This experience allowed him to see business needs from a different perspective and has provided him with insight into the challenges of managing an entrepreneurial enterprise.

Mackley graduated from Boston University with a B.S. and Columbus School of Law, Catholic University, with a J.D.

Inspired to become an entrepreneur by her two grandmothers, Pearline Scott and Delores Flowers, Tiwanna Scott Williams has grown PearlFlower catering into a premiere catering company in the Greater Cleveland area while also working full time as a Cardiothoracic-Surgical nurse.

Chef Tiwanna was a grand prize winner in JumpStart's Core City: Cleveland Impact program and one of three local chefs featured in the Launch Test Kitchen located inside of the Quicken Loans Arena for the 2018 Cleveland Cavaliers basketball season.

Each year PearlFlower donates to several organizations across the county to include:

Richmond Heights Education's signature event "Pasta with a Purpose", "A Good Christmas" celebration dinner for local families in need, Financial Literacy Programs, I CAN SCHOOLS Career Day, Alive on Purpose, WIN ministries and many other local non-profits and small businesses.

A Cleveland native, and graduate of Ursuline College, Williams is also a member of COSE, Delta Sigma Theta Sorority Inc. and was recently named the Women's Business Center of Northern Ohio's member of the year. She considers being a mom to daughter Tristan Williams as her first and most important job.

UNIVERSITY SPOTLIGHT

Ben Vinson III, PhD
Provost and Executive Vice President

Marilyn Sanders Mobley, Ph.D.
Vice President
Inclusion, Diversity and Equal Opportunity

Ben Vinson III was appointed Provost and Executive Vice President at Case Western Reserve University on July 2, 2018, and is responsible for all facets of the academic programs and research of the University. Vinson is an accomplished historian of Latin America, and served on the faculties of Barnard College and Penn State before joining Johns Hopkins in 2006 as a professor of history and founding director of its Center for Africana Studies. He went on to serve as a vice dean for centers, interdisciplinary studies and graduate education before becoming dean of George Washington University's Columbian College of Arts and Sciences.

He currently serves as Chair of the Board of Trustees of the National Humanities Center. Originally from Rapid City, South Dakota, Dr. Vinson earned a bachelor's degree from Dartmouth College and a doctorate from Columbia University. He has been awarded fellowships from the Fulbright Commission, National Humanities Center, Social Science Research Council, University of North Carolina at Chapel Hill, and the Ford, Rockefeller and Mellon foundations.

Heather E. Burton, PhD graduated from The Ohio State University with a Bachelor of Arts Degree in Journalism and African-American Studies and minor in Theater, a Masters of Social Work (University of Akron), a Masters of Public Administration and a Doctor of Philosophy in Urban Studies and Public Affairs (both from Cleveland State University).

Dr. Burton is Director of IDEAL-N and Partner Institution Faculty and Student Development at Case Western Reserve University, specializing in gender and racial equity. She is adjunct faculty in Pan-African Studies and Social Work at The University of Akron and CWRU. Dr. Burton received the 2019 Staff Diversity Award, 2019 Women of Achievement Award and 2019 Q-Grad Faculty & Staff Mentor Award.

She was a speaker for BET Foundation Girls Empowerment Summit, The Ohio State University and GAR Foundation. She is Founder of Crimson Heights Ministries, Inc., author of Crimson Heights and I'm Single: So What?, a member of Delta Sigma Theta Sorority, Inc. and has been involved in acting for over thirty years.

Her accomplishments are credited to her relationship with Christ and her family.

Ayesha Bell Hardaway, JD
Assistant Professor of Law
Case Western Reserve University School of Law

Heather E. Burton, Ph.D.
Director, IDEAL-N
Partner, Institution Faculty and Student Development

Ayesha Bell Hardaway is an Assistant Professor of Law at Case Western Reserve University School of Law. As a member of the faculty, Hardaway teaches as a clinician in the Milton A. Kramer Law Clinic in the areas of criminal justice, civil litigation, and health law. Her research and scholarship interests include the intersection of race with constitutional law, criminal law, policing, and civil litigation. Professor Hardaway is also the Director of the law school's Social Justice Law Center.

In addition to her teaching responsibilities, Professor Hardaway is currently serving as a member of the Independent Monitoring Team appointed to evaluate the progress and implementation of Cleveland Police Department reforms mandated by a settlement agreement between the City of Cleveland and the U.S. Department of Justice. In November 2017, Professor Hardaway was elected to serve on the Shaker Heights Schools Board of Education.

Prior to joining the law school faculty, Hardaway practiced in the Litigation Department of Tucker Ellis LLP. Before her time at Tucker Ellis, Hardaway was an Assistant Prosecuting Attorney for Cuyahoga County.

Heather E. Burton, PhD graduated from The Ohio State University with a Bachelor of Arts Degree in Journalism and African-American Studies and minor in Theater, a Masters of Social Work (University of Akron), a Masters of Public Administration and a Doctor of Philosophy in Urban Studies and Public Affairs (both from Cleveland State University).

Dr. Burton is Director of IDEAL-N and Partner Institution Faculty and Student Development at Case Western Reserve University, specializing in gender and racial equity. She is adjunct faculty in Pan-African Studies and Social Work at The University of Akron and CWRU. Dr. Burton received the 2019 Staff Diversity Award, 2019 Women of Achievement Award and 2019 Q-Grad Faculty & Staff Mentor Award.

She was a speaker for BET Foundation Girls Empowerment Summit, The Ohio State University and GAR Foundation. She is Founder of Crimson Heights Ministries, Inc., author of *Crimson Heights* and *I'm Single: So What?*, a member of Delta Sigma Theta Sorority, Inc. and has been involved in acting for over thirty years.

Her accomplishments are credited to her relationship with Christ and her family.

Brandon Dunbar
Student

Adrianne M. Crawford Fletcher, Ph.D., MSSA
Assistant Dean for Diversity and Inclusion
Assistant Professor
The Jack, Joseph and Morton Mandel School of Applied Social Sciences

Brandon Dunbar is a graduating senior at Case Western Reserve University (CWRU), majoring in Accounting and minoring in Music. Upon graduation he will have completed both his bachelors and masters in accounting and will be working for PricewaterhouseCoopers in Philadelphia as an auditor in the Financial Services group.

During his time at CWRU, Brandon served as the Vice President of Finance for the Undergraduate Diversity Collaborative (UDC), a student organization dedicated to enhancing and expanding diversity among undergraduate students at CWRU. In addition to the time spent working with UDC, Brandon also uses his spare time to tutor kids in the Cleveland area. Brandon has worked at the Michael R. White elementary school for the past two years and has also been a tutor with the Saturday Tutoring Program, hosted by the Church of the Covenant. Both of these experiences were built on Brandon's love for learning and teaching.

Outside of these activities, Brandon is also an active member of the Residence Hall Association, advocating for changes within the residence halls at CWRU and Case Men's Glee Club (singing group).

Adrianne M. Crawford Fletcher is the Assistant Dean for Diversity and Inclusion, and Assistant Professor at The Jack, Joseph and Morton Mandel School of Applied Social Sciences at Case Western Reserve University (CWRU). Dr. Fletcher is responsible for teaching both core foundation courses and advanced practice courses. As Assistant Dean, Dr. Fletcher is responsible for shaping the culture regarding issues of inclusion, diversity and equal opportunity. Dr. Fletcher participates in Faculty Senate for Minority Affairs, Faculty Development Council, Diversity Leadership Council, and is a mentor for the Provost Scholar Program, which serves students within the East Cleveland School District.

Dr. Fletcher holds a PhD from Loyola University Chicago and a Master's degree from the Mandel School at CWRU. Since returning to Cleveland in 2017, Dr. Fletcher has had the opportunity to engage with non-profit organizations, health care institutions and faith-based organizations regarding an awareness of implicit attitude, cultural humility/flexibility. Dr. Fletcher believes that service providers should be equipped to serve without bias, implicit or explicit. Dr. Fletcher is a member of the National Association of Social Work.

Edwin Mayes
Director
First Year Experience and Family Programs

Angela E. Miller, Ed.D.
Director, Education Abroad
Center for International Affairs

Edwin Mayes is the director of First Year Experience and Family Programs at Case Western Reserve University, a position he has held since arriving to the university in May 2012. As director, he is responsible for leadership and vision of programs for first year and transfer students and parents and families. Mayes works closely with the student success initiative, enrollment management, residence life and other internal and external partners to support students' successful transition from high school through their first year at the university.

Mayes is also co-chair of the university's award winning Sustained Dialogue Campus Network Program and a member of the Diversity Leadership Council.

Mayes has been a regular presenter on topics related to student retention and meeting the needs of students in transition. He was also an expert content author for the fifth edition of *How to Survey Your Freshman Year,* published in 2013.

Mayes is a doctoral candidate in the higher education administration program at Ohio University.

Dr. Miller serves as the Director for Education Abroad at Case Western Reserve University. In her role, she provides leadership and strategic direction for global engagement through academically rich international programs. She also serves on the Diversity Leadership Council and the Risk Management Committee at CWRU.

Dr. Miller earned her doctoral degree in Educational Leadership at Northern Arizona University. She has published research on global learning and seeks to help students gain global competencies. Throughout her career, she has mentored many professionals, and has presented on various topics in International Education, including global learning, risk management, diversity & inclusion, and women in leadership. She is a contributing author to Careers in International Education: A Guide for New Professionals by Sora Friedman and Amir Reza.

Dr. Miller is an active member of NAFSA Association of International Educators, where she chairs the Women & Leadership in International Education Member Interest Group. She is mother to two sons and enjoys reading, writing, and movies in her spare time.

David B. Miller, Ph.D., MSW, MPH
Associate Professor
Jack, Joseph, and Morton Mandel School of
Applied Social Sciences

Adrianna J. Milton
Graduate Student

Dr. David B. Miller teaches social work courses on social policy, research methods, health policy, global health and directs the International Educational Programs at the Mandel School of Applied Social Sciences. During 2019-2020, he will chair the CWRU Faculty Senate. His research foci include: cancer screening participation among minority men; effect of chronic and toxic stress on adolescents and young adults; and retirement readiness. In 2015, Dr. Miller received the John A. Yankey Outstanding Teacher Award voted on by the students of the Mandel School. In 2018, he received the Distinguished Alumni Award from the School of Social Work at the University of Pittsburgh.

Dr. Miller received his PhD and Masters of Public Health from the University of Pittsburgh and his Masters of Social Work from the University of South Carolina. He served as City Councilman-at-large in the City of South Euclid for 10 years, six of which as President of City Council.

He's an avid runner, reader, and world traveler. He is married to Alice L. Miller (Martin) and he has two children: Natasha and David.

A Florida native, Adrianna J. Milton moved to Cleveland from Texas in 2015 to earn her doctoral degree at Case Western Reserve University. This summer she will be entering her fourth year as a graduate student in the neuroscience department where she studies spinal cord injuries using rodent models.

Her graduate responsibilities include experimental design and planning, rodent surgical techniques and behavioral testing, central nervous system collection for histology, data acquisition and analysis, as well as mentoring undergraduate and high school students in research techniques in her lab. She has had the pleasure of mentoring undergraduate research interns from CWRU and Fisk University, in addition to students from East Cleveland, Berea Midpark, and Hawken.

She is a member of the Society for Neuroscience and the Ellipsis Institute for Women of Color in the Academy. In her spare time, she loves being active outdoors by biking or hiking with her boyfriend and her dog. She is a certified pole fitness instructor who also loves to cook, read and do home DIY projects.

CASE WESTERN RESERVE
UNIVERSITY EST. 1826

Brooke Odle, Ph.D.
Postdoctoral Fellow
Department of Biomedical Engineering

Oluchi Onyeukwu
Student

Brooke Odle is a Postdoctoral Fellow in the Department of Biomedical Engineering at Case Western Reserve University and conducts research in the Motion Study Laboratory (Louis Stokes Cleveland Veterans Affairs Medical Center).

In her most recent project, funded by the Craig H. Neilsen Foundation, she is developing and validating mathematical models of how individuals with spinal cord injury use their upper extremities to interact with assistive devices while standing with peripheral nerve stimulation. These models will be utilized to design advanced nerve stimulation control systems for enhancing balance during standing and walking after paralysis. She was recently awarded funding from the Paralyzed Veterans of America Education Foundation to explore the feasibility of neural stimulation to facilitate independent transfers after paralysis, which will begin in June.

Brooke received a B.S. in Bioengineering from the University of Pittsburgh, a M.S. in Biomedical Engineering from New Jersey Institute of Technology (NJIT), and a Ph. D. in Biomedical Engineering from NJIT and Rutgers University Biomedical and Health Science. Brooke is also an advocate for Science, Technology, Engineering, and Mathematics (STEM) education and mentoring.

Oluchi (Oh-lou-chee) is a Cleveland native pursuing her undergraduate degree in human nutrition at Case Western Reserve University (CWRU) in hopes of helping improve her life and the lives of others through health and wellness.

Being of Nigerian heritage, Oluchi immediately became involved in CWRU's African Students' Association (ASA) and now serves as the organization's public relations chairwoman. During her first year at CWRU she also became an office assistant at the Case School of Dental Medicine where she interacts with patients and helps to provide quality care to the CWRU and the Greater Cleveland community at large.

During her junior year, Oluchi co-founded The Sisterhood, the first organization of its kind. Now serving as the acting president, she hopes that the group's mission of providing a community, safe place, and source of empowerment for Black women at Case Western will continue even after her matriculation. Oluchi is hopeful that she will find her niche that combines her passions of nutrition, community outreach, and administration, her hobbies of cooking and traveling all while bringing people of different origins together.

Anthony C. Peebles, MBA
Director
Diversity & Corporate Relations

Levite Pierre
Student

Anthony Peebles is Director of Diversity & Corporate Relations for Case Western Reserve University. He is responsible for the identification, cultivation and solicitation of gifts, grants and contracts to support the University's Diversity Initiatives.

Tony began his career with Ameritrust Bank and was manager of Public Finance for Fifth Third Bank. He was also a Million Dollar Round Table Qualifier in 2012 with New York Life. Before joining CWRU, Tony worked as a Financial Planner with Skylight Financial Group.

Tony served as President of the City Club of Cleveland and CEO of the Ohio Minority Supplier Development Council. He is also a member of the University School Alumni Council and currently serves as Chair of the Finance & Audit Committee for the Shaker Heights Board of Education. Tony is past President of The 100 Black Men of Greater Cleveland.

Tony is a graduate of Duke University and holds an MBA from Baldwin Wallace University. Tony and his wife Tracy Martin Peebles, Esq., a magistrate with the Cuyahoga County Juvenile Court, live in Shaker Heights with their three daughters.

Levite Pierre is a Cleveland native studying at Case Western Reserve University (CWRU) in Economics & Business Management. He is set to graduate with his bachelors of arts in 2020. Levite plans on pursuing a career in public policy with the goal of working towards social justice.

Levite is the oldest of seven kids which gave him an affinity for working with youth. He has worked for Empowering Youth Exploring Justice where he brought diverse volunteers into middle schools to have discussions with youth on different topics surrounding social justice. He now works for The Ohio State Universities Cuyahoga County Extension Office (OSUE) in the Youth Advocacy and Leadership Coalition (YALC). YALC develops young adult leaders by training and supporting them in advocating for youth issues.

During his time at CWRU he has served in multiple leadership positions: the Treasurer of the African American Society, the Community Outreach Chair for the Black Student Union, and most recently, the Executive Chair of the Black Student Union. He hopes to inspire young black men & women to become positive leaders in their communities.

Ari Redcross
Student

Julian Rogers, MNO
Executive Director
Local Government and Community Relations

Ari Redcross is a May 2019 Master in Nutrition graduate of Case Western Reserve University. She completed her BS at Maharishi University of Management.

While a student at Case Western Reserve University, Ari had the opportunity to promote local farming at the Village Family Farms which aims to increase accessibility of fresh fruits and vegetables to the Hough community. She was a member of a student group that worked with Care Alliance Health Center as a part of the Interprofessional Learning Exchange and Practice.

At the Care Alliance Health Center, she identified patients' needs through interviews and worked towards alleviating gaps in care through an educational brochure designed to promote resources available at the health center. This fall, Ari will complete a dietetic internship at the Memphis VA Medical Center. In the future, as a registered dietitian, Ari is interested in applying strategies of behavior change to help individuals achieve sustainable health goals.

Julian Rogers serves as the Executive Director of Local Government and Community Relations for Case Western Reserve University. Before joining CWRU he was the Director of Community Partnerships with Cleveland State University where he managed the Office of Civic Engagement. Previously, he was an elected member of the inaugural Cuyahoga County Council where he represented District 10. Always committed to education, Julian also served as the Executive Director of Education Voters of Ohio, a nonprofit organization dedicated to improving public education and he also worked for the Cleveland Metropolitan School District, where he served as the Senior Assistant to the CEO and Liaison to the Office of the Mayor.

He formerly served on the boards of the Greater Cleveland Regional Transit Authority, the Cuyahoga Solid Waste District, NOACA and he currently serves as a trustee for Arts Cleveland. Julian was inducted into Kaleidoscope Magazine's 40/40 Club and was awarded the Emerging Leader Award from the U.S. Congressional Black Caucus. He has a degree in Political Science from Ohio University and a Master's in Nonprofit Management from CWRU.

Arlet Wright, MA
Director
Thwing Center Engagement & Operations

Arlet Wright is the Director of the Thwing Center Engagement & Operations at Case Western Reserve University (CWRU). Prior to her current position, she worked in the Office of Multicultural Affairs, the Minority Scholars Program, the Student Activities & Leadership Office and the Business Affairs Division (currently known as Auxiliary Affairs) at CWRU.

What began as merely a "job" over 20+ years ago has fostered into a passion for understanding the importance of the breath of diversity and working with all people (student, faculty, staff, and community) to create an inclusive environment at CWRU and in her life. She strives to utilize that same skill set to encourage and motivate all students, faculty, staff, friends, and family to think beyond their normal capabilities and to be lifelong learners of education and diversity. She has worked at various levels within the University and, when coupled with her education and life experience, she tries to walk in her truth so that others can walk in their truth.

Ernestine Baker-Hall
Education Chairperson

Theophilus James "Chip" Caviness Jr.
Correspondence and Social Media

Ernestine Baker-Hall is a member of the executive board of the Association of African American Cultural Gardens. As education chairperson, she ensures that programs are established for the annual Juneteenth and Kwanza celebrations. This year, the 2019 Heritage Series was held.

Ernestine graduated from John Hay in 1970. In 1974, she received a Bachelor of Science in Education degree from Kent State University, with a dual major of Elementary Education and Special Education. She received the Master of Arts degree from Baldwin Wallace College.

Ernestine was awarded the Department Chairperson of the Year - Intermediate Level, having outstanding service of a department of fifteen teachers. She received the 'Teacher of the Month' award from the Cleveland Cavaliers in recognition of the outstanding dedication to the students of the Cleveland Public School System. She continues to educate students as a home instructor tutor.

Ernestine holds a diamond life membership in Zeta Phi Beta Sorority, Inc..

Theophilus James "Chip" Caviness, Jr., is a newer member of The Association of African-American Cultural Gardens. He assists with correspondence and social media to increase national awareness of the African-American Cultural Garden.

"Chip," which has been his nickname since birth, graduated with honors from DeVry University majoring in The Applied Science of Electronics and Computer Technology. He heads up the Audio/Visual Department for The Greater Abyssinia Baptist Church, volunteers in the church office, is the website manager for the church website, is the administrator for the church's social media sites, and is a youth advocate for the G.A.B.C. WORD-in-MOTION Youth Ministry. Chip is a self-published author and writer of children's books which feature African-American characters. He is married and a father of two.

Carl Ewing
President

Tremell Yarbrough
Membership Chairperson

Carl is president of the African American Cultural Garden, a 501c3 non-profit organization dedicated to the education and development of the African American Cultural Garden. He is also a member of the executive board of the Cleveland Federation of Cultural Gardens, which oversees the 32 cultural gardens in University Circle. Carl is also instrumental in a project that will have security lights installed at the garden.

Carl S. Ewing attended Kent State University as a Political Science major and worked for over 25 years managing troubled multi-family and senior properties for Cuyahoga Metropolitan Housing Authority in Cleveland, where he possessed a strong employee leadership and tenant services. As a Certified Housing Manager, he was responsible for a 1.5 million dollar budget and maintained an operating income and expense within 5 percent of his approved budget.

Carl was inducted into the John Hay Alumni Hall of Fame in 2016 for his active involvement in Community Service throughout greater Cleveland. He is also is 2nd Vice President of the Cleveland Chapter of the NAACP.

Tremell Yarbrough is currently the membership chairperson of the Association of African American Cultural Gardens.

Tremell is a graduate of the Cleveland Public School System. He matriculated at Case Western Reserve University/Cleveland Institute of Music where he earned Bachelor of Science in Music Education with an emphasis in piano, voice, and choral conducting. He began his teaching career in the East Cleveland School District and retired from the Cleveland Municipal School District in 2014.

Tremell has been a workshop presenter for the Music of African American Spirituals, Gospel, Choral and Choral Decorum, as well as, serving as a consultant for teaching and performance styles. Tremell's awards presented in recognition of his musical talent include Who's Who of American High School Students, Ohio's 100 Outstanding Teachers by British Petroleum Amoco, The Cleveland Education Fund, and the Archbishop James Lyke African American Male Image Award.

You feel as if you've known him forever, but that doesn't mean you know everything.

Of all the women living with HIV in the United States, 66% are African American. Most of these women (87%) got HIV by having unprotected sex with a man. The good news is more women are getting tested for HIV, because they realize no one can look out for themselves better than they can. Whatever the result, there are treatment and support programs available in your community. To find out where you can get a free HIV test, visit hivtest.org/takecharge or call toll free 1-800-CDC-INFO (232-4636). If you've had unprotected sex, get tested for HIV.

Get an HIV test and look out for yourself.

   1-800-CDC-INFO (232-4636)

CORPORATE SPOTLIGHT

ARCHITECTURE, CONSTRUCTION AND ENGINEERING

Michael Chuwuonye,
SCADA
Engineer
FirstEnergy

Michael Chukwuonye works for FirstEnergy as a SCADA engineer. In this position, he works with team of analysts and engineers in support of Energy Management System and Generation Management System. He joined the company in 2016.

Michael is the chair for MOSaic a newly formed FirstEnergy Employee Business Resource Group that serves as a resource for FirstEnergy's people of color and their allies. MOSaic is an idea dear to his heart. He serves as the president of National Society of Black Engineers Northeastern Ohio (NEO-NSBE) chapter. He previously served as vice president of NEO-NSBE.

Michael received double associate degrees of general science and general arts from Cuyahoga Community College. The Washkewicz College of Engineering at Cleveland State University (CSU) awarded him a Bachelor of Electrical Engineering while Monte Ahuja College of Business also at CSU awarded him a Master of Business Administration in 2015.

As a McNair scholar, Michael encourages others about the need to be involved in scholarly activities. He also serves in many other groups like Nzuko Ndi Igbo of Northeast Ohio (NNINO) and FirstEnergy Safety committee.

Michele Crawford
Project Manager,
Capital &
Construction
Cuyahoga
Community College

Michele Crawford is a designer based in Cleveland. She attended Ohio University and The School of the Art Institute of Chicago where she studied architecture. She currently works as a project manager at Cuyahoga Community College in the Capital and Construction department where she manages multiple aspects of the college's new construction and renovation projects. Michele serves on the Rainey Institute Board of Directors as secretary and on the board of Midtown Cleveland and the Green Ribbon Coalition. She believes that design changes our world and ultimately our dreams. Michele is an ACE mentor and has led educational programs for students interested in architecture in partnership with John Hay and the Museum of Contemporary Art Cleveland. She is a member of the American Institute of Architects and the National Organization of Minority Architects. She is passionate about people, process, and the integration of art and life. Currently, Michele is exploring community engagement through the arts with local agencies.

Deona Davis
Industrial Engineer
STERIS Corporation

Deona Davis is a highly skilled Industrial Engineer with over 20 years of professional experience. She's been employed at STERIS Corporation for 9 years with an excellent track record in project management, continuous improvement, sustaining production requirements and ensuring compliance with FDA, Regulatory and ISO Standards in Healthcare and Life Sciences Business Segments.

Prior to this role, Deona held title of Senior Logistics Engineer at Penske Logistics for 2 years where she developed best practices to optimize warehousing operations and distribution systems. For 12 years, Deona was a Senior Industrial Engineer in the automotive industry working for Chrysler and General Motors Corporations. She successfully designed and evaluated integrated systems for automotive stamping and assembly processes, led business improvement projects and held supervisory roles. Deona also has experience as an Industrial Engineering Consultant.

Additionally, Deona is Senior Managing Partner at DMD Management Group and is responsible for management of administration functions, including real estate acquisitions, developments and asset management.

Deona acquired her Bachelor of Science Degree in Industrial Engineering from Cleveland State University and holds Lean Manufacturing and Project Management Certifications.

ngela M. Jones is senior governmental affairs specialist for the Northeast Ohio Regional Sewer District. A 20-year veteran in the environmental field, Angela has a vast understanding of the water and wastewater treatment industry. She works directly with key stakeholders and the community to educate and engage communities to address wastewater and stormwater issues. With servant leadership as her guiding principle, Angela is president of the Cleveland Chapter of the National Forum of Black Public Administrators. She serves as the collegiate initiative chair for the Northeast Ohio Professional Chapter of the National Society of Black Engineers. Dedicated to the education of youth on engineering as a career aspiration, she is a co-coordinator for educational outreach programs for the Greater Cleveland National Society of Black Engineers Jr. program, Student Technical Enrichment Program (STEP) and is co-lead for the Cleveland Architecture, Construction and Engineering (ACE Cleveland) Collinwood High School program. Angela received her Bachelor of Science in Civil Engineering with a minor in Environmental Science from Ohio Northern University.

Angela M. Jones
Senior Governmental
Affairs Specialist
Northeast Ohio
Regional Sewer District

aren Leak inspires young minds to develop the future as a program manager for one of Rockwell Automation's early career programs. She uses innovative approaches to engage and coach interns through real-life engineering work experiences.

Karen recognizes the volatility of the maturation process and believes in crafting individualized mentoring to lead to success. Her outreach is not limited to her recruitment efforts. She attempts to encourage all young people to consider technology in some form for their future. Helping people realize their possibilities is her goal and fundamentally, she believes there are opportunities in STEM for all.

Karen is married and shares two amazing young adults with her husband. She is a proud graduate of North Carolina Agricultural and Technical State University where she earned both a Bachelors and Masters of Science in Mechanical Engineering.

Karen Leak
Program Manager
Rockwell Automation

Kevin Madison, A.I.A. is the President of RPMI and has been with the firm for 28 years focusing on planning, programming, design, construction documents and construction support services. As an Architect and project manager, Mr. Madison has been involved and responsible for client and project team coordination, program evaluation, building design, sustainable design and quality control. Mr. Madison has a wide range of experience in the design of various building types, some of which include Sieberling K-6 School in Akron, Cleveland Brown's Football Stadium, the Great Lakes Science Center and several projects for the Cleveland Clinic. Kevin earned his Architectural degree from Howard University and is registered in the State of Maryland and the State of Ohio. He has served on the City of Shaker Heights Planning Commission and Board of Zoning Appeals, the Cleveland Restoration Society, the Greater Cleveland Habitat for Humanity Advisory Committee and the Cleveland Historic Warehouse District Design Review Board. Mr. Madison is also NCARB certified and is LEED AP BD+C Certified. He is married to Architect Sandra Madison and has two children, R. Kevin Jr. and Maya. @rpmiarchitects (instagram) @RPMadisonInt (twitter)

**R. Kevin Madison,
A.I.A., LEED AP BD+C**
President
Robert P. Madison
International

Sandra Madison, AIA, NCARB
CEO & Chairperson
Robert P. Madison
International

Sandra Madison, AIA, in March of 2016 became CEO & Chairperson of RPMI and today leads the architectural firm. She has dedicated 28 years to its success. During Sandra's tenure, RPMI has had significant roles on an array of signature projects including the Karamu House Renovation, Downtown Hilton Hotel, Cleveland Convention Center, Halle PK-8 School, Great Lakes Science Center just to name a few. She has been recognized as a top CEO by Crain's Cleveland Business in 2017, a top FBE by the OhioMBE Awards 2017, 2018 Smart Women Award Honoree, the 2018 President's Council Business Chamber Excellence Award and the 2018 Business Longevity Award. She graduated from the University of Maryland-College Park School of Architecture and attended Harvard University Graduate School of Design's Career Discovery Program for Urban Design. Her professional affiliations include the American Institute of Architects, The ACE Mentor Board of Cleveland, the Shaker Heights Architectural Review Board ,the Shaker Public Art Committee and the Euclid Corridor Design Review Board. She is married to Architect R. Kevin Madison, AIA and has two children R. Kevin Jr and Maya. @rpmiatchitects (instagram) @RPMadisonInt (twitter)

Chanel P. Murray
Vice President, Senior Process Improvement Consultant
PNC Financial Services Group, Inc.

Chanel Murray is a Senior Process Improvement Consultant with PNC. In her current role, she utilizes lean principles, data analytics and advanced technologies such as robotics automation to drive efficiency and quality improvements for the Anti-Money Laundering segment of Retail Bank Operations. Her extensive experience as a process improvement professional spans across the manufacturing, retail, supply chain and financial service industries. She prides herself on being a collaborative, critical thinker and consistently seeks opportunities to optimally solve a problem. Mrs. Murray is also an Adjunct Statistics Instructor at Cuyahoga Community College. She holds a Bachelor of Science in Industrial Engineering from Kettering University and Master of Science in Operations Research from Case Western Reserve University. Her husband and 3 sons are the center of her world outside of her professional realm.

"I am extremely grateful to have chosen a career path that feeds my passion to solve problems while impacting not only an organization's bottom line but also the quality of work for the people at the center of an organization's success."

Ruth E. Ray
Secondary Academic Coordinator
Warrensville Heights City School District

Ruth E Ray, M.Ed. currently serves as the Secondary Academic Coordinator of the Warrensville Heights City School District. A proud graduate of East Technical High School, she also received a Bachelor's of Science in Environmental Engineering (Water Resource Management & Biology) from Central State University. She later received her wetland delineation certifications and worked as an Environmental Construction Site Inspector.

Ruth quickly realized she enjoyed educating people and children about her career and the environment, so she returned to school. She completed a teacher certification program for secondary education in science grades seven through twelve and received her Masters in Education at Notre Dame of Ohio College.

Ruth's dedication and commitment has given her the opportunity to serve our youth of the North East Ohio area and beyond for almost two decades. She relishes in the opportunity to expose scholars, family, and the community to educational and career opportunities through STEAM (Science Technology Engineering Art Math).

Ruth's greatest accomplishment is being a supportive wife to Carlin D. Ray, proud mother of Carlin Dean, Cameron David, and grandmother to Carlin Dean Ray III.

Onwar Shaheer is a manufacturing process design engineer at Hendrickson, Trailer Commercial Vehicle Systems. Mr. Shaheer plays a key role in creating new manufacturing equipment, troubleshooting and resolving issues with existing equipment and supporting new plant startup. One of his strengths is his ability to learn by getting involved with projects outside of his department or even engineering. His overall experiences in materials, product design, process design and project management has allowed him to make an impact in both the automotive and aerospace industries. Onwar received his Bachelor of Science in Mechanical Engineering from Kettering University. He is an active and contributing member of the National Society of Black Engineers (NSBE) and is an advisor for the Northeast Ohio NSBE Jr. Chapter. As a mentor to not only NSBE Jr. high school students, but also undergraduate engineers, Onwar understands the potential impact he can make through his positive influence because of how others have impacted him on his journey.

Onwar Shaheer
Manufacturing Engineer
Hendrickson, Trailer
Commercial Vehicle
Systems

Lizalyn Smith is an Aerospace Engineer at the National Aeronautics and Space Administration (NASA) Glenn Research Center. Ms. Smith holds a Bachelor's degree in Mechanical Engineering from the University of Michigan, and a Master's degree in Mechanical Engineering from North Carolina Agricultural and Technical State University. In addition to her career at NASA, Lizalyn has served in various capacities for the Northeast Ohio Professionals Chapter of the National Society of Black Engineers (NSBE). She has served as president of the Chapter, as well as facilitator for the Greater Cleveland NSBE Jr. Chapter.

She is a recent graduate of the Cleveland Federal Community Leadership Institute (CFCLI), where she helped to develop and implement a program to bring Science, Technology, Engineering, Art and Mathematics (STEAM) awareness to local students.

Ms. Smith enjoys spending time with her son, writing, and teaching fellow writers the steps to self-publishing books. Her debut book, Calculate Your Savings, has helped many people discover innovative ways to save money.

Lizalyn Smith
Aerospace Engineer
NASA Glenn
Research Center

Maryanne Stone currently is a Project Manager at Cleveland State University. Her most recent overall project management responsibility includes the completion of the 100,000 square foot, $62 million Washkewicz College of Engineering Building.

Maryanne started her career in the public sector for the City of Akron Planning Department. She applied her architecture skills with Burt Hill, WTW Architects and TC Architects on the design development of several higher education facilities and public housing developments.

Expanding her career, Maryanne switched from working with design firms to construction by joining G. Stephens and SAF, Inc. As a Project Manager, she worked on significant new construction and renovation projects for local and federal government agencies throughout the east coast and the mid-west. Most notable projects includes the home of the VPOTUS, Andrews Air Force Base and Arlington National Cemetery.

She is a graduate of Kent State University's School of Architecture and has a Masters in Project Management from The Keller School of Management. She credits her love of creative arts and family for inspiring her to study architecture to complement the family construction business.

Maryanne Stone
Project Manager
Cleveland State
University

1,000 Books for 1,000 Kids

HEALTHCARE SPOTLIGHT

 Cleveland Clinic

Cleveland Clinic

Jacquelyne E. Bailey, PhD
Senior Director, Regional Community Relations

Ragina N. Bass, RN
Kidney/Pancreas Pre-Transplant Coordinator

Always fueled by passion and her strong faith focused on making an impact, Jacquelyne (Jacque) Bailey has garnered career success across industries in vastly different roles, and despite major personal health challenges. Bailey is currently the senior director of regional community relations in the Office of Government and Community Relations. The mission of the RCR is centered around establishing healthy community initiatives (group exercise and health talks on lifestyle management)—a collaborative effort between Cleveland Clinic and community partners to promote optimal health and wellness in the community.

About 10 years ago, Bailey was diagnosed with cancer, forcing her to resign from her career in business and finance, leading to her Cleveland Clinic career at South Pointe Hospital as director of the Angel Network, supporting cancer patients in the community. Bailey was successful in growing their business more than 100% in three years and built the team from four people to eight. She also raised more than one million dollars in grants over the three-year period. She left there in 2016 to join the Government and Community Relations team. As a part of the Taussig Administration Team she completed the Taussig Serving Leadership Cohort in 2015.

Nursing has been in Ragina N. Bass' blood since she was a teenager and she has wanted to be a transplant nurse even longer. Her first encounter with a transplant patient came at the early age of ten years old when her father's best friend had a transplant at Cleveland Clinic. Fast forward to the present, and you will find that she has dedicated her life to the field of nursing for the past twenty years and transplant for thirteen! When not busy helping patients pursue transplants, she enjoys writing, traveling and spending time with her family.

Cleveland Clinic

Linda D. Bradley, MD
Professor of Surgery | Vice Chair, OB/GYN &
Women's Health Institute
Director, Center of Mentrual Disorders

Kendalle Cobb, MD
Director of Diversity and Inclusion

Linda D. Bradley, MD is a professor of surgery at the Cleveland Clinic Lerner College of Medicine of Case Western Reserve University and vice chair of the Obstetrics, Gynecology, and Women's Health Institute at the Cleveland Clinic. She is also vice chair for diversity and inclusion for the Cleveland Clinic Women's Health Institute.

An internationally recognized gynecologic surgeon, Linda was president of the American Association of Gynecologic Laparoscopists and has served on the Board of Trustees for the American Association of Gynecologic Laparoscopy and the Cleveland Clinic Board of Governors.

Linda earned a Bachelor of Science degree from Vassar College and a Medical Degree from the University of Cincinnati College of Medicine.

Passionate about inspiring others to be "the best version of themselves," Linda founded Cleveland Clinic Celebrate Sisterhood®. For the past 15 years, she has hosted an annual Celebrate Sisterhood Multicultural Health & Wellness Summit, educating more than 10,000 multicultural women.

Linda believes in changing how we think about health one pot, one plate and one fork at a time. Her motto: "Every day, we can choose health."

Dr. Kendalle Cobb grew up in San Francisco. She went on to college, graduating from Harvard University with a bachelor's degree in history. She earned her medical degree from George Washington University in Washington, DC. She then headed back west where she completed her family medicine residency at Kaiser Foundation Hospital in in Fontana, CA. She takes care of patients of all ages at the Cleveland Clinic Solon Family Health Center. She also teaches at the Cleveland Clinic Lerner College of Medicine of Case Western Reserve University where she is Director of Diversity and Inclusion and advises medical students. She is the physician director of the Cleveland Clinic Physician Diversity Scholars Program that pairs underrepresented minority medical students at Ohio University Heritage College of Medicine Cleveland Campus with underrepresented minority physicians. She was awarded a one-year Chief of Staff grant in November 2016. Her project explored the successes and challenges that the Clinic faces in creating a culture of diversity and inclusion. Dr. Cobb serves on the Board of Governors of Cleveland Clinic. She and her family live in Shaker Heights.

Cleveland Clinic

Lutul D. Farrow, MD, FAOA
Staff Orthopaedic Surgeon

John Edward George III, MD, MS
Anesthesia Director of Marymount Ambulatory
Surgery Center

Lutul D. Farrow, MD is a staff orthopaedic surgeon in the Cleveland Clinic Orthopaedic and Rheumatologic Institute. He is also an associate professor of surgery in the Cleveland Clinic Lerner College of Medicine. Dr. Farrow serves as the program director for the Orthopaedic Surgery Sports Medicine Fellowship Program.

Dr. Farrow graduated from Baldwin Wallace University. He earned a medical degree at Case Western Reserve University School of Medicine and completed his Orthopaedic Surgery Residency at Case Western Reserve University/University Hospitals of Cleveland. He completed his Fellowship in Sports Medicine and Arthroscopy at the Cleveland Clinic.

Dr. Farrow has served as a team physician for the Cleveland Browns, the University of Arizona Wildcat, Pima Community College Aztecs, the Tucson Rodeo, the Arizona Diamondbacks and Colorado Rockies. Currently, Dr. Farrow serves as the head orthopaedic consultant for Baldwin Wallace University and head team physician at Brunswick High School. He has authored multiple Orthopaedic Surgery book chapters and over thirty-five manuscripts in peer-reviewed orthopaedic surgery journals.

Dr. Farrow enjoys spending time with his wife, Tenisha and their three sons, Andrew, Donovan and Jackson.

Born in Detroit, Michigan, John Edward George III, MD, MS has always been passionate about helping people and serving in his community.

Dr. George graduated from Case Western Reserve University undergraduate college and school of medicine. His medical career started in the field of plastic surgery during which he earned a Master of Science degree in applied anatomy while in training. After his plastic surgery training, he completed an anesthesia residency and fellowship, and is currently a practicing anesthesiologist at the Cleveland Clinic.

His subspecialty in anesthesiology is acute pain medicine, and his current role at the Cleveland Clinic is anesthesia director of Marymount Ambulatory Surgery Center. Dr. George also lectures at regional and national anesthesia meetings and serves on an advisory board for the American Board of Anesthesia (the credentialing body that certifies and recertifies all U.S. anesthesiologists).

Dr. George also actively participates in and enjoys giving back to the community through volunteer experiences such as serving food with his family (wife and 5 kids) a few times a year at St. Malachi Center. He also volunteers for Greater Cleveland Habitat for Humanity and serves as one of their board members.

Cleveland Clinic

Leslie Hardy
Program Manager

Uche Gordon Iheme, MD, FACP
Co-Medical Director,
Minority Men's Health Center

Leslie Hardy currently serves as program manager in the Office of Diversity and Inclusion at Cleveland Clinic. She is responsible for partnering with internal and external stakeholders to promote workforce and professional staff diversity, education, and inclusion initiatives across the enterprise. Through strategic programming and partnerships, she works to advocate for and support a workforce that is reflective of the changing demographics of our country and the multi-national landscape to provide improved patient outcomes.

Leslie completed her Bachelor of Science degree in Health Sciences at Howard University in Washington, DC, and she earned her Master of Science degree in Health Policy and Management at The New School in New York, NY. She serves on the Board of Directors at Lorain County Health and Dentistry, is on the board of the National Association of Health Services Executives (NAHSE) North East Ohio Chapter, and serves on the Diversity Committee for the National Center for Healthcare Leadership. Additionally, Leslie is passionate about accessible health and wellness practices, and will complete her 200 hour hatha yoga teacher training with the Cleveland Clinic School of Yoga in December 2019.

Uche Gordon Iheme, MD, is a physician in the department of Internal Medicine and co-medical director of the Cleveland Clinic's Minority Men's Health Center at the Cleveland Clinic. In these roles, Iheme treats patients, participates in med school and graduate medical education activities with special interest in the early detection and treatment of medical conditions that disproportionately affect minorities.

In 2017, Iheme was awarded the Volunteerism and Community Service Award by the OH Chapter of American College of Physicians, ACP. For the past decade, he has been providing care and education at health fairs at the Cleveland Clinic, churches and other locations to help close the gap in health disparities between population groups in the Cleveland area. He is a fellow of the A.C.P.

Iheme graduated from the University of Lagos College of Medicine in Lagos, Nigeria. He is enrolled in the Master of Management in Clinical Informatics graduate degree program of the Duke University School of Medicine, in Durham, NC. His special areas of interest are hypertension, medical education and minority health education.

He resident of Solon, Ohio, Iheme is married with two lovely children.

Cleveland Clinic

Dr. Stacey Jolly
Associate Program Director
Director of Ambulatory
Education and Experience

Dr. Charles Martin
Vascular and Interventional Radiologist

Dr. Stacey Jolly is of Aleut (Alaska Native; Bristol Bay Native Corporation) and Swedish ancestry. She holds a degree in biology from California Polytechnic State University San Luis Obispo and a medical degree from Stanford University School of Medicine. She completed residency in Internal Medicine and a Clinical Research Fellowship at the University of California San Francisco. Since 2009 she has been at Cleveland Clinic. She is an associate professor of Medicine at Cleveland Clinic Lerner College of Medicine and is a staff physician in General Internal Medicine. She has had a productive career in clinical research with a focus on chronic diseases such as chronic kidney disease (CKD), diabetes, hypertension, and heart disease. She has had NIH funding, is active with local and national professional organizations, and continues with clinical research related to CKD. Currently, she is the associate program director, and director of ambulatory education and experience at Cleveland Clinic's Internal Medicine Residency Program as well as the Primary Care Track Program Director. She is committed to encouraging minority youth to pursue careers in science and health fields. She is married to Dr. Emmitt Jolly, CWRU professor in biology, and they have two children.

Dr. Charles Martin (Chuck) is a vascular and interventional radiologist at the Cleveland Clinic, where he also currently serves as the director of the Interventional Oncology subgroup. He is an assistant professor at the Cleveland Clinic Lerner College of Medicine and is involved in multiple educational activities with the residents and fellows and serves as associate program director of the fellowship, and the medical students of the CCF Lerner College of Medicine. He completed his undergraduate studies at The Johns Hopkins University, and medical school at Case Western Reserve University. After completing his Diagnostic Radiology residency at University Hospitals Case Medical Center, he obtained subspecialty training in Vascular and Interventional Radiology at Yale University/Yale New Haven Hospital.

Dr. Martin serves on numerous committees, including the American College of Radiology, the Society of Interventional Radiology, the National Medical Association, the Cleveland Medical Association, and the Ohio Radiologic Society.

Currently, his research in augmented reality focuses on its applications in Healthcare. Most recently, he successfully completed the world's first tumor ablation using augmented reality. Additional AR projects are centered on patient experience and communications.

Dr. Charles Modlin, MD, MBA
Kidney Transplant Surgeon

Cleveland Clinic

Le Joyce Kaye Naylor
Chief Diversity & Inclusion Officer

Dr. Charles Modlin, M.D., MBA, is past president of Cleveland Clinic's medical staff and a kidney transplant surgeon and urologist. He is a member of the Board of Governors and Board of Trustees, executive director of Minority Health and Cleveland Clinic Physician Lead for Public Health. He founded and directs Cleveland Clinic's Minority Men's Health Center and established Cleveland Clinic's Annual Minority Men's Health Fair. He was named by The Atlanta Post as one of the Top 21 Black Doctors in America. He graduated from Northwestern University and Northwestern University Medical School, completed a six-year residency in urology at New York University, a three-year fellowship in kidney transplantation surgery at Cleveland Clinic and joined the Cleveland Clinic Staff in 1996. Honors include appointment to the Ohio Commission on Minority Health by two Ohio governors, Northwestern University Presidential Alumni Medal, MLK Community Service Award, Call & Post 100 Top Influential Leaders, Cleveland Magazine Best Doctors, Cleveland Clinic Bruce Hubbard Stewart Humanitarianism Award, and 2015 Black Professional Association Professional of the Year recognition.

Le Joyce Naylor serves as chief diversity & inclusion officer for Cleveland Clinic. In her enterprise role, Naylor champions the goal of fostering an inclusive and culturally competent work environment to better serve patients, caregivers, and underserved communities. She is responsible for partnering with key stakeholders to develop and implement the enterprise strategy for diversity and inclusion. She ensures that diversity strategies and metrics are integrated throughout the enterprise to support Cleveland Clinic's mission, vision, and values. These efforts have resulted in Cleveland Clinic being recognized as a DiversityInc Top Hospital and Health System for ten consecutive years, most notably ranking #1 in 2019.

In her pervious role, Naylor was division administrator for Human Resources. She worked with the chief human resources officer on strategic planning and process improvement, along with fiscal planning for the division.

Naylor holds a master's in human resources from Cleveland State University, a Diversity Management certificate from Cornell University, and is a Cornell Certified Diversity Professional/Advanced Practitioner. She serves on the National Center for Healthcare Leadership's Diversity & Inclusion Council, Celebrate Sisterhood Executive Committee, Member Engagement Committee for Commission on Economic Inclusion, and the Board of Directors for the American Sickle Cell Anemia Association.

Cleveland Clinic

Brain U. Nwaozuzu
Nurse Practioner, Stephanie Tubbs Jones
Outpatient Clinic

Kaine C. Onwuzulike, MD, PhD
Neurological Surgeon

Brain U. Nwaozuzu was born in Nigeria and migrated to the United States over 20 years ago. He has lived in greater Cleveland for all of those years. He is a graduate of Case Western Reserve University as well as the Federal University of Science and Technology, Owerri, Nigeria. For the past eight years, Nwaozuzu has practiced in Internal Medicine. He currently works as a nurse practitioner at the Stephanie Tubbs Jones Outpatient Clinic where he opened a cardiology clinic. In addition, Nwaozuzu has worked at University Hospital as well as Case Western Reserve University as an adjunct instructor.

Dr. Kaine C. Onwuzulike is a native Detroiter and board eligible pediatric and adult neurological surgeon at Cleveland Clinic. He specializes in various neurosurgical disorders including comprehensive pediatric neurosurgery, congenital and craniofacial malformations, complex spinal deformities, brain and spine tumors, hydrocephalus, cranio-spinal trauma, minimally invasive spine and brain surgery, neuroendoscopic surgery, Chiari malformation, spasticity and fetal repair of myelomeningocele.

He received his post graduate medical and doctoral education at Case Western Reserve University in Cleveland with a focus on neuroscience and cardiovascular disease. His doctoral degree is in Genetic Epidemiology and Biostatistics.

He is member of several prestigious specialty and philanthropic organizations including the American Association of Neurological Surgeons, Congress of Neurological Surgeons, Society of Black Academic Surgeons, American College of Surgeons, American Society of Pediatric Neurosurgeons, and International Federation of Neuroendoscopy.

He is a founding member of Legacy Associates Foundation, a philanthropic youth empowerment organization with the inherent principles of scholastic achievement, economic empowerment and community involvement and is on the Board of Directors of Boys and Girls Club of Cleveland. He currently resides in Cleveland Heights and currently practices at Cleveland Clinic Main Campus (Cleveland) and Cleveland Clinic Akron General (Downtown Cleveland).

FOCUS
CELEBRATE
PROMINENCE
RECOGNITION

COUNSELORS AT LAW

Knowledgeable and critical, the attorneys featured in this section are advocates for their corporations and communities. As they fight for justice, they stand out as pillars in the city of Cleveland.

Alexander Bolden
Associate
Squire Patton Boggs
(US) LLP

Alex Bolden is an associate in our Public & Infrastructure Finance Practice. He has experience in general obligation debt, revenue bond debt, tax increment financing, special assessments and certificates of participation. He also has experience with a variety of water and sewer revenue bonds, port authority bonds, conduit financings and 501(c)(3) bonds. Beyond the financial realm, Alex also assists public bodies by researching issues regarding their capabilities as public entities pursuant to applicable legislation.

He received his bachelor's degree from Bates College and his juris doctorate from the University of Chicago. Prior to law school, Alex worked as a judicial intern for the Honorable Rick E. Lawrence of the Maine District Court. While in law school, he was a member of the Employment Discrimination Project working on plaintiff side class-action racial discrimination litigation. Alex is an Esperanza Alumni Association Board member, helping to provide scholarships to students across northeast Ohio for postsecondary education.

Michael Bowen
Attorney
Calfee, Halter &
Griswold LLP

Michael Bowen is an attorney in Calfee, Halter & Griswold's Government Relations and Legislation and Litigation practice groups. He advises clients ranging from small, closely held businesses to large public corporations and public entities. Michael is graduate from Ohio University and Cleveland-Marshall College of Law. Notably, Michael ran the successful re-election campaign of Cleveland Mayor Frank Jackson and has advised both countywide and presidential campaigns in the past. Michael has been recognized by Cleveland Magazine as a "One to Watch," and received Crain's Cleveland Business magazine's 20 in their 20's award. He serves on numerous boards across Northeast Ohio including Engage! Cleveland, Center of Arts and Inspired Learning, and the Shaker Heights School's Foundation.

Julian Emerson
Shareholder
Reminger Co., LPA

Julian Emerson serves as co-chair of Reminger's Environmental/Mass Tort/Class Action practice group. He has represented manufacturers and suppliers in toxic tort litigation, including the representation of asbestos, silica and benzene defendants throughout Ohio. Julian handles a very diverse range of matters including general casualty, construction liability, commercial litigation, and trucking/commercial transportation in all levels of various courts in Ohio including state, federal, and appellate courts. Julian is very involved at Reminger, sitting on Reminger's Diversity Committee, Mentoring Committee, Law Clerk Hiring Committee, and the Reminger Foundation Board. Since 2012, Julian has served as an adjunct professor for Cleveland-Marshall College of Law's Mock Trial Team coaching second and third year law students in trial advocacy. He is a member of the Cleveland Metropolitan Bar Association, National Bar Association, and Norman S. Minor Bar Association. Julian also serves as one of Reminger's representatives for the Cleveland Legal Aid Society's "Partners in Justice" initiative. Julian received his juris doctorate from the Temple University Beasley School of Law and his Bachelor of Arts from Villanova University.

Gregory Guice received his juris doctorate from Case Western Reserve School of Law, and his bachelor's degree from Yale University. He is a shareholder at Reminger Co., LPA's Cleveland office and is the chair of the Retail and Hospitality Practice Group and Reminger's Diversity Committee. His practice includes retail and hospitality liability, professional liability, business/commercial litigation and employment liability. He has appeared in various state and appellate courts throughout Ohio including the Ohio Supreme Court. He has experience in Ohio U.S. District Courts, U.S. Bankruptcy Courts and Sixth Circuit Court of Appeals. Gregory serves as vice president of Diversity and Inclusion for Cleveland Metropolitan Bar Association (CMBA) and is a member of their board of trustees and executive committee. Greg serves as co-chair of CMBA's Minority Clerkship Program, chair of CMBA's Diversity Pipeline Subcommittee, and their Certified Grievance Committee. Greg has been honored numerous times by Ohio Super Lawyers magazine. He is a member of the National Bar Association, Ohio Bar Association and Norman S. Minor Bar Association.

Gregory Guice
Shareholder
Reminger Co., LPA

Joy Kennedy, Esq. is a criminal defense attorney employed in the felony division of the Cuyahoga County Public Defender Office, in Cleveland, Ohio. Joy has worked in this office for over 14 years and has handled cases that range from a simple drug possession to an aggravated murder. Joy has also provided legal representation in the areas of estate planning, probate administration, and domestic relations.

Joy graduated from Hampton University, Virginia Commonwealth University, and Cleveland – Marshall College of Law. In addition to practicing law, Joy Kennedy is also a Licensed Independent Social Worker for the State of Ohio. She has been working with families and children for nearly 25 years.

Joy is a proud member of Sigma Gamma Rho Sorority, Inc., the Cleveland Metropolitan Bar Association and the Black Women's Political Action Committee. She attends Antioch Baptist Church, is married to Antwaine, and they share two sons, Isaiah and Austin.

Joy Kennedy, Esq.
Criminal Defense
Attorney
Cuyahoga County
Public Defender Office
- Felony Division

Frederick R. Nance's legal practice focuses on sports and entertainment law and commercial litigation. His practice in recent years has included high-stakes negotiations involving community interests and Cleveland's development. He also leads the firm's Sports and Entertainment Group in the U.S. He is a member of the Executive Committee of the Greater Cleveland Partnership and has served as a director of the Cleveland Clinic for more than a decade. In 2015, Nance became one of a handful of lawyers to ever be inducted into the Cleveland Business Hall of Fame. In 2014, he received the Managing Partner of the Year Pathfinder Award by the African American Managing Partners and General Counsels' Network. He has been selected annually for professional peer recognition by organizations such as The Best Lawyers in America and Ohio Super Lawyers. A highly regarded litigator, Nance is a Fellow of the International Academy of Trial Lawyers. He received his bachelor's degree from Harvard University and his juris doctorate from the University of Michigan Law School.

Frederick R. Nance
Global Managing
Partner
Squire Patton Boggs US
LLP

Irene is a Cleveland native who used her woes with the credit system to start the only minority owned credit repair company legally operating in the state of Ohio. Growing up, she was completely unaware of how important her finances would be in adulthood. In 2014, after struggling with her personal credit, she was able to payoff existing debt with an inheritance only for her credit score to raise just 12 points. This jump-started her personal credit repair journey, where she was able to raise her score almost 400 points. Upon graduating from Baldwin Wallace University in 2016, she decided to take a chance on entrepreneurship. This resulted in the birth of Hannah Financial. Since her launch in 2017, she's been able to help over 1,000 people overcome their credit problems. Her company has removed over 2,000 inaccurately reporting accounts and helped 28 people buy new homes. She also teaches financial literacy to educate individuals on how to make better decisions that positively impact their credit. Hannah Financial has maintains an office in Cleveland and a team of five employees.

Irene Prewitt
Associate
Ulmer & Berne LLP

Marques P.D. Richeson is an experienced litigator who handles a wide range of matters from small business disputes to bet-the-company litigation. His areas of expertise include complex commercial litigation, mass tort litigation, class actions, and multidistrict litigation. He has represented clients in federal and state courts throughout the country at the trial and appellate level. Marques was recognized by Ohio Super Lawyers as promising among area litigators. He was named in Crain's Cleveland Business "40 Under 40" list. Marques serves on the board of trustees for HELP Foundation, and Center for Arts-Inspired Learning. He serves on the executive board for American Constitution Society and is a member of William K. Thomas Inn of Court. Richeson received his bachelor's degree from Vanderbilt University and his juris doctorate from Harvard Law School. Prior to returning to Cleveland, Marques worked at an international law firm in Washington DC. Before that, he served as a law clerk for The Honorable Henry Coke Morgan of the U.S. District Court for the Eastern District of Virginia.

Marques P.D. Richeson
Partner
Squire Patton Boggs (US) LLP

Samuel R. Smith II is an attorney currently in private practice. Smith's law practice consists of criminal defense and all areas of civil law except for bankruptcy, patent law and tax law. He received his Bachelor of Arts degree in Politics and Government from Ohio Wesleyan University in 1996. He received his juris doctorate degree from the Cleveland-Marshall College of Law in 2001. Smith is a former assistant attorney general for the State of Ohio and former assistant Cuyahoga County prosecutor. He is a member of Alpha Phi Alpha Fraternity Inc.; the Northeast Ohio Alumni Chapter of Ohio Wesleyan University; the board of directors for the Cleveland Heights Youth Club; the alumni board of directors for Ohio Wesleyan University; and the One Hundred Black Men. Smith is also a member of the Norman S. Minor Bar Association. In his spare time, he enjoys reading, traveling, and playing golf. He is married to Dr. Michele Heath-Smith and they have one daughter, Averie Myla Smith.

Samuel Smith II
Attorney at Law
Law Office of Samuel R. Smith II

Phillip Turner
Associate
Squire Patton Boggs US,
LLP

Phillip Turner is an associate in the financial services practice. He represents financial institutions and other entities in a variety of corporate and commercial financing-related matters. He focuses his practice on commercial and structured finance, including representing creditors and borrowers in the negotiation, documentation and management of both secured and unsecured single-bank and syndicated credit facilities. Phillip has assisted on deals across a broad range of industries, domestically and cross-border, in areas of asset-based lending, acquisition financing, equipment leasing and private equity. He received his bachelor's degree from Henderson State University and his juris doctorate from University of Michigan Law School. During law school, Phillip served as a legal counselor for Lawyers for Human Rights in South Africa, where he advised stateless individuals in Sub-Saharan Africa regarding the granting of legal statehood and citizenship. In addition, as a student, Phillip practiced in law clinics of both transactional and litigious natures in a variety of subjects.

ORGANIZATION
SPOTLIGHT

Brandie Bailey
Panzica Construction
Project Accountant

With more than 20 years of construction accounting experience, Brandie Bailey is serving the Northeast Ohio market as Project Accountant at Panzica Construction. As a liaison to the subcontractor community, she is responsible for the company's rigorous pre-qualification process which secures top-notch manpower to enable Panzica's active schedule of work. Additionally, managing the accounting and payment process, Brandie successfully keeps Panzica's $200 million project portfolio on track. Her wealth of experience and impeccable reputation for quality has earned the respect of her co-workers and industry peers. Brandie is a proud native Clevelander having studied accounting at David N. Myers University and she is a product of the Cleveland Metropolitan School District. Undertaking her very own residential construction project, Brandie recently finished a complete remodel of the interior of her home in Bedford Heights where she resides with her husband and young son.

Maya Angelou once said "Success is liking yourself, liking what you do, and liking how you do it." Baileyis proud to say that she considers herself a success because she lives by that motto.

Maia Z. Ballard
Operations Officer
RWJ Wiring, Inc.

Maia Z. Ballard is the operations officer at RWJ Wiring, Inc. which includes processing accounts, receivables, billing, invoicing and reconciling accounts. She oversees all financial and clerical services, while keeping a close eye on the internal departmental communications and resources. Prior to her current position, Maia spent several years working as a telecommunications technician for Local 38 IBEW installing low voltage systems including Wi-Fi, Nurse Call, Security, VoIP and many others. The experience helped her to prepare for a fulfilling career in the construction trades industry. When she's not keeping busy with internal reviews or site visits to various job sites, she enjoys volunteering at her church, Imani United Church of Christ, hiking, and spending time with her family.

Virginia Carter
Senior Project
Manager
Ozanne Construction
Company Inc.

Virginia Carter earned a Bachelor of Science in Civil Engineering from Cleveland State University. Since entering the construction industry over 20 years ago, Virginia has excelled in a field saturated by men. She is a highly respected individual with a strong academic background who continuously seeks to educate herself on new methodologies and critical industry-based certifications. Virginia started working at Ozanne Construction Company in 2004 where she is a senior project engineer. She is a LEED accredited professional with a LEED AP, BD+C certification. She has work on commercial, government and K-12 Education projects including Cleveland Metropolitan School District. She is commercially conscious and works hard to ensure safety for all team members. ACE Mentoring Program Cleveland at Max Hayes High School started a pilot program in 2013 which is headed by Virginia. Virginia has been instrumental in the success of the participants continued education. The 2018 ACE Mentoring Scholars awarded 30 scholarships totaling $125,000 to graduating seniors from across Northeast Ohio and $25,000 went to five Max Hayes students.

Danny Couch is Vice President & Safety Director of The AKA Team, a construction company located in Cleveland, Ohio. Danny spent 40 years with the federal government with four of those years as a member of the United States Air Force. Now that Danny has retired from the United States Postal Service, he is enjoying his second career in construction. His company provides general contracting services, construction management and commercial waterproofing. They focus on four things: safety, cost-control, timing and quality. The relationships they build with subcontractors, coupled with hands-on supervision and the ability to self-perform a variety of trades, provides them with the resources necessary to execute complex projects successfully. Danny comes from a family of entrepreneurs. His uncle and father introduced Couch's Sausage to the Cleveland area many years ago. In addition, his family were real estate developers in Cleveland; Cherry Hill, New Jersey and Atlanta, Georgia. Danny is married to Ariane Kirkpatrick and he is also the father of two daughters, Camille and Jazmine Couch and stepsons, Ali and Kristopher Kirkpatrick.

Danny Couch
Vice President &
Safety Director
The AKA Team

Shakorie Davis is president of Next Generation Construction Company, a rapidly growing general contractor currently on pace to exceed $10 million in sales for 2019.

Shakorie established NextGen in 2009. Beginning as a carpenter's apprentice, he focused on developing his skills and learning all he could as he progressed quickly to journeyman status. Always keeping his eye on the prize of business ownership and independence, Shakorie moved into the office, starting as an estimator and climbing the ladder to Project Manager.

Spending much of his apprenticeship working in local hospitals proved to be a marvelous launchpad for NextGen's growth. The company's client portfolio now includes University Hospitals, Cleveland Clinic, and MetroHealth Systems, in addition to the Cleveland Metropolitan School District.

Shakorie is a Cleveland native and committed citizen who believes in giving back, working smart, and paying it forward. An East Tech grad, he mentors at risk youth and loves to hire and develop qualified community residents. You can find him around the corner from his home, playing chess at Dewey's Coffee in Shaker Square. He is married with four children.

Shakorie Davis
President
Next Generation
Construction

Justin Dean provides field information and insight on day to day operations on construction projects to his team and assists with coordinating operations with trade contractors on work.

Mr. Dean is member of the Construction Employers Association (CEA) and active in the community by being a mentor in the Architecture-Construction-Engineering Program which reaches out to Cleveland Metropolitan School District students striking interest in the S.T.E.M. fields and prepare for college. Like many of the students he mentors, Mr. Dean is an inner-city local that graduated from Collinwood High School in 2009 then earned his Bachelor's of Science in Engineering Technology & Management from thee Ohio University in 2014 becoming a first-generation college graduate. During college, Mr. Dean joined the National Society of Black Engineers (NSBE).

On Mr. Dean's spare time, he enjoys the art of barbering and providing barber services honed throughout his college years. Encouraging others to chase their dreams and he lives by the words his late uncle gave him "Always have a backup plan for your backup plan, in case your first plan doesn't work."

Justin Dean
Field Engineer
Whiting-Turner
Contracting
Company

Marvin Echols
Construction Project
Manager
The Whiting-Turner
Contracting Co.

Marvin Echols is a construction project manager (CM) with The Whiting-Turner Contracting Co. Echols works on commercial projects in all industries with varied sizes and project costs that have exceeded a billion dollars.

Echols holds a Bachelor of Science in Mechanical Engineering. He is a member of the Cleveland Engineering Society, Construction Manager's Association of America, Construction Employer's Association, Cleveland State University's Center for Engineering Experiential Learning (CEEL) and Fenn Academy Advisory Boards, and recently became a mentor with College Now.

"Most people outside of construction, engineering, and architecture don't understand the industry or field of construction. When I mention I work in construction or as a CM, they commonly think of the construction trades like plumbers, electricians, or large-equipment operators. While those fields are worthwhile, there is an engineering side to construction that is very complex. It is a purposeful and rewarding career for those ready to accept the pressure-packed challenge. I tell students all the time how fulfilling my career is. It's tangible, it's 'green'. You're impacting neighborhoods and lives – chiefly for the good."

Margaret Hewitt,
Chief Executive
Officer
The Construction
Green Team

Margaret Hewitt, LEED AP, ENV SP is the chief executive officer of The Construction Green Team. She is a champion for sustainability in construction. Margaret has been a part of the construction industry for 30 years. She has managed more than $10 billion of construction projects and reached the Platinum level of LEED and INVEST certifications. She is a member of the Construction Employers Association, American Institute of Architects, National Organization of Minority Architects, United States Green Building Council, Institute for Sustainable Infrastructure, Black Environmental Leaders and Alpha Kappa Alpha Sorority, Inc. Margaret serves on the boards of Green Ribbon Coalition and Regional Leadership Team for USGBC Ohio. She earned her architecture degree from the University of Illinois Urbana-Campaign. Margaret is married to Edward Hewitt and has one daughter, Emilette Hewitt.

Christopher Howse
President
Howse Solutions, Inc

Christopher Howse is the President of Howse Solutions, Inc. (est. 2009), a full-service IT consulting firm. With a knack for solving problems and finding solutions, Chris has been helping companies leverage technology for over 25 years. Past collaborative projects include drone surveillance, public Wi-Fi, smartboard installation, audio-visual installations and CCTV installations.

Chris has been featured as a panelist and speaker on a variety of subject matters including entrepreneurship, skills training, workforce development and technology.

Chris is on the Advisory board for the Warrensville Heights YMCA and co-chairs the Cleveland MBEIC (Minority Business Enterprise Input Committee), the leadership group of the Ohio Minority Supplier Diversity Council. He graduated from Kent State University's Turner School of Construction, the Emerging Entrepreneurs with The Presidents' Council and the Supplier Diversity Executive Education Program with Ohio State's Fisher School of Business. He is a member of CEA (Contractor Employer Association) and CAA (Contractors Assistance Association).

Chris is married with 4 children and has coached chess, robotic, track and basketball teams.

Ariane Kirkpatrick is president of The AKA Team, a full-service construction company offering construction management, self-performance construction and commercial waterproofing. AKA's mission is to provide superior construction solutions. Ariane earned her Bachelor of Arts in Urban Studies at Cleveland State University. She is an active member of St. Agnes + Our Lady of Fatima, Presidents' Council Foundation, Construction Employers Association, and the 11th Congressional District Caucus. In 2011, Ariane had the honor to sit with President Obama at the Winning the Future Forum for Small Businesses held in Cleveland. She is the recipient of several awards including Crain's Women of Note, Presidents' Council John Bustamante Emerging Entrepreneur of the Year Award, Diversity Matters Julian Earls Community Award and Warrensville Heights High School 2013 Hall of Fame Inductee. Ariane happily sits on the board of her alma maters - Warrensville, Cuyahoga Community College and Cleveland State University. Ariane is married to Danny Couch and is the mother of sons, Ali and Kristopher; and stepdaughters, Camille and Jazmine.

Ariane Kirkpatrick,
President
The AKA Team

Taurean Spratt is a Project Manager at Turner Construction Company and has worked on recent projects including the $100M FirstEnergy Stadium Renovation and the $365M Cleveland Convention Center Project.

Taurean has played an instrumental role in Turner's community affairs efforts as a facilitator of the Turner School of Construction Management. This program offers courses to disadvantaged, veteran, small, minority and women owned businesses highlighting various principles in the construction industry. In addition to leading this program, Taurean managed Turner's inclusion program on the Cleveland Convention Center project which achieved over 30% SBE participation. As a result of Taurean's exemplary efforts at Turner, he has been the recipient of Turner's National Community Affairs Employee of the Year Award as well as several Ohio staff awards.

Taurean graduated with Honors from The University of Cincinnati with a Bachelors of Science in Construction Management. Taurean resides in Oakwood Village with his wife, Terika, and their two sons, Jayden and Camren. Taurean is a true builder at heart and is passionate about performing home renovations as well as the outdoors, motorcycle riding and boating.

Taurean Spratt
Project Manager
Turner Construction
Company

Orlando Taylor is the project manager for multiple projects at the Cuyahoga Community College Metropolitan Campus which includes the campus center renovation, and science lab upgrades. He is also providing procurement assistance for the Metro Health Campus transformation project. Orlando has worked for Turner Construction company for 22 years. He has worked on projects ranging from Paul Brown Stadium, KeyBank Integrated Branch, and Hilton Cleveland Downtown. Throughout the community, Orlando is involved in various organizations including being an ACE Cleveland board member and lead mentor at James F. Rhodes High School. He is co-chair of the Turner School of Construction Management in partnership with the City of Cleveland hosted by Cuyahoga Community College, a member of the CCC Capital, and Construction and Facilities Advisory Committee. Orlando has a MBA from Cleveland State University, and an associate degree in Civil Engineering Technology and a Bachelor of Science in Construction Management, both from the University of Cincinnati. He is a LEED AP BD+C and is OSHA 30 hour certified.

Orlando Taylor
Project Manager
Turner Construction
Company

John W. Todd
Owner
JWT&A LLC

John W. Todd is the owner of JWT&A LLC. He's owned this company since 2005. They perform Construction Management, General Contracting and Carpentry. They have performed on projects such as Cuyahoga County Juvenile Justice Center, Cleveland Hopkins Airport – BAA, Key Bank Renovation East 152nd and St. Clair, University Hospital W.O. Walker Building, Tri-C Health and Remedial School.

Todd grew up in Garfield and is a graduate of Garfield High School. Starting out with his father, he's been in construction since age 14. He entered the Plaster's Union at age 18. He completed a 4 year apprentice to become a journeyman plaster. He's taken courses at Cleveland State University and Cuyahoga Community College.

Age 28, he started his first business where he renovated homes but has since returned to commercial construction. A master plaster, Todd is a member of Construction Employers Association, Carpenters Local Union and a graduate of Turner Construction's W.O. Walker Construction Management Class.

Single with no children, Todd currently lives in Cleveland. He enjoys working out and playing golf in his spare time.

Fatima Ware
Business Owner/Sheet
Metal Worker
Fatima Construction,
LLC

Fatima Ware earned her bachelor's degree in Accounting with a minor in Business Management from Myers University in 2008. Fatima is an astute sheet metal worker with eight years of experience. Her experience in the building trades is highlighted by her accomplishments as a journeyman sheet metal worker which include National Air Duct Cleaners Association certified inspector, Aerial Work Platform certification and Infection Control Risk Assessment certification, testing, adjusting and balancing certification, as well as refrigerant transition & recovery certification. Fatima's impressive career in the construction field encompasses a myriad of projects in the Greater Cleveland Area including major projects such as University Hospital, CASE, Global Center for Health Innovation & Convention Center and Health Education Campus of the Cleveland Clinic. She established the Cleveland District Women's Committee of Local #33 currently serving as chairperson. Fatima is a native Clevelander and member of the Women in Construction Committee, Construction Employers Association, Sheet Metal and Air Conditioning Contractors Association. In recognition of her service, she received the William J. Gambatese award.

The scholars of our community aim to influence, teach and challenge. This section highlights Cleveland professionals who value education as a catalyst for success.

Roland V. Anglin
Dean and Professor
Maxine Goodman
Levin College of Urban
Affairs

Roland V. Anglin is dean of the Maxine Goodman Levin College of Urban Affairs at Cleveland State University. Recognized for his scholarly and applied work in economic and community development, he's a passionate advocate for public policy and community-based strategies that create social and economic opportunities for marginalized communities and people. Anglin was senior advisor to the Chancellor of Rutgers University-Newark, and director of the Joseph C. Cornwall Center for Metropolitan Studies. His career began at Rutgers University, then the Ford Foundation where he served as program officer responsible for community development, and deputy director for community and resource development. Anglin went on to Structured Employment Economic Development Corporation. He is the author and co-author of four books and several peer-reviewed articles. Anglin sits on several public sector, nonprofit, and private sector boards. He received his doctorate from the University of Chicago, a master's from Northwestern University, and a bachelor's from Brooklyn College. He is a fellow of the National Academy of Public Administration

Dr. Shemariah Arki
Instructor
Kent State University

Shemariah J. Arki, Ed.D. is an educator, activist and organizer. She's an instructor in the Department of Pan African Studies at Kent State University, and founder of the Ellipsis Institute for Women of Color in the Academy at Case Western Reserve University. As an auto/ethnographic researcher and creative non-fiction writer, her work centers cultural epistemologies and the construction of a #BlackCommaFeminist pedagogy. Shemariah is one of five editors for the forthcoming textbook, Teaching Brilliant and Beautiful Black Girls. Shemariah serves outside the academy as the founder and lead experience curator for Sankofa Circle Studios, engaging creative entrepreneurs with one goal - lift as you climb. Shemariah serves on the boards of Stonebrook Montessori School and Shooting Without Bullets. Shemariah's work has been recognized by the Office for Inclusion, Diversity and Equal Opportunity at Case Western Reserve University, Kaleidoscope's 40 under 40 Club, and by the Kiwanis Club at High Tech Academy. A proud Clevelander, she is mom to Solomon Tafari and Malcom Saddiq. Shemariah enjoys traveling, yoga and creating memories with her family.

Edward Banks
Executive Director
Reading R.A.M.M.

Edward Banks is the founder and current executive director of the Reading R.A.M.M. (Recording Arts Music & Media) Academy which operates five proven youth programs in Northeast Ohio. Edward has been a professional disc jockey and music producer "DJ Phatty Banks" for over 30 years. As a single parent concerned with his own children's poor academics, he developed and facilitated programs in the schools they attended to help combat the negative impact of pop culture on youth and at-risk environments they navigate through. Along with his continued relationship with entertainment, Edward has dedicated the last 14 years of his life to project-based and social emotional learning youth programming. His recent projects include - Changing The Narrative: Stories of Resilient Youth book, The Hamilton Experience, The Redline Project films, and My Young Fam radio show on WOVU 95.9 FM.

Robin Beavers is the principal of Garfield Middle School in Lakewood, Ohio. She completed her undergraduate studies in middle childhood education at Miami University. She continued her studies at Cleveland State University and earned her master's degree in education administration. While there, she became a member of Pi Lambda Theta, an education honorary. She is currently completing her dissertation in Cleveland State University's doctoral studies program specializing in urban education administration. Robin is an advocate for positive change and works to encourage students to achieve at the highest levels. She was selected as an inspiring educator by the Cleveland Area Minority Education Recruitment Association and was filmed as part of their promotional video. Recently, she was appointed by the Mayor of Lakewood as a member of the Lakewood Community Relations Advisory Council. She is instrumental in building a strong sense of community and challenging the status quo in education. Robin is most inspired by Nelson Mandela's words, "Education is the most powerful weapon, which you can use to change the world."

Robin Beavers
Principal
Lakewood City Schools

Kristin Campbell is a licensed clinical social worker and is employed by Cleveland Heights-University Heights School District as a school social worker for the last 11 years. Kristin truly believes that students are able to reach their full academic potential when non-academic barriers that have the potential to impede learning are addressed. This includes but it not limited to mental health concerns, homelessness, child abuse and neglect. Her experience, strength perspective and empathy has enabled her to assist students, families and school personnel with ensuring that all students have an equal opportunity to reach higher heights and deeper depths in the area of academia. She holds a bachelor's degree in Social Work from West Chester University of Pennsylvania and master's degree in Social Work from Ohio State University, where she was named Clinical Social Work Student of the Year. She is an active member of Delta Sigma Theta Sorority and is the proud mother of one son who she affectionately calls "Sonshine" for he brings her love and light.

Kristin Campbell
School Social Worker
Cleveland Heights
University Heights
School District

Dr. Denecia Dillard is one of Northeastern Ohio's advocates for urban education with over 18 years of leadership and team building experience. She quickly transitioned from the classroom to leading the charge as principal and serving her local community. Dr. Dillard is a graduate of Ursuline College in Pepper Pike, Ohio. She participated in a national principal fellowship program for building excellent schools designed to challenge and strengthen exceptional and early career leaders. Dr. Dillard was recognized in 2008 as a 'Rainmaker of Tomorrow' by Northern Ohio Live publication. She serves in her church community as one of the praise and worship leaders at Mt. Zion of Oakwood Village. She is a proud mother of two beautiful children, a daughter in college and son in high school. She is also a grandmother in training to Ms. Luella Simone. Dr. Dillard wears many hats. In addition to being a mother to her own birth children; she is also mother, aunt, mentor and counselor to her students.

Dr. Denecia Dillard
Principal
Lake Erie Preparatory
School

Oronde East
Education Director
Cleveland Ward 7

Mr. Oronde East is an honors graduate with a Bachelor's Degree in Elementary Education from Cheyney University. His is currently a Master's degree candidate in Educational Leadership at Strayer University. Mr. Oronde East currently works in the Cleveland Ward 7/Hough neighborhood as an Educational Consultant to Cleveland City Councilman Basheer Jones. Mr. Oronde East has introduced and facilitated tutorial, basic skills development, and GED programs for youth and adults in this community at the Hough Multi Purpose Center.

Before coming to Cleveland last year, Mr. Oronde East taught all subjects but focused heavily on Pre-Algebra, Algebra, Geometry, and Statistics & Probability to 5th-8th grade students in Philadelphia. He has created and facilitated a variety of youth programming over the years where the areas of focus were positive self-expression, self-esteem, self-discipline, and character development. His after-school and summer programming aim to close literacy gaps, as well as promote financial literacy and mathematical abilities.

Dr. Adrienne Gosselin
Associate Professor
Cleveland State
University

Dr. Adrienne Gosselin is an associate professor in the English department at Cleveland State University where she teaches African American Literature and Black Women's Studies. Dr. Gosselin received her Master of Arts and Ph.D. in English Literature from University of Cincinnati and Bachelor of Arts in Art from California State University. Dr. Gosselin's approach to teaching and scholarship is grounded in the inextricable role of African American culture in American history. She is co-author of Reflections Sweet and Sour, a manual for creating culturally relevant language arts curriculum for at-risk youth. The creative writer other achievements include 1941, a radio play on voter suppression, and Bringing Henrietta to Life, a collaborative film designed to initiate dialogue on disparities in medical education. Her latest publication is Charles Chesnutt in the Classroom, an open-access text exploring Cleveland's influence on the understudied author. She is a lifetime member of the National Council of Negro Women. Currently, she is working on her Master of Fine Arts, and writing a novel on African American soldiers in WWI.

Kenneth D. Hale
Director of Access
and Community
Engagement
Cuyahoga Community
College

Kenneth D. Hale is director of access and community engagement at Cuyahoga Community College. He provides leadership to several initiatives including High Tech Academy and Saturday Family Academy, and has managed partnerships with PNC, NASA, and First Tee of Cleveland. Hale served as campus administrator of Cleveland Metropolitan School District's high-performing John Hay Campus, which earned a rating of "Excellent" during his leadership tenure. He was the founding principal of High Tech Academy enabling more than 1,000 Cleveland high school students to earn college credit. A Cleveland and Glenville native, Hale mentors youth, and is a grant writer for Empower Communications. He has served as director of youth programs for The City Club of Cleveland, hosted radio programs, and served on numerous boards. The recipient of Cleveland Public Library's inaugural Drum Major for Change Award, Hale is a member of Affinity Missionary Baptist Church and Alpha Phi Alpha Fraternity. He is the proud father of Kiera, Kelton, Kenia and Kelvin.

Dr. Clara Jean Mosley Hall is a professor at Cuyahoga Community College in the American Sign Language and Deaf Interpretive Services department. She received her Ph.D. from Cleveland State University. Her work has been recognized by the Ohio State Senate, Phi Delta Kappa, Rochester Institute of Technology's Distinguished Teacher Recognition Program, Ralph M. Besse Award for Excellence in Teaching, and League for Innovation's John & Suanne Rouche Excellence Award in Community College Teaching and Leadership. She published work examining the construct of racelessness among African American deaf adolescents in the American Annals of the Deaf. She has traveled nationally and internationally observing various programs for deaf individuals. Dr. Hall established the J. Paris Mosley Scholarship Fund with the Cleveland Foundation providing financial support for higher education of deaf students. She is the author of Paris in America: A Deaf Nanticoke Shoemaker and His Daughter. Dr. Hall is a member of Alpha Kappa Alpha Sorority and is married to Dr. Howard Hall. They have two daughters, Ilea and Karelle.

**Dr. Clara Jean
Mosley Hall**
Professor
Cuyahoga Community
College

Bob Ivory is program director of the Students of Promise Closing the Achievement Gap Initiative in Cuyahoga County. He provides project management and program development for targeted youth in the Garfield, Maple, East Cleveland, Warrensville and Cleveland Heights-University Heights City School districts. Bob was appointed special assistant to the first Cuyahoga County executive and legislative liaison to County Council under the newly chartered Cuyahoga County government. He served as community outreach coordinator in the Cleveland Regional Office of the Governor before his promotion to Regional Project Manager in the Governor's Initiative for Closing the Achievement Gap. A native Clevelander, he attended Ohio University. Bob is board chairman of AmeriWell Pharmacy, executive committee member of the Northeast Ohio My Brother's Keeper Initiative, faith-based outreach committee chair for the Northeast Ohio American Red Cross and a member of Omega Psi Phi Fraternity Inc. Bob is the author of the inspirational book, What God Has Done. He is the producer, singer and songwriter of the CD release Sway With Me.

Bob Ivory
Program Director
Ivory Educational
Consulting Group, LLC

Franceska Jones is the career development coordinator for the Academic Support Center at Notre Dame College and freelance nonprofit consultant. At Notre Dame College, she manages employer training and career support services for students with disabilities along with being an adjunct faculty member. Franceska is a certified global career development facilitator. She is also a dedicated higher education administrator with over seven years of experience. Franceska received a Bachelor of Science degree in Business Administration from Ohio State University, and John Carroll University awarded her a master's degree in Non-Profit Administration. She is a doctoral student at Morgan State University studying Higher Education Leadership with a focus on Community Colleges. Franceska is an advisory board member for Cleveland Early College High School and very active in her community. The Cleveland Professional 20/30 Club recently acknowledged her for being a 2019 Northeast Ohio Mover & Shaker under the age of 35. A native of Cleveland Heights, Franceska is the wife of Rudolph Jones III, and the proud mother of Phoenix Jones.

Franceska Jones
Notre Dame College
Career Development
Coordinator

Mwatabu S. Okantah
Associate Professor
Kent State University

Mwatabu S. Okantah earned a bachelor's degree in English and African Studies from Kent State University in 1976 and a master's degree in Creative Writing from the City College of New York in 1982. An associate professor in the Department of Pan-African Studies at Kent State University, he also serves as director of the Ghana Study Abroad Program. Okantah is the author of Afreeka Brass (1983), Collage (1984), Legacy: for Martin & Malcolm (1987), Cheikh Anta Diop: Poem for the Living—published as a limited trilingual edition in English, French and Wolof (1997/2017), Reconnecting Memories: Dreams No Longer Deferred (2004) and Muntu Kuntu Energy: New and Selected Poetry (2013). A new collection, Guerrilla Dread: Poetry for the Heart and Mind, is forthcoming from Africa World Press this year. He has performed as griot for the Iroko African Drum & Dance Society, and in ongoing collaborations, "Collage: Music and Poetry," with the Cavani String Quartet and with Vince Robinson and the Jazz Poets.

Johnie L. Reed
Assistant Professor
Business Administration
Cuyahoga Community
College

Johnie L. Reed, MPOD, ABD, AFC®, earned a graduate degree in Positive Organizational Development and Change from Case Western Reserve University's Weatherhead School and is completing a doctoral dissertation in Business Administration at Franklin University. He is nationally certified by AFCPE as an accredited financial counselor. During his more than 30 years of experience, he has been involved in business ownership, counseling, education, and mentoring opportunities. Based on decades of engagement, he now focuses on leadership training, coaching, and speaking in the areas of diversity awareness, business and personal development, consumer debt management and credit awareness, and educational opportunities for individual development and growth. Johnie is a sought after mentor and speaker in the areas of coaching and financial literacy. As a workshop presenter, Johnie utilizes appreciative inquiry processes as a base to guide participants through the make sense decision and making process for growth and development in the areas of personal financial and credit literacy, as well as personal and professional development for use in team-based environments.

Raymon Reed
Executive Director
Walking on Water Inc.

Raymon Reed is the Executive Director of Walking on Water Inc., an organization focusing on developing people and communities in a number of different ways. Reed's life journey includes being a social entrepreneur, educator, community advocate, and a published author. This call to action began in his hometown, Cleveland, under the guidance of his father, a self-taught entrepreneur and his mother, an Olympic track star and educator. After attending Morehouse College in Atlanta, Raymon desired to return to Cleveland to begin lending his knowledge and experience gained to benefit the community. He began working as an educator in the Cleveland Public Schools, and opened the area's first vegan restaurant. With a deep, life-long passion and a call to ministry, Raymon moved to Washington D.C. and entered Howard University School of Divinity. He received his license to minister from Rev. Dr. Otis Moss Jr. in Cleveland.

Monica Starks is a sociology professor for Cuyahoga Community College. She earned a bachelor's degree in Organizational Management from Tiffin University. She completed her education at Cleveland State University earning a master's degree in Sociology. In addition to teaching sociology courses for Tri-C, Monica is a member of the Black Americans Council where she serves as a mentor for several students. Monica has been recognized as one of Who's Who in Black Cleveland for 2016. She was recognized with a proclamation from the Mayor of Bedford Heights, Ohio for her advocacy of chronic kidney disease. Monica facilitates workshops, programs, and speaks in the community for chronic kidney disease awareness. She is on the board of the Cuyahoga County Library, a member on the racism committee for the Catholic Dioceses of Cleveland and is the retreat coordinator for the Couples Club.

Monica Starks
Sociology Professor
Cuyahoga Community
College

Dr. Lemuel E. Stewart III is an associate professor/counselor at Cuyahoga Community College. He provides academic, career and personal counseling and teaches general studies courses. He served as the interim assistant dean of Counseling and Psychological Services at the Western campus. Dr. Stewart is president of the Black American Council and coordinator of the Minority Male Leadership Academy. He has served faculty senate and the AAUP as a college representative and works on numerous college-wide initiatives. He holds a Bachelor of Arts in Sociology from Cleveland State University, Master of Science in Social Administration from Case Western Reserve University (CWRU) and a Doctorate in Psychology at Southern California University for Professional Studies. Dr. Stewart is a Marshall Memorial Fellow (GMF), a graduate of Leadership Cleveland class of 2005, president of Blacks in Management Inc., member of CWRU Mandel School Alumni Board, Alpha Phi Alpha Fraternity and Christ Episcopal Church. Dr. Stewart lives in Cleveland Heights with his wife, Erica, and two daughters, Lora and Lena.

Dr. Lemuel E. Stewart III,
Interim Assistant Dean
Counseling and
Psychological Services
Cuyahoga Community
College

CELEBRATING ACHIEVEMENT IN MORE THAN 25 U.S. MARKETS

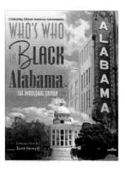  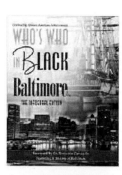  

    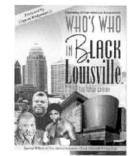

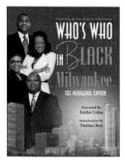  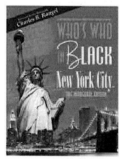  

   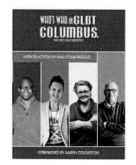 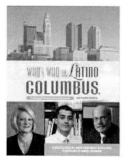

WHO'S WHO

A Real Times Media Company

www.whoswhopublishing.com

FOCUS
CELEBRATE
PROMINENCE
RECOGNITION

FUTURE LEADERS

London Arrington
Young Influencer
Troy-David PR &
Consulting

Born and raised in Cleveland, multi-talented London Arrington is an actress, singer, dancer, and model. She has a very impressive repertoire at such a young age. London has played the role of School Girl in the hit Netflix show Mind Hunters. She has a re-occurring role as young Cookie on Fox's hit show Empire starring Taraji P. Henson and Terrence Howard. London has also played the photo double for the character Raynell in the critically acclaimed film Fences starring Denzel Washington and Viola Davis. In 2017, London was featured alongside NBA star Isaiah Thomas for a Kids Footlocker commercial which received rave reviews. She was the recipient of the 2019 Humanitarian & Public Service Award from the Greater Cleveland Chapter of the National Action Network. She was honored as the "Performer of the Year" and was the co-host for the 2018 Girls Health Summit. London will be featured on the big screen later this year in her leading role as Nia in the new film project entitled Nia Knight.

Bakari Ballard
Student
Kent State University

Bakari Ballard, born and raised in Cleveland Ohio, attended John Hay High School and graduated top five in the class of 2018. Bakari is currently attending Kent State University with junior status majoring in Construction Management while minoring in Finance. He maintains a 3.3 GPA at KSU, participates in multiple students org. and is also a member of Phi Theta Kappa Honors Society. Bakari is also enjoys volunteering by going back to his high school to help coach his former baseball team and he also is an active member of the ACE mentoring program. Bakari is currently working as an intern for Sodexo construction division, working on multiple projects in University Hospital. Bakari's career goals include owning multiple real estate properties throughout the country while being a director or CEO of a construction company. Bakari will also like to give back to his community by starting a nonprofit org. that gives affordable housing to single-parent households.

Douglas Burnett III
Freshman
Morehouse College

Douglas Burnett III is an example of excellence. He is a 2019 esteemed honor graduate of Willoughby South High School. Douglas will further his education at Morehouse College. He intends to major in political science and minor in business, in hopes to become a criminal attorney. Douglas was elected in 2018 as the first African American vice president of his school's National Honor Society. Douglas participated in band, soccer, student government, mock trial, and an appointee of the Principal's Advisory Board. Douglas was chosen as one of the top three student leaders by his superintendent and principal to represent the entire school in Project SALES, a service and leadership program for model students. With Project SALES Douglas co-founded W-E Feed, a weekend meal program for underprivileged students at local elementary schools. In the summer of 2018, he was selected as one of 12 participants in the highly competitive Stephanie Tubbs Jones Summer Legal Academy and interned at the Cleveland Municipal Court. Additionally, he maintained two jobs at Calhoun Funeral Home and Giant Eagle.

Torah Faye Alexus Hudson is an aspiring artist, physician, and entrepreneur. Torah is a rising freshman who will be attending Howard University, as a Chemistry Pre-Medicine major, in the fall of 2019. Torah is an active member of the National Black MBA Association Leaders of Tomorrow Program, the National Society of Black Engineers Jr. Program, and the United Way of Greater Cleveland: Youth Fund Distribution Committee. She thoroughly enjoys serving her community and constantly expanding her capacity of knowledge. Ultimately, Torah's worldview is shaped by her love for the Pan-African collective, the expression of creativity, and compassion for our beloved planet.

Torah Faye Alexus
Hudson
Rising Freshman
Howard University

Alana N. Johns was born and raised in Cleveland, Ohio. She is currently a student at Bard High School Early College where she plans to earn her Associates Degree in Liberal Arts in 2021. Alana is very active in and outside of her school. She is a member of her school's Student Advisory Committee, a Student Ambassador, a Debate Team Leader, and a member of the Youth Forum Council. Outside of school, she spends her summers volunteering at her grandmother's non-profit summer camp in East Cleveland and she has recently joined Queen I Am, a non-profit organization whose goal is to empower young girls from the inner-city. She loves to write peculiar stories that stand out and are unique. Her writing has been published on her school's magazine site and by the Great Lakes Theatre.

Alana N. Johns
Student
Bard High School
Early College

Janae Johnson is a rising sophomore, from Euclid, Ohio, studying Finance and Management at Bowling Green State University (BGSU). During high school, she attended Villa Angela St. Joseph. Throughout her time in high school, she was senior class president, a member of the National Honors Society, and a student ambassador. She also graduated high school with a 3.98 GPA, alongside the honors diploma. During her time in high school, she set a strong foundation for her college journey. At Bowling Green State University, she is pursuing a double degree in Finance and Management. Through her time in college, her love for being actively involved has not changed. She has served as Senator for the Undergraduate Student Government, a member of the Residence Hall Council, and a member of the Business District Residential Learning Community. However, during the most recent years, she strived to dedicate her time towards organizations she felt most passionate about.

Jane Johnson
Sophomore
Bowling Green State
University

Morghan Jones
Graduating Senior
Shaker Heights High
School

Morghan Jones is a graduating senior from Shaker Heights High School. She is very involved in community outside and inside of school. Inside of school, she's involved in plenty of clubs at such has Minority Achievement Committee Sister Scholars, Secretary of Youth Ending Hunger, Bass player in school orchestra, and track. Outside of school, she is involved in a few programs such as National Society of Black Engineers Juniors where she is the Secretary. She also attended coding summer camp, Indeedwecode, for the last 4 years.

As a student, she's known as being very hardworking and works hard because she knows she must work hard for the things she wants in life. She's not like all average students. She has a learning disability, but doesn't let it stop her from following her dreams. Morghan have also been awarded with two awards, The Andrea Johnson Dare to Dream Award and the Desadre Lawson-Bullock Award. She will be attending Miami University with a major of Computer Science.

Isaiah Lucky
First Year Freshman
Cleveland State
University

Born in Cleveland, Isaiah Lucky recently finished his freshman year at Cleveland State University. Throughout his four years in Benedictine High School, he has been on the honor roll multiple times along with graduating cum laude in 2018. Isaiah has been playing the piano for 12 years, along with various recitals. Isaiah volunteers with his grandmother, Minister Dr. Bernice Washington regularly. Isaiah writes, speaks, and performs poetry. He is an active member of the "Distinguished Gentlemen of Spoken Word", a poetry group. Isaiah has won awards from Life Works Ohio for Christian Poetry writings based on biblical scriptures. In 2014, Isaiah was selected as the Black Diamonds Award recipient and was the keynote speaker for the 2016 Black Diamonds Award along with a television appearance on Kaleidoscope with Dr. Leon Bibb. Isaiah is currently choosing between English and Psychology as his major, becoming either an English teacher or a psychiatrist, potentially with a minor in music. Isaiah has been walking by faith and not by sight and knows God still has great plans for him!

Corin Manning
Senior
Shaker Heights High
School

Corin Manning is a senior at Shaker Heights High School. She is a proven leader, mentor, role-model, and teacher as evidenced by her commitment to service and volunteerism. Corin has been Junior Class President, a volunteer with Youth Ending Hunger, and a mentor with MAC Sister Scholars. Currently, she is President of Shaker's student NAACP, a peer tutor, and a member of the Student Leadership Team.

As a charter member of IndeedWeCode coding group for Black girls and NSBE Jr. (National Society of Black Engineers), Corin has managed several website creation projects and earned a paid internship with Rockwell Automation. Ms. Manning is working toward removing racial and gender barriers to success by teaching coding to younger girls to promote STEM career and financial success. It is her goal to inspire income independence and personal wealth creation which will, in turn, strengthen our communities for generations to come. Corin is also a photographer in her spare time. In fall of 2019, Corin Manning will be attending the University of Cincinnati seeking a BSIT degree as a proud Darwin T. Turner Scholar.

Jayla Evette McCoy is an AP and Honors senior at Solon High School in Solon, Ohio. She's the daughter of James E. and Richelle A. McCoy, Jr. Jayla serves as President of the Greater Cleveland National Society of Black Engineers Jr. Chapter, NASA paid summer intern in 2018 and 2019, SHS Marching Band - Clarinet Squad Leader, Varsity Bowling Team, National Honor Society, African American Culture Club President, and National Society of High School Scholars. Jayla and her family are active members of the Cleveland Chapter of Jack and Jill of America, Inc. She was 2017-2018 Regional Teen Treasurer and the 2018-2019 Regional Teen Recommendations Co-Chairman. Jayla was selected to travel with other AP language students to Barcelona, Spain and Paris, France for 8 days on an educational trip. Other honors include: SHS Comet of the Semester, Rising STAR, 2018 Look Up to Cleveland Alumna, and Honors Diploma recipient. She'll major in Engineering with a minor in Spanish. In the Fall, Jayla looks forward to being a William C. Parker Scholar in the Honors College at the University of Kentucky.

Jayla Evette McCoy
Graduating Senior
Solon High School

Javon Miller is a 20-year-old entrepreneur and life coach who is the owner and CEO of Arize Entertainment & Event Venue that recently opened in January, 2019. He attends Kent State University as a current sophomore majoring in Psychology and minoring in Entrepreneurship. Miller's additional businesses includes a handcrafted pen company, Bovazi, and his life coaching business. Arize Entertainment & Event Venue host and plans events in its venue space for Kent State organizations, greek fraternities and sororities, as well as local residents of Kent, Ohio.

Miller is a Christian ministry leader for the Impact Movement, LaunchNet Entrepreneurship Mentor, and Leadership Consultant all on Kent State University's campus. Miller enjoys being a positive influence and inspirational motivator to his peers in the areas of faith, life, and business. He aspires to glorify God in all that he does as he takes hold of opportunities given to him along the way to not only make his life better but the very people around him.

Javon Miller
CEO
Arize Entertainment &
Event Venue

From the inner city of Dayton, Ohio, Khayln Miller is an ambitious student who attends Case Western Reserve University in Cleveland and double majors in Aerospace and Mechanical Engineering. Through his affiliation and involvement with some of the nations most well known higher education organizations such as The Bill and Melinda Gates Foundation, Jack Kent Cooke Foundation, and Leadership Enterprise for a Diverse America (LEDA), as well as his hands on internship experiences, Khayln has proven to have a strong value for education and an understanding of how important it is to apply that same education to the world in which we live. Some of these internships include the Wright Patterson Air Force Base, Northrop Grumman, and Boeing. After graduating in December of 2019, Khayln plans on attending graduate school to pursue a PhD in aerospace engineering.

Khayln Miller
Student
Case Western
Reserve University

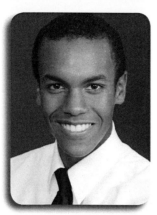

Charles Modlin III
Physical Therapy
Doctoral Student
Cleveland State
University

Charles S. Modlin III, also known as "Trey" is a Doctoral Candidate Physical Therapy student at Cleveland State University. Charles is also a United States Chess Federation Rated Chess Master who teaches chess in elementary, middle and high schools in Northeast, Ohio. He is a two-time National and four-time Ohio Scholastic Chess Champion. He graduated from Texas Tech University where he was president of the Texas Tech Chess Team. Texas Tech University recruited Trey to play on their collegiate nationally ranked chess team. Trey majored in Exercise Sports Sciences and served as a volunteer (over 400 hours) and researcher in the Cleveland Clinic Rehabilitation Institute. Charles is an honor roll graduate of Shaker Heights High School where he also lettered and earned MVP Varsity Baseball All-Lake Eric Athletic Honors, was Chess Club president and team captain, Wind Ensemble and Jazz Ensemble trumpeter and field commander of the marching band.

Wonuola Obasa
Chief Executive
Director
Fair Guide

Wonuola Obasa, an aspiring biomedical scientist, is a student at The Cleveland School of Science and Medicine. Obasa is involved with Fair Guide, a local group focused on improving the financial literacy of other students at his school. Fair Guide teaches about the importance of management, saving, and investment of money to local high school students with the purpose of empowering the youth to be financially competent as adults. Wonuola also excels in the classroom, being ranked in the top ten percent of his class, and is involved in his school community through his participation in varsity sports, including cross country, track and field, the National Honor Society, and Fair Guide. Wonuola, only a junior, is an example of dedication, perseverance, and academic excellence for all students in his school. He is regarded by his teachers as an exemplary student who enrolls in the most rigorous courses available such as honors courses and AP classes; and cares about his community, through his work with Fair Guide.

Ikenna Okoro
Chief Financial
Officer
Fair Guide

Ikenna Okoro is the co-founder of the nonprofit organization, Fair Guide. Starting in their sophomore year of high school, he and his friends developed Fair Guide into a program that addressed issues of poverty in their community through the provision of financial resources and education. As the chief financial officer, Okoro undertook the hiring of financial professionals, managing of the group's budget, completion of the grant application, and supervision of the grant allocation. As a current rising sophomore at Columbia University, Ikenna is pursuing a Bachelor of Arts in Neuroscience and Behavior on the pre-med track. He is a Kluge scholar and serves as the freshman representative of the Charles Drew Pre-medical Society. In addition to those commitments, he also belongs to the Black Student Organization and the African Students Association. This summer, Ikenna is working with Next Gen Personal Finance company in New York to plan an upcoming scholarship program for high school students in Cleveland. The total sum of the scholarships is estimated to be over $16,000.

Deyavion Washington is a second-year undergrad student at The Ohio State University on a full-ride academic scholarship. She is double majoring in Psychology and Global Studies with a minor in Spanish. She is a Northeast Ohio Diversity Center student facilitator who has volunteered numerous hours to different diversity campaigns locally and nationally. Deyavion was featured in People's Magazine in 2016 as an active member of the Say Something Campaign that shed light on bullying awareness and prevention in schools across America. She plans on using her education and experience to become a social psychologist to help with conflict intervention and peace initiatives in underdeveloped countries. Deyavion has continued to demonstrate her versatility, commitment to excellence, dedication to the common good, and emphasis on introspective growth. No matter where life leads her, Deyavion vows to use her platform to promote positive thinking, social reform, and give a voice to the voiceless.

Deyavion Washington
Sophomore
The Ohio State
University

Kendall Wood is one of the founding members of the community group, Fair Guide. He and his friends founded the group in their sophomore year of high school with the intention of teaching their peers financial literacy, a skill many had never learned before. Serving as the communications executive, Kendall attended numerous professional networking events in his junior and senior years, sent out email correspondence to the student body of his school, and created flyers for different events. Keeping in close contact with the school's principal, he made sure each event faced little to no conflict with other after school events. Now a rising sophomore at Morehouse College, Kendall is pursuing a Bachelor of Science in Psychology with a minor in Public Health. He has served as his residential hall's treasurer, does community service with a few campus organizations, and has become a certified peer counselor within a campus organization that focuses on mental health.

Kendall Wood
Communications
Executive
Fair Guide

La'Dawn Young is an entrepreneur developing her business InnHerBeautii LLC, founded in 2018. La'Dawn works in the pharmacy at Walgreens part time. She interns as an Office Assistant with Glen Shumate, Executive Director, ACE Mentor Program. La'Dawn graduated from John Adams High School in 2015. After studying Business at Central State University, she returned to Cleveland to complete an associate degree at Cuyahoga Community College. Furthering her education, she's participating in the Advanced Technology Academy program at Tri-C and numerous Dale Carnegie courses. She completed the STNA program becoming a Certified Nursing Assistant, in hopes of becoming an Independent Service Provider serving primarily in her community. La'Dawn created InnHerBeautii to provide a safe place that teaches about appropriate ways to address emotions when faced with adversities throughout life. She promotes self-confidence through beauty enhancement services. La'Dawn is a Rebellious Beauty Sales Representative, locally manufactured all-natural bath and body products. La'Dawn trust that engaging with the community creates exposure and enlightenment. Then all will see the power of unity. La'Dawn Young is the change she hopes to see in her community.

La'Dawn Young
Founder
InnHerBeautii LLC

CORPORATE
SPOTLIGHT

RADIO
ONE
THE URBAN MEDIA SPECIALIST

Denzel J. Brand
Promotions Director
Radio One Cleveland

Ahmaad Crump
On-Air Personality
93.1 WZAK FM
In-Arena Host
Cleveland Cavaliers

Denzel J. Brand is the Promotions Director for Radio One Cleveland. Born and raised on the eastside of Cleveland, Denzel has always had a passion and love for music, entertainment and the media industry. Denzel received an undergraduate degree in Communication Studies from Kent State University in 2014.

Denzel began his career with Radio One Cleveland in 2013 as a station intern. He quickly discovered a passion for the Promotions/Marketing department and acquired a position as a part-time promotions assistant. In 2016, Denzel was promoted to Promotions Coordinator and then in 2017 to Promotions Director. In this position, he manages the station campaigns, events and client activation for the cluster. He is also a key player in the development and execution of Z107.9's marquee events, "Summer Jam" and "White Out." .

Ahmaad Crump is an on-air personality for 93.1 WZAK and in-arena host for the Cleveland Cavaliers. A native of Cleveland, Ahmaad graduated from Cleveland Heights High School and later attended Central State University. His contagious personality became noticed with everyone on the campus, and that's where he began hosting various talent shows, greek step shows and various parties on the campus and local clubs. When he returned home, he had no clue that his hometown NBA team had an opportunity he couldn't turn down. In 2005, Crump became In-arena host for the Cleveland Cavaliers and hasn't looked back. He has been voted by the NBA 2 times to host the NBA All-Star Weekend festivities. He also is the host of SportsTime Ohio/Fox Sports "Beer Money" a show where you win cash money for knowing Ohio Sports Trivia.

January 2014, Crump joined Radio One Cleveland as an on-air personality and brings the same energy that he exhibits on the court to the Cleveland airwaves.

RADIO ONE
THE URBAN MEDIA SPECIALIST

Rochelle "Ro Digga" Frazier
On Air Personality
Assistant Program
Director - Z1079 WENZ FM
Radio One Cleveland

Eddie Harrell, Jr.
Vice President
General Manager
Radio One Cleveland

Rochelle "Ro Digga" Frazier is the midday host on Z1079 and Assistant Program Director for WENZ FM.

She started her career in radio with an internship with Radio One Cleveland. Her hard work helped her land a position in promotions after she graduated from the Ohio Center for Broadcasting. She held several positions, including national sales coordinator, while working as a part-time on-air personality.

In 2011, Frazier was named midday host and assistant programming director for WENZ-FM. She's also the corporate liaison for Radio One's internship program. Most recently, Frazier was promoted to co-host of WENZ-FM's afternoon drive program.

In addition to her work in Radio, she is a strong supporter of youth initiatives. Frazier's energy and tireless push to motivate and inspire troubled teens can be seen through her blog "RoDigga's AdoLessons" on zhiphipcleveland.com

Eddie Harrell, Jr. is the Vice President & General Manager of Radio One. Before leading the Cleveland market, Mr. Harrell served as VP/GM of the company's Columbus market. Before joining Radio One, Mr. Harrell served as chief operating officer of the Columbus Urban League as well as Chairman of the Ohio Civil Rights Commission.

Harrell graduated from Otterbein University and earned a Master of Business Administration from Ashland University. Harrell and his wife, Valerie, are the parents of Kayla and Eddie III.

CORPORATE SPOTLIGHT

Rohnesha Horne
Marketing Director
Radio One Cleveland

Haz Mathews
On Air Personality
Production Director
93.1 WZAK FM
Radio One Cleveland

A native of Cleveland, Ohio, Rohnesha Horne began her career in radio as the Assistant Marketing Director for Radio One Cleveland in 2008. In 2010, she was named Promotions Director for Radio One Cleveland properties: WENZ-FM, WZAK-FM, WERE-AM and WJMO-AM. In this position, she managed the station campaigns, events and client activation for the cluster. Rohnesha is also the local liaison for Radio One's legal department. In the spring of 2017, Rohnesha was promoted to Marketing Director.

An event planner at heart, Rohnesha dedicates her free time to several passion projects. She's the creator and host of The Power Shower, a free event designed to encourage single women to know that they are powerful. Rohnesha has also served as a wedding planner and consultant on events for several new businesses, DJ's and local recording artists.

A native of Havre De Grace, Maryland, Haz Mathews' career in radio began in 1999 with an internship for Radio One's 92Q Jamz in Baltimore. His hard work did not go unrecognized. After his internship ended, he was quickly hired as DJ and on-air personality. While there, Haz discovered his passion for production and in 2004, he was promoted to Production and Image Director for Radio One's Baltimore cluster.

In 2008, Haz joined Radio One Cleveland as an on-air personality and production assistant for 93.1 WZAK. In 2013, he was promoted to production director where he oversees production services for the Radio One Cleveland market.

In addition to radio, Haz Matthews has experience in front of the camera. In addition to several appearances in top-rated shows including the HBO TV Series "The Wire," Matthews host a weekly entertainment segment for Dish Nation that can be seen locally on WBNX- TV the CW.

RADIO ONE
THE URBAN MEDIA SPECIALIST

Jared "Incognito" McGriff
On Air Personality
Imaging Director - Z1079 WENZ FM
Radio One Cleveland

Sam Prewitt
Digital Sales Manager
Radio One Cleveland

Incognito's start in radio is rather unique. A frequent caller into his local station's night show, the on-air personality at 105 WFXE-FM recognized his natural ability to command an audience and introduced him to the program director. With that introduction, he started his career in media. Incognito worked at several stations in rural Georgia until 2013, when he landed a position at Atlanta's Streetz 94.5-FM. His hustle and drive did not go unnoticed. Shortly after joining Streetz, Radio One started courting him to join their team. In 2015, Incognito made the transition from WENZ-FM to host the new formed "Posted on the Corner" night show and quickly lifted the 7p-12a time slot to number one.

Sam Prewitt is the Digital Sales Manager for Radio One-Cleveland responsible for overseeing nearly 400 client-focused marketing programs, which include customized promotions, local and national advertising programming while developing and managing the sale efforts of a team of account executives. Since joining Radio One in 2008 before his current role, Sam worked in a variety of capacities for Radio One-Columbus and was a popular On-Air Personality in Columbus and Cleveland known by listeners as "SPdaCoolKid."

Considered as one of the radio industry's brightest and rising stars, he has been featured in numerous print and non-print magazines including Columbus Alive, Who's Who in Black Columbus, and Radio One Columbus affiliate 107.5's Top 30 under 30 in Columbus.

Sam is a Cleveland, Ohio native and holds a Bachelor of Arts in Communications from Ohio Dominican University. While a student at the University he served as the Programing Director and an On-Air Personality for RadiODU. He remains active in his community and is a member of Alpha Phi Alpha Fraternity, Inc and the American Heart Association Young Professionals Board.

CORPORATE SPOTLIGHT

Robin "Bijou Star" Sadler
On Air Personality
Z1079 WENZ FM
Radio One Cleveland

Sam Sylk
On Air Personality
93.1 WZAK FM
Radio One Cleveland

Robin "Bijou Star" Sadler is a multimedia personality, motivational speaker, entrepreneur and philanthropist. Bijou received an undergraduate degree in Broadcast Journalism from Howard University's prestigious John H. Johnson School of Communications. It was there that she cultivated her gift for the media arts, working with and learning from numerous media trailblazers in several mediums.

Bijou can be heard daily 10a-3p as the Midday Host on WENZ Z107.9FM in Cleveland OH. She exudes poise and passion, as she connects and captivates audiences through a unique communication style formulated from experience, education and just being herself. Bijou is affectionately known as "Glam Star" by friends and fans alike because of her love for fashion and everything GLAM!

Bijou is a strong believer in her faith. She lives every day in her true purpose using her platform and resources to promote and expose people to all things positive. Her goal is to motivate and empower individuals to also live purposeful lives and most importantly to remember it's never too late to answer your calling and live your dreams.

With a career that spans more than two decades, Sam Sylk is one of the most versatile talents working in media. Since starting his career in broadcasting in 1992, Sylk has worked all over the country including New York, Philadelphia and Chicago. He's worn several hats including TV show host, morning and afternoon drive radio personality and news reporter in several major markets.

While working in Chicago at WGCI-FM, Sylk picked up a weekend shift in Cleveland at Z1079 WENZ-FM. He commuted between Chicago and Cleveland for several years gaining a loyal fan base in both cities.

In 2013, Sylk was named the midday host for 93.1 WZAK and has maintained solid ratings. In addition to hosting middays in Cleveland, Sylk can also be heard middays on Radio One Cincinnati's Old School WOSL-FM.

Most recently, Sylk has added entrepreneur to his list of accomplishments. Last year he opened a restaurant in Cleveland, Sam Sylk's Chicken and Fish, and will expand to a second location in Cleveland Heights by the end of the year.

RADIO ONE
THE URBAN MEDIA SPECIALIST

Keenan "DJ K-Nyce" Williams
On Air Personality
Mixer - Z1079 WENZ FM

DJ Steph Floss
DJ for Z1079 WENZ-FM
Radio One Cleveland

Few disk jockeys display creativity and versatility in a DJ set like Keenan "K-Nyce" Williams. This Cleveland, Ohio native starting mixing in 2005 and already had a strong following on the club scene before joining WENZ-FM's roaster of mixers in 2010.

In 2014, he added air personality to his responsibilities and began to make his mark as a media professional. In 2015, he was name interim host of WENZ-FM's afternoon drive program and named permanent co-host, alongside Ro Digga, in 2016.

A father of two, K-Nyce is passionate about children's causes. In April 2016, he defied his fear of heights by riding the I-X Center's Ferris wheel for 55 hours to raise funds for the Boys & Girls Clubs of Cleveland.

There's a short list of DJ's that are versatile enough to rock 20,000 seat arenas, club events and high-profile parties across the country. Z1079's DJ Steph Floss does this in his sleep. A native of Cleveland, DJ Steph Floss AKA "the Prince of the City", already had a strong following on the club scene before joining the Z1079 team in 2010 where he currently serves as the DJ for the 9pm Mix and host of the Saturday Night Pre-Game show.

DJ Steph Floss has been able to extend his brand beyond Ohio through his affiliations with the Cleveland Cavaliers and his strong personal relationships with a host of celebrities. Floss travels several times a month to DJ club events around the country, earning respect in the club and among his peers. He won Best Mix Show DJ in 2015 at the Ohio Hip Hop Awards and continues to be the #1 DJ in the city - shape the way we experience entertainment in Cleveland.

Derek Forrest
Sports Reporter

Moreen Bailey Frater
Director
Community Relations

News 5 Sports Reporter Derek Forrest joined the station in April 2018. In prior years, he worked at WLWT in Cincinnati, WLKY in Louisville, and WYMT in Hazard, Kentucky.

Derek enjoys telling stories about people. "In sports, I love knowing how an athlete got to where they are now. There is always something that drives someone to be where they are today. Whether it was a bad or good experience," he adds.

Derek loves playing baseball, working out, and listening to podcasts. He's enthused and amazed at Cleveland's passion for the Indians, Cavs, and Browns!

Moreen Bailey Frater is Director of Community Relations at the local ABC affiliate, WEWS News 5. She worked in local radio as a reporter, talk show host and news & public affairs director prior to joining News 5 as a reporter/producer. Moreen then moved into the role of community relations director at News 5 and later spearheaded the station's diversity program in addition to her duties in community relations.

She currently serves on the boards Apprisen and the Cleveland based Barbershop Literacy Project.

Moreen holds a B.A. in Journalism from The Ohio State University and a M.Sc. in Organizational Development and Analysis from Weatherhead School of Management, Case Western Reserve University.

Danita Harris
News Anchor

Jade Jarvis
Reporter

News 5 Anchor Danita Harris encourages people to go for their dreams. Indeed, she has. Harris has received local and national recognition for her work on the air and in the community. She's been honored by Black Women in Sisterhood for Action and has also received the prestigious "Women of Vision" award from the National Coalition of Black Women. Additionally, Harris was recognized as one of the Outstanding Women in Clergy by the National Council of Negro Women and has been inducted into the Ohio Broadcasters Hall of Fame.

Recently, she was named "Journalist of the Year" by the Public Children's Services Association of Ohio for her stories on foster care and adoption.

Harris has conducted scores of memorable interviews including with Oprah and Robin Roberts.

Before joining News 5 in 1998, she worked for Black Entertainment Television Network.

Her off-hours are devoted to her husband, son and daughter. Harris claims she's a 'homebody' and can make a mean Spam sandwich!

In April of this year, Jade joined News 5 as a reporter following journalism stops in Scranton and Philadelphia.

Some of her most memorable reporting work includes covering weeks of extensive flash flooding in Northeastern PA, which resulted in millions of dollars in damage.

Jade enjoys getting to know Cleveland and describes it as "a big city and small town all wrapped into one"!

Terrence Lee
News Anchor
Good Morning Cleveland

Remeisha Shade
Power of 5
Meteorologist

Multimedia Journalist Terrence Lee has a simple philosophy when it comes to his reports on News 5 and that is, "Don't just expose wrongs, but also report on what's good about our community."

Terrence was born, raised and educated in Maryland. He joined News 5 in February 2013 and is Co-Anchor of Good Morning Cleveland. In his short career, Terrence has already received awards for Outstanding Spot and Public Affairs News Reporting. His role models are his parents and Journalist Ed Bradley.

Terrence is an avid concert and moviegoer and claims he can do the "Matrix" back bend without the help of wires, like Keanu Reeves!

Power of 5 Meteorologist Remeisha Shade joined the News 5 team in September 2018. You can Remeisha regularly on News 5's weekend 6pm and 11pm newscasts, and she also fills in on other newscasts during the week. Her career path has taken her to television stations in Texas and Alabama as well.

In her spare time, Remeisha can most likely be seen at one of the Metroparks, a yoga studio, working out at the gym, or at one of the local ice skating rinks.

An interesting fact about Remeisha is that she competed in the Miss Alabama Teen USA pageant and also won Miss Florida State University while a senior at Florida State. She then went on to compete in the Miss Florida pageant and performed a jazz dance performance that included a weather forecast at the beginning!

Frank Wiley
Anchor
Reporter

Lauren Wilson
Multimedia Journalist

Frank Wiley is an Emmy Award winning journalist who has a passion for telling stories and building relationships.

He is half of the News 5 at 5 Anchor Team at NewsChannel 5 in Cleveland.

In The spring of 2015 he and his family moved to Cleveland. He has three children: Iceis, Sophia and Jaxx. Prior to moving to Cleveland, he and his wife, Karli lived in Atlanta, where Frank anchored the morning show at CBS46.

Before moving to Atlanta, Frank spent two years in his hometown of Tulsa, Oklahoma as the weekend anchor. Prior to moving to Tulsa, Frank worked in St. Louis, at KSDK as an anchor/reporter, and before that spent time in Tulsa as a reporter, but his career began in Lawton, Oklahoma at KSWO.

Lauren Wilson was born in Shaker Heights, and raised in Akron, Ohio. After graduating from the Performing Arts Program at Firestone High School, she went on to study Broadcast Journalism at Bowling Green State University. During her time there, she interned at WBGU/PBS in Bowling Green, Ohio, WTOL/CBS in Toledo,Ohio and E! Entertainment in Los Angeles, California. Before graduating with a Bachelor of Science in Journalism in 2009, she also was the General Manager of BG24 New, the news station on campus.

After graduation, Wilson became the associate producer, On-Air Talent and eventually producer at 90.3 WCPN/ NPR & WVIZ/PBS ideastream for nearly 5 years. While employed at ideastream she created a local foodie series called 'Beyond the Dish' for which she won three Emmy awards, a Gracie Award and other honors for her producing and on-air talents. She is now the Multi-Media Journalist/ reporter for The Now Cleveland on WEWS News 5.

Wilson loves connecting with people and telling their stories and is glad to be in Cleveland.

ORGANIZATION
SPOTLIGHT

The Greater Cleveland
Alumnae Chapter of Delta Sigma Theta, Inc

Sara Corprew
Recording Secretary
.

Sara Corprew has more than 20 years of experience in customer service, sales, supervision, management and recruitment with a variety of for profit and nonprofit. Sara specializes in helping organizations with early talent identification which will strengthen their pipeline for future employees. Sara also assists corporations with their diversity and underserved needs.

Sara has been engaged with clients such as Deloitte & Touche, KPMG, PwC, Verizon Wireless, PNC, American Eagle Outfitters, KeyBank, Cleveland Clinic Foundation, Medical Mutual, Eaton Corporation, Federal Home Loan Bank of Pittsburgh, and Moen. Her human resources management experience includes: client account management, interview preparation, talent acquisition, planning career fairs and informational sessions, professional coaching, development and training, professional workshop facilitator professional mentor, professional event planning, standard operating procedures (SOP) for continuous improvement, new technology implementation.

Sara was initiated Theta Eta Chapter Spring 2005 and is currently an active member of Delta Sigma Theta Sorority, Inc., Greater Cleveland Alumnae Chapter where she serves on the executive committee as recording secretary. She holds B.S. David N. Myers University Master's Degree in Management Ursuline College.

Dr. Nicole Y. Culliver
President

Dr. Nicole Y. Culliver is the President of the Greater Cleveland Alumnae Chapter of Delta Sigma Theta Sorority, Inc. Dr. Culliver brought the vision of "Transcending the Path: Community Eminence through Innovative, Inspiring, and Invigorating Service." This vision brought new community collaborations that garnered local, regional, and national awards in the areas of Political Awareness and Involvement, Physical and Mental Health, Educational Development, International Awareness, A NANN Community Leader Award, A NCNW contributor award, and a Regional Chapter of the Year Award. She is a Diamond life member of the sorority who directs her chapter's 80 committees, 500 chapter members, and more than 1000 members throughout Greater Cleveland.

Nicole is a proud HBCU graduate from Lincoln University, PA., and received her PhD in Early Childhood Education from Walden University. She enjoys spending time with her husband Devlin Culliver and is the proud mother of Alexandria and Eric.

Cheri Coleman Daniels
Corresponding Secretary

Cheri Coleman Daniels is a lifetime member of Delta Sigma Theta Sorority, Inc., a charter member of the Bermuda Alumnae Chapter and corresponding secretary of the Greater Cleveland Alumnae Chapter. A graduate of Central State University, with a B.S. in Business Administration majoring in management. Cheri has over 35 years of financial experience and leadership positions including Finance Manager at Cleveland Job Corps, Vice President of Operations at the Call & Post, Assistant Manager-Commercial Loans at National City Bank. Cheri lived in Bermuda for 13 years and worked for Bank of Bermuda, Exxon Financial Services and Esso Bermuda, both divisions of ExxonMobil.

She is president of Cleveland Alumni Chapter of Central State University, a member of the NAACP, Lee Harvard Community Center and St. James A.M.E. Church. She has served as a member of the Cleveland Orchestra Community Relations Committee and AHA Power to End Stroke. Cheri has been awarded the YWCA Greater Cleveland Professional Woman of Excellence.

Cheri is the proud mother of Alexandria, Courtney and Ronald Jr. and the proud daughter/caregiver of father, Theodore Coleman.

Phyllis A. East, MBA, M.Ed.
Financial Secretary II

P hyllis A. East is a graduate of Cleveland Public Schools from Jane Addams Business Careers Center with a major in Legal Secretary. She attended Cleveland State University and David N. Myers University, obtaining her Masters in Business and Masters in Adult Education. Currently, she is Assistant Treasurer with East Cleveland City School District.

Phyllis A. East is the mother of five and grandmother of five. Enjoys singing in the church choir, line dancing and karaoke. East is the current President-Elect of Parent Advisory Committee with Open Doors Academy for the 2017-2019 school year and member of Delta Sigma Theta Sorority, Incorporated, initiated in the Spring of 2007. She served as chair of EMBODI for the 2015-2017 Sorority year. Currently, she serves as Financial Secretary II with Delta Sigma Theta and newly re-elected for the 2019-2021 sorority year.

Melonie M. Frazier
2nd Vice President and Membership Chair

M elonie M. Frazier is a retired teacher from the Cleveland Metropolitan School District and currently works part-time as an Early Childhood Educator Supervisor for Lakeland Community College.

As a retired teacher, she successfully educated generations of students in CMSD and her in-depth organizational and management skills have transferred to her position as a part-time adjunct faculty member successfully guiding and supervising student teachers.

As Second Vice President and Membership Chair, she is responsible for leading and providing intergenerational activities to retain and reclaim chapter members and is responsible for the intake of new members for the Greater Cleveland Alumnae Chapter.

Recently elected by the chapter as the First Vice President for the 2019-2021 term, her responsibilities will include managing the chapter's programs that provide philanthropic activities for the Greater Cleveland community.

Melonie holds a Bachelor of Science Degree in Education from Kent State University and a Master of Education Degree from Cambridge College. Her daughter is also a Delta.

Teresita Jones-Thomas
Treasurer

M s. Jones-Thomas has been with PK Management, LLC, since its inception. Specializing in acquisitions, management and development of multifamily real estates, she is primarily responsible for overseeing the financial operations, assisting in HUD Financial Reporting and Compliance of PK Management. Ms. Jones-Thomas was previously employed by Associated Estates Realty Corporation (AERC), Cleveland, Ohio, which is a publicly traded Real Estate Investment Trust (REIT).

She holds a Bachelor of Business Administration in Accounting from Cleveland State University, a Master of Business Administration in Human Resource Management from Keller Graduate School of Management of DeVry University and a Doctor of Business Administration in strategy and Innovation, to be conferred by Capella University

Ms. Jones-Thomas is a current member of Delta Sigma Theta Sorority, Incorporated where she serves as Treasurer (Greater Cleveland Alumnae) and Midwest Accounting Coordinator (Midwest Region).

LauraAnn T. Moore, M.Ed.
Financial Secretary

LauraAnn is the Special Education Program Manager for the Cleveland Metropolitan School District (CMSD). In this role, she manages eighteen schools within one of seven networks. LauraAnn services each school under her leadership through the guidance CMSD's Portfolio Strategy, Theory of Action, Central Office Support Plan, and The Cleveland Plan. Within the CMSD school district, LauraAnn serves on the Strategic Priority task force, collaborating to make CMSD a first choice school district.

LauraAnn is a member of of Delta Sigma Theta Sorority, Inc. and holds the office of Financial Secretary in Greater Cleveland Alumnae Chapter. She is also a member of The National Sorority of Phi Delta Kappa, Gamma Rho Chapter in Cleveland, Ohio. LauraAnn holds a Bachelor's Degree from the University of Akron, Master's from Cleveland State University and seeking her Doctoral Degree in Education from Lipscomb University in Nashville, Tennessee. LauraAnn is a native of Cleveland, Ohio. She has a daughter serving as her light. LauraAnn lives by the notion of, "to thine ownself be true."

Ruth Price Rollins
1st Vice President/
Program Chair

Ruth Price Rollins is a 50 year Diamond Life Member of Delta Sigma Theta. She currently serves as the 1st Vice President/Program Chair of the Greater Cleveland Alumnae Chapter and is the President Elect. Ruth is retired from a successful 36 year career as a Sales Specialist in the Pharmaceutical Industry. During her career with Abbvie, she won numerous sales awards including All Star.

Ruth currently serves as a Director on the Board of the Greater Cleveland Delta Foundation Life Development Center and is a member of the Board of Diversity, Equity and Inclusion at Kent State University. She has been a member of East Mt. Zion Baptist Church for forty years where she sings in the choir.

Ruth holds a B.A. in Psychology and an M. Ed. in Educational Administration both from Kent State University.

Ruth is married to Raymond Rollins, with whom she makes wine as a hobby. Ruth is a new grandmother to Ryann Elizabeth, has a passion for music, collects elephants and enjoys Zumba and water aerobics.

Daina White
Internal Audit Chair

Daina White is a Claims Examiner for the U.S. Department of Labor. Daina holds a Bachelor of Science degree in Business Administration from Florida A&M University and a Master's Degree in Business Management from the University of Phoenix. Daina is the Internal Audit Chair for the Greater Cleveland Alumnae Chapter of Delta Sigma Theta Sorority, Inc. and will be serving as Financial Secretary I for the upcoming fiscal year. She is passionate about serving her community and showing love through action as she works tirelessly on various committees within the chapter. Daina is also co-founder, director and coach for the North Collinwood Thundercats Youth Organization, a non-profit, all-star cheerleading team committed to building strength, character, and relationships for girls ages 4 - 18. A native Clevelander, Mrs. White is also a dedicated wife and mother of two college students. She enjoys reading, traveling and mentoring youth in the community.

CORPORATE SPOTLIGHT

Margaret Bernstein
Director
Advocacy and Community Initiatives

Kierra Cotton
Digital Content Producer

A Los Angeles native, she earned her bachelor's degree in Journalism from the University of Southern California. She worked as a reporter and columnist at The Plain Dealer from 1989 to 2013. A recipient of many journalism honors, Margaret won the Ohio Society of Professional Journalists' first-place award for minority issues reporting in 2011 and 2012, for a series of profiles about the 11 Imperial Avenue victims.

Well known for her passion about mentoring, Margaret was named National Big Sister of the Year in 2000 for her work with two Cleveland girls, Cora and Ernestine, through Big Brothers Big Sisters.

She is also the writer of The Bond, a memoir on fatherlessness by the famed Three Doctors. That experience led her to write her most recent book, a storybook titled "All In A Dad's Day" that is designed to tighten the bond between fathers and their young children.

Margaret is married to Shaker Heights Chief Prosecutor C. Randolph Keller, and is the mother of two children, Randy and Alexandria.

Kierra Cotton joined the WKYC team in 2016 as an audience engagement specialist. After honing her skills, she joined the digital team in her current role as a content producer.

Cotton discovered her passion for digital media while interning for WBNS-10TV in Columbus.

Before joining WKYC, Cotton attended Ohio University obtaining her Bachelor of Science in Journalism with concentrations in visual communications and communication science disorders.

She was active in the university›s entertainment news show, Straight Up! in various behind the scenes and on-air roles. She is also a member of Phi Sigma Pi honor fraternity.

Cotton›s strength lies in her ability to cover a wide range of topics. She›s traveled to cover Hurricane Irma but also enjoys entertainment and feature reporting.

A Cleveland native, Cotton is happy to be in her hometown embracing the city of Cleveland from a fresh perspective.

Dorsena Drakeford
Reporter
WKYC-TV

Michael Estime
Meteorologist

orsena Drakeford is a reporter for Channel 3 News in Cleveland. She started her career a few years after graduating from Valdosta State University in Georgia with a bachelor's degree in Journalism. Her first job in broadcast journalism took her to Texas where she learned how to operate behind-the-scenes equipment before stepping in front of the camera. At that time, she discovered her niche: covering the crime and courts beat. Drakeford then moved to Iowa as the Criminal Justice reporter before settling down in Cleveland in 2017. Her passion for the truth and storytelling has kept her excited about the future of journalism and the need for accountability. Drakeford believes the look of broadcast journalism might change for the viewer, but the integrity should remain the same.

Though she calls Georgia home, she has enjoyed her time in Cleveland telling your stories, learning about the city and getting more involved with the community.

efore joining the Channel 3 family, Estime served for 4 years as the Morning, Midday & Noon Meteorologist at WTVQ in the "Horse Capital of the World" - Lexington, Kentucky.

While in Kentucky, his forecasts of crippling snowstorms, record shattering cold, devastating flooding and violent tornadoes helped earn our weather team the title of "Most Accurate Forecast in Central Kentucky" by WeatheRate. Your safety before, during and after a storm is his number one priority. Rain or shine, day or night, Estime's passion for the weather, commitment to his community, and optimistic outlook are qualities that you can count on.

He is a proud graduate of Central Michigan University (CMU) and earned degrees in both Meteorology and Mathematics. During his time at CMU, he worked for MHTV News Central 34, and was awarded "Best Weathercaster" in 2006, 2007 & 2008.

Estime started his career working behind the scenes at WWJ-TV CBS Detroit through the Emma L. Bowen Foundation (EBF) and was awarded a 5-year work/study scholarship with CBS News.

CORPORATE SPOTLIGHT

Jasmine Monroe
Morning Show Reporter

Brandon Simmons
Multimedia Journalist

Jasmine Monroe studied at Clarion University, where she became the first African-American female news director, anchor, reporter and cohost director to report local on-campus news at WCUCFM radio and WCUB TV news. She was also a part of Alpha Kappa Alpha Sorority, Inc.

After earning her Bachelor of Science degree in broadcast journalism, Monroe moved to Washington, D.C. and served as an assistant intern at BET Networks. While there, she worked on the pre-production, production, and post-production of the 2012 BET Awards. Monroe also created questions for the red carpet show Mad Swagg and aided in the commercial placement for the Pink Luster's promotional advertisement during BET's 106 & Park.

Before coming to Youngstown, Ohio, Monroe interned at KDKA-TV and Radio in Pittsburg, helping produce KDKA Radio's Inside Story with Marty Griffin.

While at WFMJ, Monroe reported on everything from Youngstown State University Board of Trustees, to Jim Tressel's inauguration, to presenting the Ringling Bros. showcase.

Monroe continued her education at Clarion University and reported local news at the campus tv and radio station as the first African-American freshman woman to hold the position of a news director, anchor, reporter and cohost director at WCUCFM radio and WCUB TV news, And also a strong woman of Alpha Kappa Alpha sorority Incorporated.

Brandon Simmons is a multimedia journalist at WKYC-TV (Cleveland NBC affiliate).

A self-proclaimed "utility man" of the newsroom, Mr. Simmons is capable of working in many facets of the news industry. Positions he has covered include database manager for election coverage and school closing systems, videographer, special projects editor, and multimedia journalist.

From basic newsgathering to dealing with highly technical computer-related issues, Mr. Simmons has experience in multiple areas of news media.

Some of Mr. Simmons' recent work includes travel to Tampa, Fla. and Charlotte, N.C. to cover the Republican and Democratic National Conventions, respectively.

Mr. Simmons is a graduate of Cleveland State University and holds a B.A. in Communications with a focus in Digital Media.

Ray Strickland
News Reporter

Tiffany Tarpley
Multimedia Journalist

Ray Strickland is an Emmy-nominated journalist, who worked at two different television stations before joining WKYC-TV Cleveland in June of 2018. He was born and raised in Akron, or what he likes to call "Home of LeBron James." Ray earned his degree in broadcast journalism at Kent State University. Before returning home, Ray spent a year in Dickinson, North Dakota where he worked at KXMB-TV. He covered the Standing Rock protest, where thousands of Native Americans protested against the construction of the Dakota Access Pipeline. Ray's coverage landed him a job in St. Louis at KSDK. Again, Ray found himself on the front lines of one of the nation's most compelling stories. He covered the Jason Stockley protest where people in St. Louis protested for weeks after a White police officer was acquitted in the fatal shooting of an unarmed Black man. Ray has also worked as a sports reporter at the Akron Beacon Journal, and as a news/traffic reporter for 1590 AM WAKR.

Tiffany Tarpley joined the Channel 3 news team as a Multimedia Journalist in March of 2014. The Lorain native is thrilled to be back in Northeast Ohio reporting primarily for the morning newscasts.

Prior to WKYC-TV, Tiffany worked in a variety of roles, behind the scenes and in front of the camera, for news outlets in Milwaukee, WI, Toledo and Lima, Ohio.

As weekend anchor and producer for WUPW-TV (FOX affiliate) in Toledo, Tiffany and the rest of the weekend team earned two regional Emmy awards and a regional Emmy nomination for Best Weekend Newscast, three years in a row. In 2008, Tiffany's co-workers voted her FOX Toledo's employee of the year which landed her a spot in Lin Television's Circle of Excellence. Tiffany received an all-expense paid cruise to Nassau, Bahamas where she accepted her award.

Tiffany attended Lorain County Community College for two years and later graduated from Bowling Green State University with a bachelor's degree in broadcast journalism and the honor of Broadcast Journalism Student of the Year.

Before returning to Northeast Ohio Tiffany wasn't a morning person but now when the alarm clock goes off at midnight she has no choice but to rise and shine.

Monique Jackson
Producer
Director
WKYC-TV 3

Danielle Wiggins
Reporter

Monique is a multi-talented Producer/Director at WKYC-TV 3 in Cleveland, Ohio. She has been responsible for creating high-end and effective marketing campaigns on WKYC's air for a number of years.

Recently, Monique was promoted from Creative Service Director to Director of Brand Strategy in connection with the station's See The Possible brand. Forward-thinking, good leadership, and empowering people are just a few of the traits Monique believes to be impactful and ultimately successful to any organization." I AM CREATIVE, THEREFORE I MAKE A DIFFERENCE", is her approach to problem solving and brand messaging. Monique's passion for creativity has won her several Emmy's, a Best of Gannett Award, as well as an honorary certificate of excellence from the US Coast Guard.

She is a native of Cleveland, Ohio and graduated from Kent State University with a Rhetoric and Communication degree and ended up in the best place in television: Marketing. Monique is currently a member of NAPW, NABJ, NATAS and PROMAX.

Danielle Wiggins is the morning traffic reporter for WKYC-TV, Cleveland's NBC affiliate. Before joining WKYC in 2013, she was the main producer and correspondent for "The Regina Brett Show" on 89.7 WKSU, Northeast Ohio's regional National Public Radio (NPR) affiliate.

The Regina Brett Show won multiple state and national awards under Danielle's leadership; including an Ohio Excellence in Journalism award for best radio show.

Danielle is passionate about using her love for media to empower others. She spent four summers serving as an instructor at Kent State's Upward Bound program. In the summer of 2010, Danielle and her students won a national Trio Quest Award for a commercial the class wrote and produced promoting Upward Bound programs.

Danielle is an ordained minister at the Shepherd's Pasture for All Nations church (SPAN Ministries) and a member of Delta Sigma Theta Sorority, Inc. She holds a bachelor's and master's degree from Kent State University. Danielle is married to Chris Wiggins. The two are the proud parents of Jeremiah and Christen Wiggins.

ORGANIZATION
SPOTLIGHT

Brian R. Webster, MPA
Polemarch
Kappa Alpha Psi,
Cleveland Alumni
Chapter

Brian R. Webster moved to Cleveland in 2007 to study Sociology and Communication Sciences at Case Western Reserve University; later receiving his Masters in Public Administration from Cleveland State University in 2013. A Cleveland Bridge Builders Graduate, Webster serves as Site Coordinator at Anton Grdina School for Burten, Bell, Carr Development Inc. Webster assists in securing resources and organizing various programs for the scholars and their families to utilize. Organizing a mini step show, ensuring every scholar receives a Christmas gift, and taking every 3rd - 8th grader to see the film "Black Panther" are just a few of the service projects organized by Webster. Webster also serves as a mentor, program facilitator for Neighborhood Leadership Institute's youth leadership programs. Webster manages registration logistics for All About Your Health's annual boys and girls summits.

Webster consistently volunteers at The American Heart Association, and with Manna Food from Heaven. As a proud member of Kappa Alpha Psi Fraternity Incorporated, he serves as Polemarch of the Cleveland Alumni Chapter. He is featured in the 2017 edition of "Who's Who in Black Cleveland."

Derek S. Funderburk, MBA
Vice Polemarch
Kappa Alpha Psi,
Cleveland Alumni
Chapter

Derek S. Funderburk was born and raised in Cleveland, and is committed to serving Northeast, Ohio professionally and personally. Mr. Funderburk serves as the Vice Polemarch or Vice President of the Cleveland Alumni Chapter of Kappa Alpha Psi Fraternity Inc. and is a member of the Cleveland Chapter of the NAACP.

Mr. Funderburk has held multiple management level positions. Mr. Funderburk worked for America's Body Company/Leggett and Platt, in St. Louis, MO and Washington, D.C. as Quality Manager and Operations Manager. Currently, Mr. Funderburk serves as Production Specialist with American Axle Manufacturing located in Twinsburg, Ohio. In his current position, Mr. Funderburk is responsible for the effective and successful management of labor, productivity, quality control, operational procedure, systems and principles and enhanced management reporting.

Mr. Funderburk received his Master of Business Administration from the University of Phoenix in 2019, Green Belt Six Sigma Certification and Design of Engineering certification from the University of Akron. Mr. Funderburk enjoys watching his son D.J. Funderburk play as the starting forward for N.C. State University Men's Basketball team.

Martez M. Glenn
Keeper of Records
Kappa Alpha Psi,
Cleveland Alumni
Chapter

Martez M. Glenn was born in Cleveland, Ohio. Martez, graduated from South High School and continued his studies to later obtain a Master of Education degree from Tiffin University in Higher Education Administration. He is currently employed by Cleveland State University as a Sr. Admissions Counselor / Multicultural Recruitment Counselor, where he recruits scholars from Cleveland Metropolitan School District primarily, Mahoning County, and 19 Southeastern Ohio counties. He is an active member of Kappa Alpha Psi Fraternity, Inc. Cleveland (OH) Alumni Chapter where he was initiated. Martez is the current Keeper of Records for the chapter and he is also active on several committees. Martez loves giving back to the community by volunteering many hours of community service hours throughout the City of Cleveland. In his free time Martez is preparing to pursue his PhD in Urban Education at Cleveland State University fall 2020. Martez is the proud father of KarLy and Riayn.

Thomas Pipkin is the Specialized Dockets Manager for Cuyahoga County Juvenile Court. His capacities include coordinating the delivery of restorative treatment services for at-risk court involved youth populations, including Drug Court, Reentry Court and Human Trafficking Docket participants.

Thomas has worked professionally in fields geared towards youth with special needs and court involvement for the better part of 19 years. Decreasing barriers to resources for youth involved in the juvenile justice system, and acknowledging the impact trauma plays in their homes, schools and communities are his primary goal. Thomas is a certified trainer in the Effective Practices of Community Supervision and also Co-Chairs the Youth Advisory Council initiative amongst other things.

Outside of the professional setting, Thomas is a dedicated father of two sons and understands the importance on maintaining strong relationships with family and friends. Thomas is a proud member of Kappa Alpha Psi Fraternity Inc. He is a member of the local Alumni Chapter and has served in many different capacities. Currently, he holds positions on its Board of Directors and Property Directorate.

Thomas Pipkin
Board of Directors,
Members
Kappa Alpha Psi,
Cleveland Alumni
Chapter

Ifeolu A.C. Claytor is a campaign and community engagement professional. A native of Shaker Heights, Ifeolu matriculated from Shaker Heights High School to Miami University. While there, Ifeolu earned a Bachelor's degrees in Political Science and Social Justice Studies, served as the student representative on the search committee that found Miami University's current president, and joined the Kappa Delta chapter of Kappa Alpha Psi Fraternity, Inc.

After graduating, Ifeolu returned home and has worked with ACLU of Ohio, the LGBT Community Center of Greater Cleveland in HIV-Prevention Education, as the Regional Field Director for the Safe & Healthy Ohio Campaign (Issue 1), and as the campaign aide to Justice Michael P. Donnelly. Now, Ifeolu works as a Research Associate with Burges & Burges Strategists.

Within the Cleveland (OH) Alumni Chapter, Ifeolu has served as the Chair of the Community and Social Action committee. In this role, he has expanded community partners, secured grants for the chapter, and educated the public about numerous important issues affecting our community. Ifeolu is excited to sit on the chapter's Board of Directors this coming year.

Ifeolu A.C. Claytor
Board of Directors,
Members
Kappa Alpha Psi,
Cleveland Alumni
Chapter

Wm. Eric Hills is a social service management professional. He Eric graduated from Cleveland's East High and Wittenberg University, earning a Bachelor of Arts in History and Sociology. He was an active member of The Black Student Union and worked as a Peer Advisor. He was initiated into the Mu Xi Chapter of Kappa Alpha Psi Fraternity Inc. his freshman year.

Eric has been employed by Cuyahoga County for the last 27 years. He served as a Senior Supervisor for the Job & Family Services division for the last nine. In his free time, Eric works as a mentor in the True2U program assisting 8th and 9th grade students, and College Now mentoring program, helping incoming freshmen complete the Baccalaureate degree.

Within the Cleveland Alumni Chapter of Kappa Alpha Psi, Eric has served on the Social Committee and Board of Directors. He currently holds the following offices in the chapter: Strategus (Sargent of Arms), Member of the Property Directorate Board and Co Advisor of the Kappa League/Guide Right program which mentors young men ages Middle school through High School.

Wm. Eric Hills
Strategus
Kappa Alpha Psi,
Cleveland Alumni
Chapter

KAPPA SPOTLIGHT

A. Cory McDaniel
Keeper of Exchequer
Kappa Alpha Psi,
Cleveland Alumni
Chapter

Born and raised in the Mt. Pleasant neighborhood of Cleveland, A. Cory McDaniel graduated from John F. Kennedy High School in 2002 and subsequently graduated from Bowling Green State University with a Bachelor's in Communication. After spending 10 years as a Financial Consultant and Educator, his love for children and his desire to see them properly educated brought him back to education. He initially began his career as a 1st Grade teacher and with the successes he achieved in and outside the classroom, A. Cory McDaniel then became Principal after one year. McDaniel is now heading into his third year as Head of School for a charter school on Cleveland's east side as well as completing his Masters in Curriculum and Instruction with a focus in K-8 Mathematics. One of his greatest achievements is being able to establish a successful school culture and increase its academic performance levels.

McDaniel serves the Cleveland Alumni Chapter of Kappa Alpha Psi as Keeper of Exchequer.

CORPORATE
SPOTLIGHT

Ohio | Development Services Agency

Annette Chambers-Smith
Director Ohio
Department of
Rehabilitation and
Correction

Annette Chambers-Smith was previously the General Manager of Payment Services for JPay Incorporated, A Securus Technologies Company in Miramar Florida, which works to connect friends and family with incarcerated loved ones through a variety of corrections-related services in 35 different states. She has also served as the Chief Operating Officer (COO) of the same company.

Chambers-Smith served for over two decades in the Ohio Department of Rehabilitation and Correction, most recently as Deputy Director in the Office of Administration. In that role, she managed the business organizational operations. During her time at ODRC, she worked to create a more efficient environment in the department, reducing staff resource needs by 55 percent and cutting millions in waste from the operating budget.

Kenyatta Chandler
Chief Financial
Officer
Ohio Development
Services Agency

Kenyatta Chandler is the Chief Financial Officer of the Ohio Development Services Agency. Chandler manages the agency's $1.3 billion capital and operating budget, through accounting, asset management, auditing, and procurement. Unique to the Development Services Agency, he oversees fiscal services for the agency's grants, loans and tax credits. His extensive public and private sector experience provides accountability for taxpayer dollars and transparency of operations.

Chandler has more than 25 years of public and private experience in financial management and technology implementations. He is a former business manager from the Ohio Office of Budget and Management. Chandler also served as the administrator of treasury management services at the Ohio Treasurer's Office.

Chandler is active in the government finance community, and has served a member of the Association of Financial Professionals (AFP), Government Finance Officers Association (GFOA) and the Association of Government Accountants (AGA). He has a Bachelor of Science degree in organizational leadership from Franklin University. He earned a Masters of Business Administration in management information systems from Franklin University.

Kimberly Hall
Director
Ohio Department
of Jobs and Family
Services

Kimberly Hall previously served as senior vice president of administration and general counsel at Columbus State Community College. Hall joined Columbus State in 2012, and she provides executive guidance on College policy, administration and strategic initiatives. Her leadership portfolio includes supervision of the Legal Office, Human Resources Department, Equity and Compliance Office, Police Department, Facilities Management Division and the Shared Governance Office. She also serves as liaison to the Board of Trustees for the development and implementation of board policy.

Prior to joining Columbus State, Hall served as deputy chief counsel for Attorney General Mike DeWine. Kim has served as deputy chief counsel for the Ohio Department of Education and, early in her career, she practiced as a labor and employment attorney with the Vorys, Sater, Seymour and Pease firm and the Littler Mendelson firm. She serves on the Board of Directors for the Columbus School for Girls and the YWCA of Columbus.

Kim is the founder and president of the Olive Tree Foundation for Girls, a non-profit organization that provides mentoring, enrichment programs and scholarships for young women. She received her Bachelor's degree from Columbia University and her Juris Doctorate from Fordham University School of Law.

Major General John Harris served as the Assistant Adjutant General for Army since January 11, 2011. He began his military career in 1981 when he enlisted in the Ohio Army National Guard. He received a commission in 1984 through Officer Candidate School.

General Harris has commanded at the platoon detachment, company, and squadron levels while serving in staff assignments at the battalion, squadron, and joint force headquarters level. Recent assignments include Chief of Staff (Joint Force Headquarters), Deputy Chief of Staff for Personnel (Joint Force Headquarters), and Commander of Task Force Lancer in Kosovo.

**Major General
John C. Harris, Jr.**
Adjutant General
Ohio National Guard

Jeffrey Johnson is the Chief of the Minority Business Development Division of the Ohio Development Services Agency. In this role, he is responsible to lead the state's efforts to help develop and grow Ohio minority-owned businesses. Johnson works closely with the Ohio Minority Business Advisory Council and fourteen Minority Business Assistance Centers around the state to support the agency's efforts.

Prior to joining the Ohio Development Services Agency, Johnson was the Vice President of Government and Non-Profit Lending at JP Morgan & Chase where he provided expertise on municipal bond underwriting and analysis. In his more than 30-year career, almost 15 years has been as an institutional investor, dealing primarily with municipal transactions. He has years of experience working with government municipalities and community organizations.

Johnson is also an active member in his community, where he has served as a board member to the New Albany Joint Park District, New Albany Plain Local School District and the Columbus Urban League.

Jeffrey Johnson
Chief of the
Minority Business
Development Division
Ohio Development
Services Agency

Jack Marchbanks was previously the assistant director for business and human resources at the Department of Transportation where he was responsible for the management of the department's 5,000 employees and the development of ODOT's $3.3 billion dollar budget.

Jack is responsible for the strategic direction of the agency's finance, human resources, IT, legal and communications divisions and the opportunity, diversity and inclusion programs. In addition, he has served as the department's district six deputy director twice.

Previously, Marchbanks worked in the private sector as a Marketing Director for PRIME AE Group, a minority-owned architectural and engineering firm.

Jack Marchbanks
Director
Ohio Department of
Transportation

Ursel McElroy
Director
Ohio Department of
Aging

Ursel McElroy has a wealth of experience in both local and state government with specific focuses in eldercare and programs aiding those in poverty. Her career began at the Franklin County Department of Jobs and Family Services and was also a Case Management Supervisor for the Franklin County Office on Aging.

McElroy served as the Chair of the Ohio Coalition for Adult Protective services through 2008 and worked in the Office of the Ohio Attorney General for 10 years as the Deputy Director of Education and Policy where she managed the establishment of the Ohio Elder Justice Initiative. She has also held key roles at the Ohio Department of Youth Services and the Ohio Department of Job and Family Services.

McElroy earned a Bachelor's Degree in Psychology and a Master's Degree in Public Administration, both from The Ohio State University. She resides in Columbus.

Alisha Nelson
Director
RecoveryOhio

Alisha Nelson currently serves as the Director for RecoveryOhio, a new initiative designated within the Office of the Governor to fight Ohio's public health crisis focusing on mental health and addiction prevention, treatment and recovery support services.

Before her time in the Governor's Office, Nelson served as the Director for Substance Use Policy Initiatives in the Ohio Attorney General's Office. While at the Attorney General's Office, Nelson co-chaired the Ohio Joint Study on Drug Use Prevention Education which developed the Drug Use Prevention Education Resource Guide, which has been shared with schools and community prevention organizations statewide. She has also served on Attorney General DeWine's Insurer Task Force to assist in the development of recommendations to help eight of Ohio's largest healthcare insurers address the opiate epidemic.

Prior to her state work, Nelson worked for the Alcohol, Drug and Mental Health (ADAMH) Board of Franklin County.

Michele Reynolds
Director
Faith-Based and
Community Initiatives
Office of Ohio
Gov. Mike DeWine

Michele Reynolds is the Director of the Governor's Office of Faith-Based and Community Initiatives.

Reynolds is the founder and Chief Executive Officer of NISRE, Inc. – a faith-based, nonprofit community development organization that provides affordable housing solutions and economic development initiatives to help revitalize neighborhoods in low- and moderate-income communities throughout the state. In addition, she is the First Lady and Executive Pastor of Common Ground Destiny Center Church.

Her education includes a Bachelor of Science degree in Criminal Justice from the University of Cincinnati, Master of Arts in Public Administration and Urban Studies from the University of Akron, Master of Law from Thomas Jefferson School of Law, and Honorary Doctorate of Philosophy from CICA International University and Seminary, and "All but dissertation" for her earned doctorate degree in Business Administration from Northcentral University.

She and her husband Pastor Uhleric (Rick) Reynolds live in Central Ohio with their family.

Ervan Rodgers II
Chief Information
Officer
Ohio Department of
Administrative Services

Ervan was recently appointed as the State of Ohio's Chief Information Officer and Assistant Director of the Ohio Department of Administrative Services. As state CIO, Ervan is responsible for the strategic direction and efficient use of information technology across the state and for oversight of state IT activities.

Prior to his appointment, Ervan served as the CIO at the Ohio Attorney General's Office where he focused on developing IT strategies to help better serve and protect Ohioans. Ervan has experience providing IT consulting to global Fortune 100 companies and a successful track record of leading teams and leveraging technology to position companies for growth. This includes hands-on experience with digitizing core business processes, e-business, developing value-added solutions, change management, and mentoring management teams.

He served on the board of directors for Ohio Geographically Referenced Information Program, an organization that encourages the creation of digital geographic data of value, State of Ohio CyberOhio advisory board and the Franklin University Cybersecurity and Public Safety advisory board.

Eric M. Seabrook
Deputy Director and
State EEO Coordinator
Ohio Department of
Administrative Services

Eric M. Seabrook is the recently appointed Deputy Director for the Equal Opportunity Division of the Ohio Department of Administrative Services. As such, he is responsible for implementing and enforcing the State of Ohio's affirmative action and equal employment opportunity policies, and implementing and monitoring the state's procurement preference programs for minority-owned, women-owned, and socially and economically disadvantaged businesses.

Eric has over 25 years of experience in public service including technology transfer and commercialization, lobbying health and human services issues, and addressing the legal challenges of election law and election administration.

Eric has served as Chief Counsel for the Ohio Secretary of State, Technology Transfer Officer with the Thomas Edison Program, Technology Assessment Coordinator with the United States Senate and as a public affairs consultant with Bass Public Affairs.

Ronald C. Todd II
Minority Affairs Liaison
Office of Ohio
Gov. Mike DeWine

Ronald C. Todd II currently serves as Governor DeWine's Minority Affairs Liaison. Ronald is the point person for the State of Ohio on topics including minority business development, economic development, K-12 educational establishments and colleges, faith-based initiatives, and government access. He works to inspire and connect diverse Ohioans to a government that works for them by creating a platform to voice their concerns.

Before his appointment, Ronald served as the Minority Affairs Liaison in the Ohio Secretary of State's Office under then-Secretary Husted where he advised the Secretary of State's Office on all matters of import to Ohio's minority communities.

Ronald has been a keynote speaker for various organizations throughout the country. He has served as a panelist at the Congressional Black Caucus and the National Press Club in Washington, D.C.

Ronald is very active in his community. Ronald was honored in 2013 as Top 10 African American Males of Dayton, Ohio, listed as a leader in Who's Who Black Cincinnati/ Dayton and Success Guide (Cincinnati/Dayton).

CELEBRATING ACHIEVEMENT IN MORE THAN 25 U.S. MARKETS

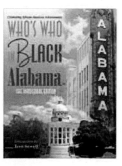  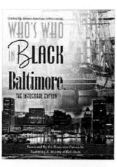  

  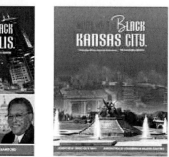  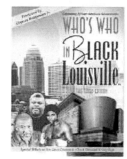

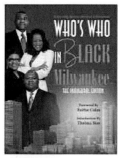    

   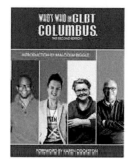 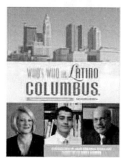

WHO'S WHO

A Real Times Media Company

www.whoswhopublishing.com

ORGANIZATION
SPOTLIGHT

Lamar T. Cole
Assistant Vice President
Business Banking at
Huntington National
Bank

Lamar T. Cole is a Life Member of Omega Psi Phi Fraternity, Inc., and was initiated through the Psi Theta Chapter on June 2, 1989. He is a native of East Cleveland, Ohio and graduate of St. Joseph High School. Lamar furthered his education at the University of Cincinnati where he earned a Bachelor of Arts Degree in Marketing & Management. He returned to Cleveland and attended Case Western Reserve University's Weather School of Management where he obtained an MBA in Banking & Finance.

Lamar is an Assistant Vice President in Business Banking at Huntington National Bank. He serves on the Scholarship Committee for the Cleveland Foundation. Lamar has also conducted financial literacy workshops for the Consortium of African American Organizations, Christian Business League, Minority Business Assistance Center, Grandville Academy, Junior Achievement, and several Cleveland area School Districts.

Lamar serves Omega Psi Phi Fraternity as its 4th District Representative (Ohio & West Virginia). He was honored as the 2014 Fourth District Omega Man of the Year.

Lamar, his wife Lisa and son Tillman reside in Shaker Heights, Ohio.

Rev. Theopolis Washington II
Manager of Vehicle
Fleet Maintenance
United States
Postal Service

Rev. Theopolis Washington II is a twenty year employee of the United States Postal Service. His current position is Manager of Vehicle Fleet Maintenance. He manages and controls operating cost, budget, and oversight for vehicle maintenance operations for territory in Northern Ohio. He is a native of the city of East Cleveland where he graduated from Shaw High School in 1984. He is an Army Veteran and a graduate of Cleveland State University, where he obtained a Bachelors of Art in Religious Studies.

Rev. Washington is an Associate Minister at The Historic Greater Friendship Baptist Church and the serving Chaplain of the Glenville High School Football, Basketball, and Track teams.

He is a member of Omega Psi Phi Fraternity Inc. Zeta Omega graduate chapter, and serves the fraternity as the 4th District Chaplain for the states of Ohio and West Virginia. He was initiated into the fraternity in 1989 through the Psi Gamma chapter at Kent State University.

His wife of 24 years, Cleveland Heights High School teacher Shawn Washington, is a proud member of Delta Sigma Theta Sorority Inc.

Darryl G. Moore
Owner
Alice's International
Salon and Spa

Darryl G. Moore is a native of East Cleveland, Ohio, where he graduated from Shaw High School. He furthered his education at Kent State University where he earned a Bachelor of Arts Degree in General Studies. After graduation, Darryl began his career in Education with the Cleveland Metropolitan School District where he taught and assisted with development of an entrepreneurial curriculum.

Darryl is a successful entrepreneur. He has been in the beauty salon industry for over 20 years. He is the owner of Alice's International Salon and Spa (named after his mother). With an interest in the empowerment and safety of low income communities, he founded his construction company, 3 D Moore Enterprises, LLC. 3 D Moore Enterprises, works on community improvement projects in low income areas throughout the county.

Darryl is a 30 year member of Omega Psi Phi Fraternity. He serves as the International Chairman of the Reclamation and Retention Committee and as the 4th District's Northeast Ohio Area Representative. He was recently honored as the 2018 Zeta Omega Chapter and 4th District Omega Man of the Year.

Antwaine Kennedy graduated from Cleveland Heights High School. After high school, he attended Alabama State University and received a Bachelor's degree after transferring to Cleveland State University. At Cleveland State University, Antwaine was initiated into Omega Psi Phi Fraternity Inc. by way of Phi Theta Chapter. Antwaine obtained his MBA from the University of Phoenix.

Antwaine is currently a substitute educator for CMSD while owning and operating Antwaine's Catering. Antwaine acquired a Senior Home Health Care Franchise called Acti-Kare in May of 2019.

Antwaine has earned several awards such as District Undergraduate Omega Man of the year. In 2009 and 2012, he earned Zeta Omega's Omega Man of the Year award. Under his direction as Basileus, Zeta Omega was awarded the 4th District Large Chapter of the Year as well as the Social Action International Chapter of the Year. Antwaine is currently the Fourth District Undergraduate Advisors Chairman and a member of the International Undergraduate Advisors Committee.

Antwaine and his wife Joy, who is a dedicated member of Sigma Gamma Rho Sorority Inc., have two sons, Isaiah and Austin

Antwaine Kennedy
Educator for CMSD
Owner
Antwaine's Catering

Anthony Scott, Esq. serves as the Assistant Director of the City of Cleveland's Building and Housing Department. In this role, he supports the City's mission of assuring that all structures in the city are maintained and constructed in a safe and habitable manner. Anthony graduated from Shaw High School in East Cleveland, Ohio. After graduation, he served 8 years in the United States Marine Corps. Upon being honorably discharged, he returned to Cleveland and completed his Bachelor's degree in English, his Master's degree in Public Administration, and Juris Doctorate at Cleveland-Marshall College of Law.

Anthony is the Basileus (President) of the Zeta Omega Chapter of Omega Psi Phi Fraternity, Inc., where he was recently honored as the Chapter Man of the Year. He prides himself on the uplift and support his organization provides to the Greater Cleveland community. Anthony also serves as a Trustee for the Black Professional Association Charitable Foundation (BPACF). Finally, he serves as mentor to several students in high school, college and graduate/professional level programs.

Anthony Scott, Esq
Assistant Director
Building and Housing
Department
City of Cleveland

Grover Brown is the UAW Local 573 World Class Logistics Specialist with the Mopar Division of Fiat-Chrysler Automotive at the Cleveland Parts Depot Center. As the WCL Specialist, Mr. Brown is skilled on the multiple manufacturing pillars that aim towards the quality and production of the employees, and how to make their job's safe and more productive. Mr. Brown also sits on the Executive Board of Local 573 as a Trustee.

Mr. Brown is an active Life Member of the Zeta Omega Chapter of Omega Psi Phi Fraternity Incorporated, where he holds the office of Vice Basileus (Vice President). Mr. Brown believes in uplifting the community by participating in various activities that give back. He was awarded the 2017, Zeta Omega Superior Service Award in appreciation of his commitment to service. Mr. Brown is a proud Clevelander who attended Lincoln West HS. He furthered his education at The University of Toledo, earning his Bachelor of Arts and Science in English Literature while working full-time at Toledo Jeep.

Mr. Brown has a daughter that he loves dearly, Emon.

Grover Brown
WCL Specialist
Mopar Division
Fiat-Chrysler Automotive
Cleveland Parts Depot
Center.

Kendric Jackson
Accountant
Defense Finance and
Accounting Service –
Enterprise Systems and
Solutions Division

Kendric Jackson serves as the Accountant for the Defense Finance and Accounting Service – Enterprise Systems and Solutions Division. In this role, he is responsible for reporting and analysis of Department-wide financial statements, cross-component budget execution analysis, and oversight of Treasury reporting operations for the Department of Defense. He is also an adjunct Accounting Professor at Bryant & Stratton.

Kendric completed his Bachelor's degree in Accounting and Business Administration with a concentration in Management from Elizabeth City State University in Elizabeth City, NC. Thereafter, he completed his Master in Accountancy from the Weatherhead School of Management at Case Western Reserve University.

Kendric was initiated into Omega Psi Phi Fraternity, Inc. through the Lambda Gamma Chapter on November 20, 1993. He has dutifully served Omega Psi Phi for more than 25 years. Currently, he serves as the Zeta Omega Chapter Keeper of Records and Seal (Secretary), addressing the administrative needs of more than 200 chapter members. He also serves as a Referee for the Cleveland Football Officials Association and an Umpire for the Eastern Cuyahoga County Umpires Association.

Jeffrey Maxwell, Sr.
Senior Accountant
Defense Finance and
Accounting Service
(DFAS)

Jeffrey Maxwell, Sr. works as a Senior Accountant for Defense Finance and Accounting Service (DFAS). In this role, he ensures the men and women of the United States Navy have the supplies and resources needed to properly protect the United States' lands and shores. He is also a veteran of four years with the United States Army. As a decorated Desert Storm Era Veteran, he prides himself on being able to continue to serve his country by assisting service members through DFAS.

Jeffrey graduated from Cleveland Heights high school in 1985. After completing his military service, he returned to Cleveland and obtained his Bachelor's and Master's degree from Lake Erie College in the Accounting field.

Jeffrey is a proud member of the Zeta Omega Chapter of Omega Psi Phi Fraternity Inc. He has served as the chapter's Keeper of Finance (Treasurer) for two terms. He also continues to serve as a member of the Brothers Organization. The Brothers are an organization formed at Cleveland Heights High School that continue to give back by providing annual scholarships to students.

Michael J. Fordham
Social Service
Coordinator
ABC Management

Michael J. Fordham is a native of Youngstown, Ohio and a graduate of The Rayen School. Michael attended the University of Akron. He started a career of helping children and families with a particular interest on strengthening the role of the father in the household.

Michael has served as the Family Involvement Administrator with the Centers for Families and Children. He has also served as Family Liaison with the Cleveland Municipal School District. Michael was charged with increasing parental involvement, family engagement, and providing resources to assist families. A collaborative effort within the community resulted in several successful and well-attended fatherhood programs.

Michael has served as the Chapter of the Zeta Omega Chapter of Omega Psi Phi Fraternity, Inc. since 2007. He is active with several other organizations that share his passion for strengthening families; including, Bethany Baptist Church where he serves as a Deacon and Minister in Training, and the Cuyahoga County Fatherhood Initiative. Currently Mr. Fordham is currently employed with ABC Management as a Social Service Coordinator.

Mr. Fordham has two children and three granddaughters.

Kendrick Cloud is a General Engineer in the Public & Indian Housing Division of the Department of Housing and Urban Development. In this role, he is responsible for overseeing over $40M+ annually in Capital Fund Program funds used to develop and modernize housing for low income residents in public housing throughout the state of Ohio. Prior to his position with HUD, he served as the Lead Mechanical Engineer/Project Manager for Laughlin AFB in Texas.

Kendrick has a Bachelor of Science degree in Mechanical & Manufacturing Engineering from Tennessee State University and a Master of Science degree in Civil Engineering from The University of Alabama at Birmingham. During his matriculation through Tennessee State, he was initiated into Omega Psi Phi Fraternity, Inc. via the "Mighty" Rho Psi Chapter in the spring of 2000.

He serves as the Keeper of Peace (Sergeant at Arms) for Zeta Omega Chapter. He participates in numerous community service activities with the chapter, including voter education and registration, food basket giveaways, and highway clean up.

Kendrick is married and a father of two beautiful young ladies.

Kendrick Cloud
General Engineer
Public & Indian Housing
Division
Department of
Housing and Urban
Development.

WHO'S WHO

A Real Times Media Company

FOCUS
CELEBRATE
PROMINENCE
RECOGNITION

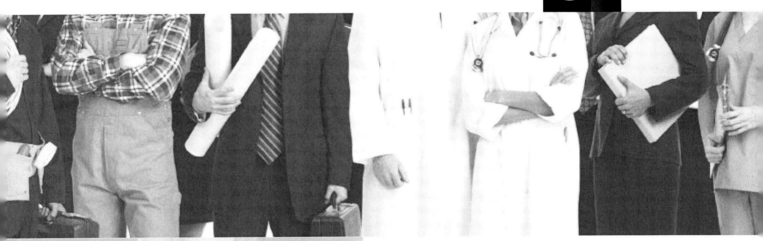

The professionals of Cleveland are the oil that keeps the engine of the city going. These individuals of various fields collectively serve as role models and are highly regarded for their work ethic.

Ericka L. Abrams
Principal and Agency
Manager
Legacy42 Insurance
& Financial

Ericka L. Abrams is the principal and agency manager of Legacy42 Insurance & Financial, a life, health, and financial services brokerage serving clients in several states. She has over 20 years of experience in health education, financial literacy and wealth advocacy. Ericka holds a Bachelor of Science in Community Health Education from Clark Atlanta University, Master of Public Health from Case Western Reserve University, and is in pursuit of a Doctor of Philosophy in Public Health from Walden University. Her belief and understanding are that health and wealth are inextricably linked; therefore, she made the conscious decision to further her knowledge in financial services by earning a license in insurance, and certifications in long-term care, Medicare and annuities. Ericka also supports the health of senior citizens with her homecare agency, Honor & Compassion Home Care, LLC.

Dr. Lachaka Askew
Chief Executive Officer
20 Second
Intercessor Inc.

Dr. Lachaka Askew is an author, actress, and chief executive officer of 20 Second Intercessor Inc., a 501c3 nonprofit that works with charities to serve the homeless. With its focus on advocacy, the agency spearheaded efforts with its "Free Soup for Conversation" campaign and Baptist-Muslim dialogue workshops. Lachaka maintains a global ministry, speaks at Interfaith vigils, is a member of Cleveland Committee of Foreign Relations and reports advocacy news in its newsletter. She has three published books about intercessory prayer and one short-story fiction book. Using her research about Alzheimer's and health, she has written articles for MedCrunch Magazine, Inspiring Woman Magazine, and the Bedford Tribune. She reignited her love of acting through productions at Karamu House. Lachaka received her Doctor of Ministry degree from South University, Master of Science and Bachelor of Arts degrees from Cleveland State University. Her educational achievements include outstanding research recognition from Cleveland State University and memberships in four national and international honor societies. She is happily married with three children.

Rodney L. Brown
Chief Executive
Officer/Principle
Photographer
Rodney L. Brown
Photography

Rodney L. Brown is one of the most accomplished corporate photographers in Northeast Ohio. With his diverse background in photographic specialties, he engages in digital studio, commercial, and PR/marketing with a special emphasis on special events. Rodney presently works with such clientele as Western Reserve (OH) Chapter of The Links Incorporated, Women of Color Foundation, Dominion East Ohio, University Hospitals and The Urban League of Greater Cleveland. Rodney has earned among his peers and clientele the reputation for being reliable, a perfectionist and professional. In fact, a client gave him the moniker, "Professionals Professional" which is currently his business motto. A graduate of John Adams High School, Rodney learned the basics of photography from classes taught at the Karamu Camera Guild, and later continued his studies at the New York School of Photographic Arts. Rodney is a native Clevelander and a member of Olivet Institutional Baptist Church. In 2003, Rodney joined the 100 Black Men of Greater Cleveland, Inc. and he currently serves on their board of directors.

Rosetta Brown-Murphy is the office manager and assistant to the executive director of the Buckeye Shaker Square Development. A member of the National Association for Female Executives, Rosetta strives to uphold the vision of the organization to provide a unique opportunity for residents, institutions, merchants and stakeholders for a better understanding and improvement of the community. Rosetta worked with the Ohio State Extension Summer Sprout Program for the past four years planting gardens to help eliminate food deserts within the community. Collaborating with a Metro Health Hospital doctor, she teaches healthy cooking classes to neighboring families, while utilizing food from the garden to prepare meals. Rosetta volunteered her time with the Tax Assistance Program (VITA) for over 12 years, preparing tax returns for low to moderate income families. She is a member of Mount Sinai Baptist Church where she serves in several capacities and leads the deaconess ministry. Rosetta studied at Capital University. She is married to Keith V. Murphy.

Rosetta Brown-Murphy
Office Manager and
Assistant to Executive
Director
Buckeye Shaker Development Corporation

Evette Jackson Clark is founder and executive director of The Phenomenal Foundation, a nonprofit community outreach organization. She has two master's degrees from Cleveland State University in education and psychology. Evette is an adjunct professor at Bryant & Stratton College; and chief executive officer of Moving Forward, a workforce development consulting firm. Her clients include the Cleveland Clinic and the Black Professional Charitable Foundation. She published the inspirational book Wait on the Platform, a compilation of life lessons and comparing life's journey to an amusement park adventure. Evette is the recipient of numerous awards including the National Action Network – Woman Empowerment Award, Bryant & Stratton College Woman Who Rocks, and the Everyday Hero Award.

Evette Jackson Clark
Founder and
Executive Director
The Phenomenal
Foundation, Inc.

Laura C. Cowan is the resident services liaison with Cuyahoga Metropolitan Housing Authority (CMHA) working in resident services as the domestic violence advocate. She assists CMHA residents by empowering, advocating and educating them on prevention to end domestic violence and child abuse and providing workshops, materials, guidance and emotional support. She is a member of Coalition for a Better Life, Black on Black Crime Inc., and National Action Network Cleveland Chapter. She volunteers at the Domestic Violence and Child Advocacy Center of Greater Cleveland and is an ambassador at the Rape Crisis Center of Greater Cleveland. She was awarded Crain's "Women of Note", and Women of Color Foundation's "Courage Award". Laura has appeared on Anderson Cooper Live, Meredith Vieira Show, ID Investigation Discovery "House of Horrors", TVOne's: Justice By Any Means, Dr. Phil, CNN, Huffington Post, Los Angeles Times, and local Cleveland media for her advocacy work in domestic violence. She's also a radio host on VoiceItRadio.com with Laura Cowan's Empowerment Hour.

Laura C. Cowan
Resident Services
Liaison/Domestic
Violence Advocate
Cuyahoga Metropolitan Housing Authority

Wayne Dailey
Creator Director
Rhonda Crowder &
Associates LLC

Wayne Dailey is an award-winning creative director. He worked as an art director for the Los Angeles Times for more than 20 years. Wayne's Fortune 500 brand identity experience allows him to create campaign experiences to print online to broadcasting and interactive media. His client list includes Cleveland's United Black Fund, Hough Reads, Construction Employer Association, Taste of Shaker Square, Cleveland Indians and numerous Los Angeles clients including Tribune Company, Times Mirror, Horne Entertainment, Chaka Khan, Steven Segal and many more. Wayne provides creative solutions for events and high-end book/magazine/newspaper publishing, entertainment, advertising, marketing, direct sales, product packaging and presentations. He began his career as a graphic designer with Channel Communication/WCLQ TV 61 in Cleveland and relocated to southern California in 1985. Wayne is a graduate of John F. Kennedy High School and the University of Cincinnati where he received a Bachelor of Arts in Communications.

Cydney Davidson-Bey
Founder
Technology in Color

Cydney Davidson-Bey (formerly Gillon) obtained a bachelor's degree in Information Technology and Network Security from Eastern Michigan University in Spring 2017. Her company, Technology in Color (TIC), was born out of her passion for IT and her shock as she walked across the stage as the only Black woman in her field. The mission of TIC is to support, advance, and grow the number of inner-city young women of color in the IT field. After teaching as a coding instructor for United Black Fund of Greater Cleveland and Richmond Heights Schools, Cydney decided to take Technology in Color to her alma mater, MC2 Stem High School in Cleveland. She is also a board member at the high school actively advocating for the students and educating them on the sciences behind emerging technologies impacting today's industry and consumer markets. Cydney is heavily involved in charitable acts such as providing clothing and other essentials to families in need during the winter months.

Dr. Tyffani Monford Dent
Psychologist
Monford Dent
Consulting &
Psychological Services,
LLC

Dr. Tyffani Monford Dent is a licensed psychologist and founder of Monford Dent Consulting & Psychological Services, LLC. She was named Wilberforce University's Outstanding Alumnus and an ATSA Fellow for her significant contribution to the field of prevention and response to sexual violence. Dr. Dent was named a National Sexual Violence Resource Center Visionary Voice for her work addressing the needs of Black and Brown women and girls and other marginalized communities impacted by sexual violence. Dr. Dent serves on several boards addressing issues of mental health, sexual violence prevention and intervention, and human trafficking. She has presented all over the United States on sexual violence prevention and intervention on the continuum, the role of intersectionality in the lives of Black and Brown girls/women, and culturally informed work with those within the juvenile justice system. Dr. Dent is the author of several books addressing issues of emotional wellness in women and girls. She is a member of Delta Sigma Theta Sorority and Jack & Jill of America.

Jacqueline Goodrum is the chaplain, the Black History chair, and field liaison for the National Action Network Greater Cleveland Chapter. She has been the early childhood educator at Superior Elementary School in East Cleveland for nine years. Currently, she is an executive committee member of the Cuyahoga County Democrat Party, vice president of the East Cleveland Citizens, City-Wide Organization, and Spiritual Development Sunday School instructor at Universal Liberty in Christ Temple Church. She has five children, nine grandchildren and has written two books. The late, great, Rev. Dr. Martin Luther King, Jr. once said, "Our lives end the day we become silent about the things that matter." Jacqueline says she calls herself a modern-day Harriet Tubman when it comes to early childhood education. "I don't have a shotgun, but I have a wealth of knowledge that I pass on to children." As the saying goes, "You are either part of the problem, or part of the solution and action speaks louder than words."

Jacqueline Goodrum
Chaplain, Black History
Chair, and Field Liaison
National Action
Network Greater
Cleveland Chapter

Joe "Flash" Gordon is currently a transportation consultant at Central Cadillac, located in Downtown Cleveland. In his position, he provides consulting services to Clevelanders on their luxury automotive needs to be leased or purchased. Joe started his career in the automotive industry in 1954 when he worked at his father's service station. Two years later he became the manager of that station, and in 1963 was able to open his own Super Sohio station.

In 1972, Joe became a dealer candidate with General Motors in the newly created minority dealer development program. Throughout his career he has sold many makes of vehicles including Pontiac, Chevrolet, Chrysler, GMC, Buick, Rolls Royce and finally Cadillac. Even after 60 years in the industry, Joe still enjoys selling and driving luxury cars!
In his spare time Joe enjoys music, particularly jazz, golf, traveling and fine dining.

Joe "Flash" Gordon
Transportation
Consultant
Central Cadillac

Loretta Gray is president of the Cuyahoga County Section of National Council of Negro Women, Inc. where she oversees operations. She transforms vision into reality through strategy development and led the chartering of the Cuyahoga County youth section. Loretta spearheaded strategic shifts for transitioning the organization to an enabler of innovation to support STEM scholarships. She is a respected, credible voice in decision-making, collaboration, and establishing partnerships. The educator and author earned a Bachelor of Science and master's degree in Education from Cleveland State University where she supervises for the Office of Field Services. Loretta is a Neighborhood Leadership Development Program graduate and founder of TeensLINKS, a social media/Internet network to helpline suicide prevention, domestic violence, counseling, mentoring, and youth support services. A member of the National Sorority of Phi Delta Kappa and Top Ladies of Distinction, she serves on the Northeast Ohio Black Health Coalition Advisory Committee. Loretta is mother to Shajuan, grandmother to Devin; and a life member of Temple Baptist Church.

Loretta Gray
President
National Council of
Negro Women, Inc.
Cuyahoga County
Section

Yvonka Hall
Executive Director
Northeast Ohio Black
Health Coalition

Yvonka Hall is the executive director of the Northeast Ohio Black Health Coalition and co-founder of the Cleveland Lead Safe Network. The 1974 murder of her mother dramatically changed her life. Yvonka's childhood promise to use her life to help others, has led to the creation of cutting-edge programs and impacted thousands of people's lives. She is nationally recognized and serves on the Ohio Healthy Homes Network; Health & Human Services Region V Health Education Advisory Committee; Multi-Ethnic Advocates for Cultural Competency boards and the United Way. She is a member of the National Council of the Negro Women CCS, Cuyahoga County Progressive Caucus and Top Ladies of Distinction Greater Cleveland Chapter. She was elected to the Cuyahoga County Democratic Party Central Committee representing District N. She is a mother, grandmother and activist deeply involved in social justice activities including Stop the Inhumanity at the Cuyahoga County Jail; Cleveland Lead Advocates for Safe Housing; Clevelanders Organized for Regional Development; Pregnancy and Infant Loss Committee and Ohio Lead Free Kids Coalition.

Felicia C. Haney
Founder
Beech Street
Publicity

Felicia C. Haney was born with the gift of gab and has since re-gifted it serving as a multi-media and PR professional who has rubbed elbows and walked red carpets with Hollywood's elite. The Ohio Excellence in Journalism award-winning reporter by day and superhero by night has taken flight, covering everything from major studio film junkets to major network awards shows.

Using her professional knowledge, Felicia gives back by molding adolescents to build life skills and become more influential in their communities. She is also the co-founder of #CLEfigHT-Shunger – a monthly grassroots initiative to end homelessness.
She sits as an Advisory Board member for the historic E.F. Boyd and Sons Funeral Home. She is also a member of the Press Club of Cleveland, the National Association of Black Journalists and the Greater Cleveland Association of Black Journalists. Felicia is featured as one of 130 subjects in the book "Black in Cleveland" and was named as an Emerging Leader in "Who's Who in Black Cleveland," the tenth edition.

Felicia owns and operates Beech Street Publicity, a communications firm that brings the beat of the world to the ear of the local listener.

Pastor Courtney Hauser
Executive Director and
Therapist
Healing Care
Counseling Center

Pastor Courtney Hauser is a wife, mother, counselor, pastor and author. After experiencing domestic violence, physical and sexual abuse early on in life, Courtney discovered that pain could be used as a springboard into purpose and passion. She has a master's degree in clinical mental health counseling from Ashland Theological Seminary. Courtney has used her clinical and spiritual education to bring healing and mental health awareness to the Black community. She is the owner and executive director of Healing Care Counseling Center, a private practice where those who are struggling with everyday life concerns can receive professional counseling sessions. Courtney is the founder and conference host of From Victim to Survivor (V2S), a therapeutic program for women survivors of abuse. V2S partners with local sponsors to provide free access to the conference for women survivors. Courtney can also be found serving alongside her husband, Pastor Mario, as the student ministry pastor of Church on the Northcoast. Together they are the proud parents of Faith, Taylor and Josiah.

Rachel L. Hill is a graduate of Shaker Heights High School, The Ohio State University (OSU), and Cleveland State University. She was a member of The United States Army National Guard. She goes by the moniker "The First Lady of Sports," and currently hosts Her, in the Huddle! Rachel is also a co-host on the political affairs talk show, The Forum: with Mansfield Frazier on WTAM 1100 AM for iHeartRadio. She covers sports for Cleveland.com, Voice It Radio, and television appearances. Rachel was a field hockey and lacrosse coach at her alma mater, Shaker Heights High School, winning the Ohio State High School Field Hockey title as a coach in 2014. Rachel is a member of Delta Sigma Theta Sorority Incorporated and serves as the treasurer of the Cleveland chapter of the National Association of Black Journalists. She loves Cleveland, Shaker Heights, OSU, and her hometown sports teams. Rachel aspires to be an inspiration to anyone that wants to follow in her footsteps and show that women can be intelligent about sports.

Rachel L. Hill
On-Air Talent
iHeartRadio

Margo Hudson is a tutor, a motivational speaker, an outspoken champion for adult education, and an advocate for literacy. She is also a GED graduate. Margo completed it in 2012 at the age of 52, after taking the exam six times and studying for 11 years. Her perseverance did not go unrecognized. In 2016, she was named National Adult Learner of the Year and received Governor Kasich's Courage Award. That same year, she led the Pledge of Allegiance at a session of the Republican National Convention. A year later, she was named one of Cleveland Magazine's "Most Interesting People". This year, The Cleveland Foundation has recognized her as a "Place Maker", someone who has made the community a better place. To kick off Cleveland Book Week, she recently spoke at Creative Mornings. The formerly shy student is now fearless, calling up governors, Congress, and celebrities to advance the mission of Seeds of Literacy.

Margo Hudson
Graduate-
Tutor-Speaker
Seeds of Literacy

Magistrate Judy Jackson-Winston is a post decree magistrate for Tonya R. Jones, the first African American elected judge in the history of Cuyahoga County Domestic Relations Court. Magistrate Winston is the author of The Anniversary and The Anniversary Behavioral Health Guide and Workbook and writes under the pen name JJ Winston. Magistrate Winston's literary works were created to educate the African American community about the importance of mental health treatment. She has participated in numerous community events aimed at eradicating stigma and educating the community on this important worthwhile subject. Magistrate Winston holds a bachelor's degree in social work, a master's degree in social service administration and a juris doctorate. Magistrate Winston is a licensed independent social worker with supervisory designation, and a licensed attorney in Ohio. Magistrate Winston is a member of Alpha Kappa Alpha Sorority Inc., Top Ladies of Distinction, Cleveland Metropolitan Bar Association, Norman S. Minor Bar Association, and Association of Family and Conciliation Courts. She is married to Douglas Winston, Esq. and has two adult children.

**Magistrate Judy
Jackson-Winston**
Cuyahoga County
Domestic Relations
Court

PROFESSIONALS

Jenifer Jay
Owner
Premier Virtual
Assistance, LLC

Jenifer Jay is the founder of Premier Virtual Assistance LLC. She eliminates the chaos that prevents business owners from growing and scaling their companies by teaching them how to streamline systems and processes to gain more clients and get paid seamlessly. Jenifer has worked across several business industries helping anyone from corporate clients to small business owners including University Hospitals' Case Medical Center, Breen School of Nursing at Ursuline College, and a host of outstanding local businesses. In addition, she lends her knowledge and expertise to improve the internal structure of businesses as a process consultant. Business is Jenifer's DNA as she secured her first business management job at the age of 14 with her family-owned construction company. By age 19, she was a fully developed office manager and bookkeeper. Jenifer obtained a computer information systems degree from Purdue University in 2010. Premier Virtual Assistance continues to stand out in its industry with an A+ rating from the Better Business Bureau since it opened in 2015.

Jeffrey Jemison
Owner
JEM Relations, LLC

Jeffrey Jemison is the owner of JEM Relations, LLC., a marketing, advertising and public relations firm in Cleveland and Akron; and the publisher of the Ohio Life News newspaper. He was a member of the East Cleveland Board of Education for 13 years where he served as president for three terms overseeing a $200,000,000 building project and the district's rise in student achievement. Jeffrey is the former vice president of the Ohio Black Caucus of School Board Members. He was the first chaplain of the Cuyahoga County Democratic Party for 12 years; and the first chaplain of the Ohio Democratic Party for eight years. He served as pastor of St. John Baptist Church, in Painesville, Ohio for nine years. He is married to Lori Jemison and they have five children. Jeffrey has been on numerous boards including the NAACP, United Way, United Pastors in Mission, and E.C. Concerned Pastors. He is a graduate of Electronic Technology Institute in Cleveland; Moody Bible Institute in Chicago; and Ashland Theological Seminary's Black Studies Program.

Audra T. Jones
President & Chief Executive Officer
Krystal Klear
Communications, LLC

Audra T. Jones hails from Cleveland, Ohio where she lives and serves as an author, speaker, entrepreneur, and educator. Audra received her Bachelor of Arts in English Arts from Hampton University. She also holds a Master of Business Administration from Baldwin Wallace University. Audra serves as founder and chief executive officer of Krystal Klear Communications, L.L.C., a full-service communications firm specializing in creating successful branding and marketing platforms through events, workshops and coaching. She is also the author of three books. Audra is an active member of Mt. Zion Church in Oakwood Village, and serves on the board for several area schools. Audra is a college educator and received the 2016 John H. Bustamante Emerging Entrepreneur of the Year Award. She has served as the 2016 Keynote Speaker for the Claude E. Watson Scholarship Fundraising Banquet and spoken around the country on entrepreneurship, marketing and financial literacy Audra enjoys traveling, cooking, writing, music and golf.

Rudolph Jones III is a real estate agent with Keller Williams Greater Cleveland and small business owner of Tax Solutions, Inc. As a real estate agent, Rudolph serves buyers and sellers of a diverse population. Rudolph is a certified negotiator and a rising talent in his profession. Keller Williams of Greater Cleveland named Rudolph a "rising star" in an office of 350+ agents for 2018. Rudolph is also a small business owner of Tax Solution Inc., a tax preparation service that offers professional tax preparation for affordable prices since 2014. Rudolph received his Bachelor of Science in Business from Kentucky State University, and John Carroll University awarded him a master's degree in Nonprofit Administration. Rudolph is active in his community through the Cleveland Alumni Chapter of Kentucky State University and volunteers annually with the Cleveland Council of Black Colleges Alumni Association. Rudolph is a member of William T. Boyd Lodge #79 P.H.A. Rudolph is the husband of Franceska Jones and proud father of Phoenix Jones.

Rudolph Jones III
Real Estate Agent
Keller Williams
Greater Cleveland

The Rev. Dr. Leah Lewis serves as Founder, CEO & Chief Creative Officer of Three Butterflies LLC. She is a filmmaker and creator of original content for TV, film, and new media. Leah also serves as Executive Director of Little Lumpy's Center for Educational Initiatives: Learning, Literacy and Technology, which the United Black Fund, Omnova Solutions Foundation, and the Cleveland Foundation have supported.

Through Little Lumpy's Center, she creates educational opportunities in multicultural education and literature, including, but not limited to the Great Lakes African American Writers Conference. Dr. Lewis employs all of her capacities in her art, projects, and programs.

Dr. Lewis' approach is to skillfully demystify communities that are rarely seen or experienced in mainstream media. Her projects celebrate the genius that every human being embodies. She also serves as Adjunct Faculty at Cuyahoga Community College in the College of Liberal Arts where she teaches Religious Studies. Dr. Lewis is graduate of Ashland Theological Seminary (OH) (D.Min.), Yale Divinity School (M.Div.), Howard University School of Law (J.D.) and Bowling Green State University (B.S.Ed.).

The Rev. Dr. Leah Lewis
CEO
Three Butterflies, LLC

Greg Lockhart, started his broadcast career after graduating from Kent State University over thirty-five years ago at WEWS TV5. For the last twenty-five years, WJW Fox8 has benefited from his extensive experience and immense talent. Greg brings a unique perspective to his role as a videographer covering the news. While negative news is unavoidable, it is important to Greg to promote and cover positive stories that deserve to be told. Through his production company, Frame By Frame, he has produced, filmed, and edited various projects including live events, marketing videos, web-based content and documentaries. Greg is passionate about his work and continues to seek new and innovative ways to deliver the best results. Greg continuously receives recognition for his work including several Emmy Awards, Telly Awards, and multiple Ohio News Photographer awards. He is a member of the National Association of Television Arts and Sciences, The National Association of Black Journalists, NAACP, and, the 100 Black Men of Greater Cleveland, where he has served as a mentor and on the board of directors.

Greg Lockhart
Videographer
WJW

Kevin O. Lowery
Founder
The Urban Exposure
Company

A native Clevelander, Kevin O. Lowery graduated from John F. Kennedy in 1988. Kevin's life is a testament of positive change! Kevin's history spans from the streets of Cleveland to Cleveland Marshall Law School, where he graduated with his Juris Doctorate in 2013.

Kevin's mission, through the Urban Exposure Company that he founded in 2007, is to reach and enlighten at-risk-youth to prevent them from making some of the turns made in his life. The company's vision is to expose at-risk youth and the ex-offender, in the urban community, to people, places, and things. Kevin believes that through mentoring, educational assistance, social programming, economic enlightenment, and exposure to environments outside of their norm, that the company's target groups will be positively motivated to become productive citizens in our society.

Kevin is married with three children. He and his family are members of Mt. Olive MBC, where he and his wife serve as Adult Youth Leaders of the youth ministry. Kevin is a member of the Lucasville Five Defense Committee advocating against the alleged wrongful death sentence for his childhood friend Keith Lamar.

Chanelle R. McCloud
Chief Executive
Officer
Professional
Inspiration, LLC

Chanelle R. McCloud, M.Ed. is the founder and chief executive officer of Professional Inspiration, LLC, a personal and professional development company, and has been inspiring youth and adults in the Greater Cleveland Area and other parts of Ohio for over a decade. The mission of the Professional Inspiration, LLC is to inspire people to greatness through words and education. The Kent State University and Notre Dame College graduate has ten years of experience as a language arts teacher in urban schools. In addition, Chanelle designed Motivational Experience Workshops for several organizations - The Literacy Cooperative of Greater Cleveland, Euclid Council of the International Reading Association, Youth Opportunities Unlimited, San's Sacred Circle, Twelve Literary Arts and Euclid City Schools. Most recently, Chanelle has authored professional development curriculum that is set to launch nationally in 2019. She will release her first book, Letters from a Healing Heart, in June 2019.

Cassandra McDonald
Founding President
Euclid NAACP

Cassandra McDonald is a civil rights activist and public figure. She made history as the first African American female to establish an NAACP branch in Cuyahoga County and Euclid, Ohio. She is the founding president of LAWRS Foundation which employs legal advocacy for underserved populations. Cassandra is on track to becoming a licensed sports agent for the NFL. Recognition for her service include The Undefeated Award in Re-entry, Women's Trailblazer Award, Emmett Till Leadership Award, WEA Achievement Award, Stiletto Boss Award, and Maltz Museum of Jewish Heritage Civic Award. She is a graduate of Cleveland State University and Cleveland Marshall College of Law, Ashbrook Scholar of Ashland University, a former student of Akron University's Bliss Institute of Applied Politics, and post-graduate Ph.D. student of Law & Policy at Walden University. Cassandra is a member of the Black Women's Political Action Committee, Criminal Justice Executive Committee of the Ohio State Bar Association, American Bar Association, National Action Network, and Universal Negro Improvement Association. She says her children are the highlights of her many blessings.

The Power of I Am. After 17 years in the corporate arena of human resources (HR) and project management in engineering, she took a leap of faith. Nicky Miller is a dynamic self-esteem builder, breakthrough coach, motivational speaker and social entrepreneur.

She is the founder of I AM: Mirror Messages, Inc. A cultural movement and multiplatform designed to rebuild the self-esteem and positive mindset of women and girls facing domestic violence. Her catchy and unique hashtag #iammirrormessages is seen across all social/media networks.

As a social entrepreneur Nicky serves a dual role as board of Economic Development and the first chairwoman of WIN (Women in the NAACP) Cleveland, Ohio. Nicky was honored by Radio One as Cleveland's Future History Maker 2018 for her passionate advocacy for community progress.

Nicky holds a Bachelor of Science from Wilberforce University, Master of Business Administration from University of Phoenix and currently pursuing a Doctorate in Organizational Leadership from University of Phoenix and is certified in lean six sigma green belt (2016).

She's a proud member of Alpha Kappa Alpha Sorority, Incorporated, National Congress of Black Women and Mom Rising.

Nicky Miller, MBA
Founder
I AM: Mirror Messages, Inc.

Deonna Moore Taylor is a best-selling author, award-winning professional, motivational speaker, executive consultant and certified life and mindfulness coach. Deonna has delivered training solutions, worked with Fortune 500 companies, colleges, and nonprofit organizations. Her professional portfolio includes Cleveland Clinic, Progressive Insurance, Rockwell Automation, CVS Caremark, Smithers Quality Assessments, Case Western Reserve University, Cuyahoga Community College, Girl Scouts USA, NASA, and Maximus. In 2016, Deonna started Dempsey Consulting Group and in 2018 founded The Leader Style Lifestyle Movement, a nonprofit organization. Deonna's specializations are information technology services and education which provides strategic and operational leadership consulting, change management, organizational psychology, branding, and client relationship management. She has co-authored three bestselling books. Deonna is a contributing writer for several magazines, blogs and online publications. Deonna's life mission is to improve the lives of women and girls. She hosted a domestic violence (DV) forum that changed the conversation about DV and saved five women that were in DV situations. This forum has been branded as "Sister2Sister: I AM My Sisters Keeper."

Deonna Moore Taylor
Chief Executive Officer
DMT Consulting & Coaching

Karen Murray is an Adult Reference Associate at the East Cleveland Public Library in East Cleveland, Ohio. Ms. Murray provides information and resources to the community she serves. Her strong attributes includes working on special projects and outreach. She is devoted to promoting literacy to all ages by utilizing interactive programs whenever possible. She holds a Bachelor's of Science Degree in Nutrition, a Geriatric Certification from Cuyahoga Community College and a Mediation Certificate from the Cleveland Mediation Center. She is a member of the Friends of the East Cleveland Public Library and the Heritage Park Community Association. She also works with FOR SPECTRUM SAKE, an organization committed to educating people about Autism Disorder Spectrum. Ms. Murray has received several awards and honorable mentions from organizations such as the City of East Cleveland, Cleveland Clinic and Project Love. She has two sons who who inspire her daily with love and words of encouragement.

Karen Murray
Adult Reference Associate
East Cleveland Public Library

Stephanie Morris Nunn
CEO
The Nadira Collection

Stephanie Morris Nunn is a former employee of Cleveland Clinic, multi-award winning designer, and CEO of the Nadira Collection. Her clothing line can be seen on the streets of California, New York, Washington and Cleveland. The Nadira Collection has been showcased in fashion-fairs all across the United States. Stephanie's clothing line is designed for fashion conscious women of all sizes who are particular about making a statement of class and sophistication.

Stephanie completed her Bachelor's Degree (BS) and Master's Degree (MPA). She is a volunteer on the executive team for Prevent Blindness, speaks to groups about vision loss, depression, engaging in the basic sensorial and having faith through it all. She produces an annual fashion show and networking event to bring awareness of the visually impaired. She is also a member of the NAACP Cleveland and enjoys her ministry, singing in the Praise Team at Mt. Sinai Ministries.

Stephanie is the wife of Michael Nunn, mother to two sons, Jahi and David, and a doting "Nana" grandmother. She also volunteers at the Intergenerational Community of Ohio.

Eryka Parker
Founder
Lyrical Innovations,
LLC

Eryka Parker is a ghostwriter, writing coach, and the founder of Lyrical Innovations, LLC. Courtney has partnered with Cuyahoga County Community Public Library to host multiple Vibe Sessions which offers free coaching and supportive resources for aspiring Cleveland writers and entrepreneurs. Her goal when creating Vibe Sessions was connecting the right people and providing the resources and best practices needed to do amazing things with their talents and gifts. Eryka's passion for investing in others has also resulted in the launch of her writing podcast, Penpoint Your Perspective, which serves as a platform to promote Cleveland authors. Born and raised in Cleveland, she earned a Bachelor of Business Administration from Kent State University and her Master of Business Administration from University of Phoenix-Beachwood. She is a member of the Chagrin Valley Chamber of Commerce and volunteers regularly with Love on the City Cleveland. Parker enjoys making an impact behind the scenes as a college mentor and scholarship judge and is committed to helping the community.

Lindy Peavy
Founder and Chief
Executive Officer
LiPav Consulting, LLC

Linda Peavy is owner of LiPav Consulting, LLC, a marketing, literary, grant writing, and communications company. LiPav is the PR firm for the Miss America Organization. With 21 years of marketing experience, Linda develops strategies for events, plays, schools, books, religious leaders, and major conferences. Clients have appeared with Essence, Tom Joyner Morning Show, D. L. Hughley Show, Ebony, and Guideposts. She has worked with Danny Glover, Delroy Lindo, Cathy Hughes, Nicole Ari Parker, Boris Kodjoe, and Charlie Ward. Her grant writing has secured funding and business development of $17,000,000.00. As a professional publisher, she helped create over 500 books for authors. Linda serves as the communications director for At the Well Young Women's Leadership Academy, From the Fire: Leadership Academy for Young Men, and minority teen programs at Princeton University. Linda earned a bachelor's degree in Marketing and MBA/Management degree from University of Akron. She is single and resides in Willoughby, Ohio. Linda founded the blog, Cultured Curves: Sophisticated Style, Fashion, and Beauty for Curvy Women over 50.

Stephanie Phelps began in radio news, as a talk show host and interviewer. After 30 years, she continues to impact radio, print, television and the digital landscape. Throughout her career, she has worked as a newspaper reporter, magazine columnist, editor, traffic reporter, and public information officer. Stephanie is best known as lead host and co-creator of AnotherLook which aired on Time Warner Cable for more than 12 years, featuring prominent local and nationally known guests. Stephanie is proud to have served as emcee and speaker for several special events including the Who's Who in Black Cleveland unveiling ceremony. Currently, she is producing a new generation of TV, radio and other programming, under the AnotherLook brand to promote emotional wellbeing and spirituality. Stephanie is a member of several journalistic and media organizations including the Greater Cleveland Association of Black Journalists and is assistant editor of the Society of Professional Journalists Writer's Week. She is long time member of The Olivet Institutional Baptist Church and proud mother of two exceptional adult sons.

Stephanie Phelps
Journalist
AnotherLook Ventures

Brittny Pierre is a journalist and pop culture writer for PopEd World, a Detroit based site based on unique critiques and observation into the entertainment industry. She has been published in numerous publications including The Village Voice, Bustle, L.A. Weekly, Complex magazine and many more. Her writing is centered around music, personal essays and pop culture analysts. Although she was born and raised in New York, Cleveland has embraced her as her current home. You can often catch her pieces on what's she's listening to or the adventures she is on around the world on her lifestyle blog. She has a bachelor's degree in Women's Studies and Journalism and Media Studies from Rutgers University. When she is not writing, Brittny enjoys attending concerts, volunteering at animal shelters, calligraphy writing, and traveling.

Brittny Pierre
Journalist
Pierre Into My Life

Tracie Potts is founder and publicist of Troy-David PR & Consulting. Ambitious, entertaining and outgoing are just a few attributes that describes this tenacious and talented individual. Tracie is the fun-loving co-host on Chill Talk Radio. She was named Publicist of the Year at The Ohio Entertainment Awards and is a native of Cleveland. She enjoys traveling, reading and motivational speaking. She is a graduate of Central State University where she attained a bachelor's degree in Communications/Journalism. She has a master's degree in Business Administration and certification from The Ohio Media School. Tracie has worked on several popular television shows such as The Queen Latifah Show, Saturday Night Live, Late Night with Conan O'Brien, American Idol and BET Entertainment Television. Tracie has been the publicist of a number of major media events and public service projects throughout Cleveland. She is a proud member of Delta Sigma Theta Sorority, Inc., and The National Association of Black Journalists.

Tracie Potts
Publicist
Troy-David PR &
Consulting

PROFESSIONALS

Everett Prewitt
President
Northland Research
Corporation

Everett Prewitt is president of Northland Research Corporation, a real estate consulting firm. He is an alumnus of Leadership Cleveland, a former army officer, and a Vietnam veteran. Everett received his Bachelor of Arts in Business Administration from Lincoln University in Pennsylvania and his Master of Science in Urban Studies from Cleveland State University. He received the Distinguished Alumni Award from both universities. Everett has served on over 15 boards, was president of both the Cleveland Association of Real Estate Brokers and the Cleveland Area Board of Realtors where he received the Realtor of the Year award. He also received the Award for Civic Service from the Citizen's League of Greater Cleveland. Prewitt is the award-winning author of three novels, Snake Walkers, A Long Way Back, and Something About Ann. Everett is a native of Cleveland and a proud graduate of Glenville High School.

Fatimah Satterwhite
Hospital Contract
Manager
United Healthcare

Fatimah Satterwhite is a health insurance professional with more than 20 years of experience in the industry. She currently is the hospital contract manager for United Healthcare, managing contractual relationships with hospital systems. Prior to working with United Healthcare, Fatimah spent most of her career at Medical Mutual where she served in multiple roles under network contracting. She serves on the board of directors for Towards Employment a nonprofit agency in Cleveland, committed to giving community members second chances in their career through vocational training, job readiness, and life skills development programs. Fatimah also serves as secretary on the board of trustees for Affinity Missionary Baptist Church. In her spare time, she enjoys teaching others financial literacy and how to be better stewards of their money and time. Fatimah earned her bachelor's degree in Healthcare Administration from Ursuline College, and earned her master's degree in Business Administration from Ashland University. Fatimah and her husband, Vincent Satterwhite Jr., reside in Twinsburg, Ohio. They have one adult son.

April R. Scott
Office Manager/
OAKS Compliance
Specialist
AGM Energy Services

April R. Scott is the office manager and OAKS compliance specialist of AGM Energy Services. April is civic minded and active in her community where she serves on the executive committee for Richmond Heights. She has a passion for empowering youths by positively impacting, encouraging, and uplifting them through SOS: Strengthening Our Students mentoring program, and mentoring interns who are interested in the trades through ACE (Architect, Construction and Engineering). April has received numerous awards for her commitment of exceptional service to others. She graduated cum laude with a bachelor's degree in Public Relations, Corporate Communications, and Social Media from Ursuline College. She is a member of Alpha Kappa Alpha Sorority, Alpha Omega Chapter, Phi Theta Kappa, Honor Society, president of The Cleveland Drifters, Soup 4 The Soul Fundraising co-chair, UCAP Alumnae Committee board member, Cuyahoga Democratic Women's Caucus, NAACP, associate of Jack and Jill of America, and Public Relations Society of America. April has been married for 27 years to Richard "Zoom", they have one son, Demetrius.

Aseelah Shareef is Director, Operations and Community Programs at Karamu House, the nation's oldest African-American theatre. At Karamu, Aseelah curates and develops culturally responsive programming and facilitates arts education for lifelong learners. As a Dancer, she performed with Cleveland Contemporary Dance Theatre under the leadership of Michael Medcalf, and toured the world with Washington DC-based, Step Afrika! She continues to be both artist and administrator.

Her previous experience includes former Dance Director of Cleveland School of the Arts, Project Manager for Cleveland Metropolitan School District's Department of Arts Education, Adjunct Professor of Dance at Cuyahoga Community College and master-teaching artist for the Center for Arts-Inspired Learning. Aseelah is an Ohio Citizens for the Arts Board Member, a member of the Society for Human Resource Management (SHRM) and a proud member of Delta Sigma Theta Sorority, Inc. She is a graduate of The Florida State University (Master of Arts in Arts Administration, a Bachelor of Science in Exercise Science).

Aseelah Shareef
Director, Operations
and Community
Programs
Karamu House, Inc.

Billy L. Sharp is president of Urban League of Greater Cleveland Guild. Prior to becoming president of the Urban League, he founded Billy Sharp OmniMedia, (BSOM) a company that produces, publishes and sells books, documentaries and educational DVDs. BSOM created Community Benefit Consulting Division, with clients such as McDonald's, InstaRide Cle, Central Towing & Auto Service, and Fat Boy Donuts. Billy has worked in the private sector as a top management administrator in the fast food industry. He has worked with McDonald's, Burger King and Wendy's, where he worked with youth by helping them prepare for work in an ever-changing job market. Billy has dedicated his time and energy to the betterment of citizens not only in Northeast Ohio but across the state. He has also volunteered and headed several community-based organizations such as the Urban League of Greater Cleveland Guild, Mastering Generosity Unlimited, Ohio Young Black Democrats Northeast Ohio Chapter, Cleveland Stonewall Democrats and Organizing for Action - Cleveland Chapter.

Billy L. Sharp
President
Urban League of
Greater Cleveland
Guild

Myra Simmons is a resident of the Kinsman neighborhood and is very passionate about her neighborhood. Since 2003, she has served as the lead planner of the annual Marshall Avenue Back-to-School Safety Fair supplies, safety resources, food fun activities to youth and families on Marshall Avenue and surrounding neighborhoods. Simmons is an active member of True Gospel Missionary Baptist Church and serves on the Pastor's Aide and Willing Workers ministry. For her years of dedicated volunteer service, Simmons was awarded the key to the City of Cleveland by Mayor Frank Jackson in 2010. She has resided on Marshall Avenue since 1969. She is a retired steelworker of 42 years with Arcelor Mittal Union Local 979, a member of Women of Steel Hard Hatted Women, and Women on the Rise. Myra is also a member of National Action Network, Neighborhood Leadership Development Program, Police Athletic League, Big Brother-Big Sister, Order of Eastern Star, and many more organizations.

Myra Simmons
Humanitarian
Retired

Teresa M. Stafford
Chief Advocacy
Officer
Cleveland Rape Crisis
Center

Teresa M. Stafford serves as the chief advocacy officer at Cleveland Rape Crisis Center, the largest independent rape crisis center in the nation. Teresa has over 20 years of experience providing direct service to both offenders and victims of crime, with a specialization in sexual violence, domestic violence and families of homicide victims. Teresa advocates for system change needed to create a climate that is trauma informed for all survivors. She is the founder and principal consultant for Inspiring Change, LLC where she is dedicated to shifting thoughts through transformative conversations that inspire individuals and organizations to flourish. Stafford is also a contract consultant with the International Association of Chief of Police and RTI International. She has received several awards including the Gloria Pointer Award for Supporting Families of Victims, Peter DeMarco Exemplary Service Award, National Sexual Violence Resource Center Visionary Award, and 2018 Robert Denton Achievement Award. Teresa is a member of Sigma Gamma Rho Sorority and graduated from Tiffin University majoring in Criminal Justice Administration.

Dr. Tameka L. Taylor
President
Compass Consulting
Services, LLC

Dr. Lachaka Askew is an author, actress, and chief executive officer of 20 Second Intercessor Inc., a 501c3 nonprofit that works with charities to serve the homeless. With its focus on advocacy, the agency spearheaded efforts with its "Free Soup for Conversation" campaign and Baptist-Muslim dialogue workshops. Lachaka maintains a global ministry, speaks at Interfaith vigils, is a member of Cleveland Committee of Foreign Relations and reports advocacy news in its newsletter. She has three published books about intercessory prayer and one short-story fiction book. Using her research about Alzheimer's and health, she has written articles for MedCrunch Magazine, Inspiring Woman Magazine, and the Bedford Tribune. She reignited her love of acting through productions at Karamu House. Lachaka received her Doctor of Ministry degree from South University, Master of Science and Bachelor of Arts degrees from Cleveland State University. Her educational achievements include outstanding research recognition from Cleveland State University and memberships in four national and international honor societies. She is happily married with three children.

Delvis Valentine
Host
The Sports Brothers

Delvis Valentine is currently the sports director at WNVW 107.3 FM (The Wave). He hosts a sports talk show and a romantic music show on WOVU 99.5 FM. Delvis covers the Cleveland Browns and Cleveland Cavaliers. He has provided college football analysis on ESPN 3 and was the television ringside boxing announcer on TV 20 in Cleveland and Vuuzle Fight Network worldwide for the recent Next Generation Boxing Card. Delvis received his Bachelor of Arts degree from Malone College and his Master of Business Administration degree from Indiana Wesleyan University. Delvis is a graduate of John F. Kennedy High School and Cuyahoga Community College. Valentine is an avid supporter of Cleveland area singers and musicians and features their music on his radio show. Occasionally, he performs with some of the bands at venues around the city. He provides mentoring for young men and women that wish to enter broadcasting.

Sherry D. Ward is a North Carolina native and a product of Cleveland County school system. She joined William A. Gaines Funeral Home in 1982. Sherry brings with her a background in political science and holds a funeral director and insurance license in the state of Ohio. Sherry has worked with such organizations as V.O.I.C.E.S., a community activist group; and as past president for the Lady D. Drill Team. She is a member of The National Funeral Directors Association, the Buckeye State Embalmers and Funeral Directors Association, and the Cleveland Embalmers Association. She also is very personal, compassionate, and willing to share her wealth of knowledge. Sherry touches each and every family's heart that she meets.

Sherry D. Ward
Funeral Director
Gaines Funeral Home

Nicole Wells is a behavioral and social scientist. A traditionally trained academic, Nicole has earned a bachelor's degree in Sociology from John Carroll University, and dual master's degrees from Cleveland State University in Business Administration and Sociology. She also earned a third master's degree in Organization Development from Bowling Green State University. Nicole distinguished herself as a change agent early in her career by first serving as an educator in several local school systems, and multiple colleges and universities. She then focused on the private sector where she worked with several organizations to assist in the training and development of workforce leadership. Nicole is affiliated with organizations such as Case Western Reserve University, Deloitte, Eaton Corporation, and NASA. Nicole further improved our community via real estate development when she purchased properties and transformed them into homes for east side families. She has since been featured as a panelist in several state panel discussions aimed at developing solutions to issues impacting northeastern Ohio families.

Nicole Wells
Behavioral and
Social Scientist
Independent
Contractor

Melvin L. White is the chief executive officer and co-owner of Legacy Builders Speakers Consulting Group, an organization that he founded in 2011 and now operates with his daughter in an effort to create social change in the community. He is an award-winning author, entrepreneur, and motivational speaker. Melvin's book, Breaking the Cycles of Abandonment, has served as an inspiration to thousands of community members. He hopes his latest book due for release this summer, Disconnected: The Controversial Issues in Relationships will garner the same enthusiasm. Melvin's focus is bringing awareness to the challenges mental health presents in the Black community. He hopes that his direct work with mental health clients will break the stigma associated with the illness. He facilitates Boot Camp for new dads at Cleveland Clinic and Metrohealth Melvin serves on Men in Early Childhood, Cuyahoga Fatherhood Initiative Committee, and Healthy Fathering Collaborative. Melvin earned an AAS degree in Early Childhood Education, a BBA degree in Organizational Management and a MS degree in Leadership.

Melvin L. White
Chief Executive
Officer/Co-Owner
Legacy Builders Speakers Consulting Group

Taylor White
President and
Co-Owner
Legacy Builders
Speakers Consulting

Taylor White is the co-owner of Legacy Builders Speakers Consulting Group, an organization that her father created in 2011 in an effort to create social change in communities. As a social entrepreneurial, Taylor's focus has been to create safe zones for her peers to openly communicate and seek advice on sexuality, bullying, conflict resolution and many other issues that often pressures our youth into silence. Taylor is a peer educator for Planned Parenthood where she often models positive youth behavior, affecting social norms, as well as model constructive relationships between adults and young people. When discussing sex or the nuances of teen culture, Taylor has proven she can achieve a level of comfort and trust that is difficult for adults to match. Taylor is a junior at Trinity High School where she serves as student ambassador, honor student and change agent. Taylor plans to attend college to pursue a career as a child life specialist.

Sharron Murphy-Williams
Executive Director
The Phe'be
Foundation

Sharron Murphy-Williams is the founder and executive director of The Phe'be Foundation. She has over 25 years of experience in the credit/debt management and homebuyer education industries. She began her career with Dun & Bradstreet prior to becoming an independent credit counseling specialist. She has implemented and developed innovative programs that enhance housing and economic empowerment opportunities, some of which have proven to be models for Cleveland-area banking institutions, curriculums and agencies.

Murphy-Williams has been featured in Essence Magazine, Ebony and on BET as well, recognized by Kaleidoscope Magazine, The Plain Dealer, Call & Post, Cleveland Board of Education, The City of Cleveland and others for the work she has done as it pertains to financial empowerment.

In addition to serving as leader of The Phe'be Foundation, Murphy-Williams gives back to her community by serving as a member of several civic and professional organizations including The National Association of Female Executives, Cleveland Metropolitan Schools, Department of Aging, Rotary International, United Black Fund (UBF), Founding Member of Society of Urban Professional (S.O.U.P.) and the Predatory Lending Task Force.

Dr. Eric Kevin Wood Jr.
Dentist
Bright Now! Dental

Dr. Eric Kevin Wood Jr. is the lead dentist of two locations of Bright Now! Dental – the Steel Yard Commons location in Cleveland and Belden Village location in Canton, Ohio. Dr. Wood served as the lead dentist for two years in Canton before partnering with Bright Now! Dental to open its first Cleveland location in the Steel Yard Commons. He completed general practice and pediatric dental residency programs at Metro Health Medical Center of Case Western Reserve University. Dr. Wood established himself as a pediatric dentist in his community on the west side of Cleveland. He has called Cleveland home for over six years. He earned his Bachelor of Science degree in Psychology from University of Tennessee-Knoxville, and his Doctor of Dental Surgery degree from Meharry Medical College in Nashville, Tennessee. He is a third generation dentist, following his late grandfather and late father. Dr. Wood uses his long line of experience and fun style of care with each patient to ensure they are happy with their visit

With over 20 years of experience, S. Carlton Betts Jr. is a leader in the health care field. Carlton currently serves as the Executive Director of Acute Clinical Operations at Centers for Dialysis Care. His responsibilities include clinical oversight of acute dialysis services for 9 facilities.

Carlton has earned a Master of Business Administration from Cleveland State University, as well as a master's in Nursing from Indiana Wesleyan University. He is a veteran of the US Navy and has continued to serve on various committees and boards. He currently serves on the NEONI Legislative Committee, Greater Cleveland Organization of Nurse Executives and the Ohio Renal Association. Carlton was also appointed to the Ohio Board of Nursing Advisory Group where he will serve until December 2018. Carlton has obtained his Nurse Executive Advanced Certification through the American Nurses Credential Center. Carlton and his wife reside in Orange Village with their three children. They are faithful members of Oakwood Village Church. Carlton believes in using his knowledge and skills to enhance service delivery and promote positive outcomes in his community.

S. Carlton Betts Jr.
Executive Director of
Acute Clinical
Operations
Centers for Dialysis
Care

Gateway is a RN and minority owned skilled home healthcare agency with offices in Cleveland. Akron, Canton and Lorain. Gateway employees over 200 people and specializes in providing care to our inner city elderly and disabled residents. Gateway is one of the largest minority employers in Northeast Ohio.

Tracy is a Registered Nurse and native of Akron, Ohio. She is a graduate of Central-Hower High School and Idabelle Firestone School of Nursing in Akron, Ohio. She holds a Bachelor of Science in Healthcare Administration from Wilberforce University. Tracy has been a scholarship recipient and member of the Akron and Columbus Black Nurses Association. She was a recipient of The Phenomenal Woman Award of Akron. Tracy enjoys administering Gateway's scholarships along with Dennis and Desmond Cox.

Tracy has been married to Dennis Cox for 29 years and is the mother of Desmond and Javay Cox and currently resides in Bratenahl, Ohio.

Tracy Cox
Chief Executive
Officer & Owner
Gateway Healthcare
Service, LLC.

CELEBRATING AFRICAN-AMERICAN ACHIEVEMENT
IN MORE THAN 25 U.S. CITIES

ALABAMA • ATLANTA • BALTIMORE • CHARLOTTE • CHICAGO • CINCINNATI
CLEVELAND • COLUMBUS • DALLAS • DETROIT • HOUSTON • INDIANAPOLIS
KANSAS CITY • LAS VEGAS • LOS ANGELES • LOUISVILLE • MEMPHIS
MILWAUKEE • MISSISSIPPI • NEW YORK CITY • PHILADELPHIA • PHOENIX
PITTSBURGH • RALEIGH-DURHAM • ST. LOUIS • SOUTH FLORIDA • WASHINGTON, D.C.

WHO'S *Who*

A Real Times Media Company

University Hospitals
Cleveland Medical Center

CEDI

community impact, equity,
diversity, and inclusion

Nathaniel McQuay Jr. MD FACS
Associate Professor of Surgery
Case Western Reserve School of Medicine
Chief Acute Care Surgery

Dr. Ogechi Muoh
Staff Rheumatologist, Director of David
Satcher Program at the Office of Community
Impact, Equity, Diversity and Inclusion

Dr. Nathaniel McQuay Jr. is a native of Richmond, Virginia. He received a B.S. degree in Biology from Hampton University and a medical degree from the Medical College of Virginia. He then completed a general surgical residency at Eastern Virginia Medical School and a Trauma/Critical Care fellowship at the R Adams Cowley Shock Trauma Center.

Dr. McQuay was the first African American faculty member in the division of Trauma at the University of Pennsylvania. Following his seven year tenure in Pennsylvania, Dr. McQuay was recruited to Johns Hopkins Bayview Medical Center as the Director of Trauma, Critical Care & Acute Care Surgery. He was then recruited to Cleveland to serve in his current role as the Chief of Acute Care Surgery at University Hospitals Cleveland Medical Center overseeing the successful initial verification of its Level I trauma center.

He has authored several scientific manuscripts and is a member of many regional, national and international professional societies.

Dr. Ogechi Muoh is a Staff Rheumatologist at the University Hospitals of Cleveland. Her specialty focus is on autoimmune and connective tissue diseases like Lupus and rheumatoid arthritis.

She has recently been named the Director of the David Satcher program, which focuses on cultivating and advocating for minority medical students, residents and fellows at University Hospitals. The goal is to help in retaining and growing a diverse pool of minority physicians at University Hospitals.

Dr. Muoh has lived in Ohio for most of her training, graduating from Kent State and obtaining her medical degree from Ohio University. She is married with three children and loves trying diverse cuisine and travel.

University Hospitals
Cleveland Medical Center

Kwadwo Asare Oduro Jr. MD PhD

Hematopathologist, Asst. Prof. of Pathology
University Hospitals Cleveland Medical
Center, Rainbow Children's Hospital, Case
Western Reserve School of Medicine

Khendi White-Solaru MD

Cardiologist, Division of
Cardiovascular Medicine University
Hospitals, Harrington Heart and
Vascular Institute (HHVI)

Dr. Kwadwo Asare Oduro Jr. is a hematopathologist at the University Hospitals (UH). In his work, he utilizes a variety of classical and novel techniques to diagnose malignant and non-malignant blood diseases. He is also involved in training medical students, residents and fellows and conducts research to advance our understanding and ability to diagnose hematologic malignancies.

He has received several awards including a Prince of Wales Scholarship, John Harvard Scholarship, American Heart Association research grant and United States & Canadian Academy of Pathologists Stowell Orbison Certificate of Merit Award. He recently received a Minority Faculty Development award from UH.

Kwadwo received a bachelor's degree in Biochemical Sciences and a Master's degree in Chemistry from Harvard University. He subsequently received MD and PhD degrees from Washington University in St Louis. He completed Anatomical pathology residency and Hematopathology subspecialty fellowship at the Massachusetts General Hospital, before arriving in Cleveland. He is board certified in both specialties.

A native of Ghana, in West Africa, Kwadwo is the husband of Stephanie Oduro and the proud father of two daughters, Nathania (Nattie) and Ruth (Ruthie).

Dr. Khendi White-Solaru a native of Silver Spring, Maryland, relocated to Ohio where her husband Adebanjo Solaru is a native of Cleveland Heights, Ohio. She is a board-certified cardiologist and vascular medicine specialist at University Hospitals in Cleveland, Ohio. She is also an academic researcher as an assistant professor of medicine affiliated with Case Western Reserve University School of Medicine. Khendi is a 2019 nationally selected participant of the Program to Increase Diversity in Cardiovascular Health-Related Research (PRIDE) institute sponsored by the National Institutes of Health.

Dr. White-Solaru graduated from Swarthmore College with Bachelor of Arts degree and a double major in biology and psychology. After graduating from Howard University College of Medicine where she received her doctorate, she then completed a postgraduate medical training with an internal medicine residency at Brigham and Women's hospital. Dr. White-Solaru completed a fellowship in Cardiology and Vascular medicine at the Cleveland Clinic.

visit us at
www.realtimesmedia.com

Our Brands:

WHO'S *Who*
A Real Times Media Company

THE MICHIGAN **FrontPage**

^{NEW}
Pittsburgh Courier

RTM Digital Studios

TRI-STATE **DEFENDER**
A REAL TIMES NEWSPAPER
The Mid-South's Best Alternative Newspaper

CHICAGO **DEFENDER**

VOICE OF THE COMMUNITY SINCE 1936
MICHIGAN CHRONICLE

ADW
Atlanta Daily World

RE TIM ME

ENTREPRENEURS

FOCUS
CELEBRATE
PROMINENCE
RECOGNITION

With charisma, smarts and courage, the entrepreneurs of Cleveland are carving their own way into the business of the city.

Honey Bell-Bey
Director
Honey From A Rock
Empowerment
Institute

Honey Bell-Bey is a motivational poet, published author, community advocate and experienced trainer in the field of substance abuse, youth work, culture, and the integration of science innovative practice. A graduate of the historic Bethune-Cookman University, she has a degree in broadcast production technology. Honey has been employed with NBC affiliates, Sports South at CNN, and the Atlanta Olympic Games. She is a motivational poet who employs creative arts strategies, engaging youth and adults. Honey is a trainer for the Mandel Center at Case Western Reserve University, Cuyahoga County Youth Work Institute, and a master trainer for Ohio Mental Health and Addiction Services (SAMHSA- Substance Abuse Prevention Skill Training), and Regional Training Liaison for North Central Ohio's Institute for Human Services. Honey has presented at conferences throughout the nation. She is the founder, director and writer for international performance group, The Distinguished Gentlemen of Spoken Word. She has won numerous awards and Congressional recognitions for her innovative programming strategies engaging youth from high-risk environments.

Mike Berry
Owner
Release The Pressure
Foundation

Mike Berry is a writer, filmmaker and motivational speaker. Realizing that his life was spiraling into a downward path at an early age, Berry turned to the arts as a way of channeling his energy. His various accomplishments include recording a Top 100 Billboard album and a Top 20 Billboard single as a rapper under the stage name of "Big Gank". He was one of the first unsigned artists to tour with MTV's Rock-the-Vote campaign. In 2011, he began producing and directing award-winning screenplays including If You Knew Better, You'd Do Better; Banger; Hey Mr. Postman and most recently celebrated the official selection of his short film Blanket Blessings in the 43rd Cleveland International Film Festival. In 2017, he re-launched his highly acclaimed novel, The Dangerous Times through Oasis Publishing. Diagnosed with depression early in life, Berry established his nonprofit organization Release the Pressure Foundation in 2016. He is committed to providing awareness and support to individuals suffering from depression by assisting anyone who is seeking help.

Debaneise Byrd
Artist
Debaneise
Entertainment Group

Debaneise Byrd is a native of Cleveland. She is a soulful vocalist, actress, dance teacher, and Karamu House Theater veteran. Her textured tones have their roots in jazz and gospel music but shifted into R&B soul after hearing artists such as Patti LaBelle, The Temptations, Eddie LeVert, Gladys Knight and Phyllis Hyman. She has performed with several groups in the Cleveland area. Her first single, Eyes Don't Lie debut on Cleveland's WZAK 93.1 FM. The single peaked at number one on the charts and was even charted overseas in London. Debaneise also had the opportunity to sing background for Dennis Edwards of The Temptations. She was part of the singing group The Deltons backing him on his Don't Look Any Further tour. Debaneise has just released her new single entitled, It's You streaming now on all media music hosts platforms.

Tammara Caldwell-Willis is the founder of Visions Revealed Inc. and has been practicing the methodology of vision boards for 12 years. Tammara has a Bachelor of Science in Business Management from Myers University and holds a Case Western Reserve University Women in Leadership Certification. Presently, she is teaching a vision board/goal-setting class for the students of "School of One" at the Cuyahoga County Juvenile Detention Center as part of their curriculum. She has facilitated various workshops for incarcerated adults at Grafton Correctional Institution and the Northeast Reintegration Center. Tammara currently works in collaboration with other nonprofit organizations which possess a strong mission to improve their communities. She has assisted many fundraising efforts and events that benefit various philanthropic entities. Tammara developed and continues to lead, an annual toy drive for the Original Harvest Missionary Daycare in Cleveland for the past 12 years as well as homeless and community drives.

Tammara Caldwell-Willis
Founder
Visions Revealed Inc.

Victoria L. Davis is a retired special education teacher who touched the lives of many students over a 30-year career. Her former students commended her for the patience and encouragement she provided to them. As a child, Victoria struggled with reading. She wanted to make a difference, and that she did. She is currently inspiring others as a Bible Study facilitator in which she is a faithful member of Garfield Memorial Church. After retirement, Victoria explored the hobby of creating unique jewelry. With the encouragement from a dear friend, she began creating exquisite specialty pieces under her brand Juss B Jazzie Jewelry. Victoria also co-owns a thriving business with her husband called Computer Jazz where he repairs computers. Victoria operates the corner store while selling the infamous "walking tacos" and cookie bottom brownies! Her motto is, "I Want To Serve You In Peace". She is a proud 1981 graduate of Kent State University, and member of the Alpha Kappa Alpha sorority.

Victoria L. Davis
Creator and Founder
Juss B Jazzie Jewelry

Arikka Diamond always dreamed of opening a clothing boutique. She was elated when the dress she designed for her senior prom appeared as a season's best on many of the popular internet forums. That is when she knew it was time to put some plans into place. On January 1, 2019, her online store, Sparks Fly Fashion, hit the internet. At the age of 19 and a freshman at Kent State University, Arikka finds herself juggling a busy life as a young adult, college student and entrepreneur. Sparks Fly Fashion consists of three segments - urban fashion, hair, and accessories. Arikka works with distributors and manufacturers across the globe to select and design products that are affordable and fashionable. Products are updated continuously to reflect the latest fashion including what is hot with influencers and at the same time reflecting Arikka's personal "fly" style, thus the name Sparks Fly Fashion. As her business grows, she hopes to connect with talented young designers looking for a platform to showcase their work.

Arikka Diamond
Entrepreneur and
Owner
Sparks Fly Fashion

Jay.R Fogle
CEO
FoGO355

Jay.R Fogle is the Chief Executive Officer of FoGo365, a Cleveland based tech/lifestyle company whose motto is "Nothing's Impossible," embodying Jay's vision and creativity. Jay.R's hands on approach to management and his never ending fight to give a voice to the underdog is what makes him stand out amongst his peers. From writing & producing a broadway quality production Karma, which was full of some of Cleveland's best talent, to coding an app that's sure to change the world, Jay.R is truly a renaissance man.

Jay.R is no stranger to hard work and constant innovation. As a single father of two (Geoffrey & Makai), Jay.R has managed to launch a magazine (G3 All Access), clothing line (Boasts & Bragg), host a radio show (The Goonies), as well as develop "LoKul," the National Black Business Directory app. "Times are changing and you have to be able to evolve as those changes take place… stay tuned."

Larry H. Gardner II
Owner/Executive
Producer/Media Personality
Voice It Radio.com/
Nerve DJ's/
G Productions Inc.

Larry H. Gardner II is the executive producer of Headlines and Headaches on Voice It Radio.com and the Nerve DJ's network. Larry is involved in his church and community with the Cleveland Clergy Coalition and the Greater Cleveland Association of Black Journalists. He has also worked with other organizations. Larry has a strong worldwide audience who listen in to the real issues that affect us daily. He is a proud graduate of John Marshall High School. His post education is coursework in communications with a minor in construction at the University of Cincinnati and Cuyahoga Community College. Larry started working with Voice It Radio.com in February 2016. In a short time of producing the community and political broadcast, Larry has achieved worldwide success having local and national figures on his show. Larry credits his faith, his family and his only child, Jalen Gardner, for his success.

Lady Gilmore
Entrepreneur
Follow Your Dreams
Daycare Palace

Lady Gilmore has been an entrepreneur since the age of eight. She is a community leader that has been active in several organizations that help and encourage others. Lady Gilmore is the owner and president of Follow Your Dreams Daycare Palace. She is a community activist and has volunteered her time encouraging others. Lady Gilmore has a weekly radio show called Queen on the Scene. Her weekly show features various members of the community. She is a person that demonstrates compassion towards others. Lady Gilmore has a positive attitude and spirit. Other community leaders and entrepreneurs have been inspired by Lady Gilmore to "follow your dreams." Lady Gilmore has a radiant personality that shines for everyone. She is a person of faith.

Daveda Hayes-Cunningham was introduced to modeling at the tender age of ten to combat extreme shyness. She quickly grew from student to teacher becoming responsible for delivering instruction to children, teens and adults. Daveda was soon incorporating choreography and eventually producing fashion shows. At the University of Akron, she produced fashion shows for the local charter of the NAACP and the Black United Students. There, her passion for fashion intensified. In April of 2003, she incorporated Segami International, Inc. and led the organization successfully as president and chief executive officer for seven years. In 2014, Daveda entered the world of pageantry celebrating her fourth successful event this past November. The mission of the pageant is to build self-esteem and self confidence in young ladies ages three to 17 by exposing them to basic pageantry and offering an outlet for creativity and self-discovery. The organization recently had its second adult pageant, Grown & Sexy, for women ages 25 and up.

Daveda Hayes-Cunningham
Owner
B'Elite Pageants

Tina Hobbs is a casting director and film producer in Cleveland, Ohio with a focus on independent films. Since 2011, her company has cast numerous movies, web series, commercials, television programs and stage plays. Projects in her portfolio include Swing Lowe, Sweet Chariotte, 3rd Floor West, Pressure, Heights Girl, Banger and most recently, Hey Mr. Postman featuring Omar Gooding and Paula Jai Parker and premiered in the summer of 2018. Tina has dedicated her time and efforts to nurturing the growth of Ohio's independent film market by partnering with film festivals and other organizations to host various casting workshops. She also teaches a media and arts class at Cuyahoga Community College for aspiring filmmakers. She is a member of African American Women in Film as well as Women in Film and TV Ohio. Twice a year she organizes a series of networking events called "The Schmooze". This widely attended event brings together actors, crew, filmmakers and professionals. Tina's expertise in casting and producing makes her a valuable hometown resource.

Tina Hobbs
Owner & Chief
Executive Officer
HobbsStyle Casting &
Productions

Tracy Lamar Johnson Jr. is the founder of Voice By An Angel Outreach which is an organization that provides resources, support, and advocacy for those in the community that are impacted by HIV and AIDS. He just recently opened a nonprofit organization called Sickle Angels which focuses on advocacy for people with sickle cell and HIV. Johnson Jr. has great stage presence and has starred in numerous plays in the community. In August 2020, Johnson Jr. will be starring in a self-produced stage play about his life story and the many struggles and strongholds he has overcome. He works as an assistant manager at many local group homes in Cleveland and helps support those with mental health challenges in his community. Johnson Jr. volunteers at his local church regularly and is a doting father of three children.

Tracy Lamar Johnson Jr.
Founder
Voice By An Angel
Outreach, Inc.

James Johnson
Founder/CEO
U.G. Digital Media &
Publishings

James Johnson is the Founder and CEO of U.G. Digital Media & Publishings. Developed here in Cleveland in 2013, UGD spans multiple industries, including media; public relations, and fitness & wellness. Through UGD, James works as a magazine publisher, journalist, and personal trainer. He recently launched an online radio station under the brand, via which he hosts multiple shows and podcasts. James' true passion is media. He carries 16 years of experience, having worked for such companies as Radio One, WKYC TV 3, and BET. He's built a strong resume and background, standing firmly on the principles of following his passion as all costs.

In addition to James' colorful background in media, he has also devoted 17 years to the healthcare industry, having worked his way to middle management at University Hospitals before pushing to devote more time to his passion of media and entertainment. He's currently penning an autobiography he plans to self-publish in 2020.
James is the proud father of one son.

Mary Johnson
Owner & Creator
Vitiman Kandie, LLC

Mary Johnson is a personal training coach who has lost over 120 lbs. She holds several degrees and certifications that include business arts, private investigations, personal training, rock mechanic engineer, industrial machine operation, data processing and decoding, and First Aid CPR/AED. Mary is the owner of Vitiman Kandie, LLC where she provides positive transformations to the hopeful spirit seeking a lifestyle change, juices, vegetarian supplements, healthy meal plans, physical therapy, and VK fitness apparel. Mary has participated in the Natural Muscle Association Bodybuilding Competition placing in three categories and landing the front page of the Cleveland Rite Aid Marathon website. Mary is a member of the Women's Business Group & Young Black Democrats. Mary is motivational speaker, authoress of From This to That, and community volunteer. Mary is very passionate about helping youth and adults gain more knowledge on obesity and has partnered with Cleveland Clinic Wellness Program. Mary held positions at Cargill Deicing Company, Cleveland City School District, Cleveland Public Library, and The Center for Health Affairs & Champs.

**Ruth H.
Johnson-Williams**
Executive Director
Pneuma Life Foundation

Ruth H. Johnson-Williams has evolved as a sage voice of leadership in the African American community and beyond as founder and chief executive officer of the Pneuma Life Foundation for the Prevention of Abusive Family Environments, a nonprofit tax-exempt organization. She earned her Associate of Arts degree from Cuyahoga Community College in Cleveland, and a Master of Business Administration at the Ohio Christian University in Canton. She is certified as a chaplain by the Veterans Administration, and a chemical dependency counselor assistant (CDCA). She is a member of good standings with the Domestic Violence Coordinating Council (DVCC). Ruth is licensed by the National Christian Counselors Association (NCCA) as a pastoral counselor, and by the American Christian Counselor Association (ACCA) as a licensed counselor in crisis and trauma. As an author an inspirational speaker, she seeks to expose and eradicate sexual/domestic violence against men, women, and children. Ruth promote advocacy, education, and awareness by uniting faith-based and community organizations for one common purpose.

Allan Jones is the fun-loving, outgoing and energetic co-host and executive producer of In the Ring with Tarver & Jones, on VoiceItRadio.com. The weekly two-hour sports broadcast is hosted by five-time Light-Heavyweight Champion of the World, and United States Olympic medalist, Antonio Tarver and sports analyst, entrepreneur, boxing enthusiast and trainer Allan Jones. A native of Cleveland, Jones is a successful businessman with ventures in Cleveland and Atlanta. He is the co-owner of Torch Smokes N Vapes, and Chariot Auto Sales. He played football at Shaw High School and later attended Cleveland State University where he attained a bachelor's degree in Political Science. Jones is a multi-talented individual. He displayed his acting ability while appearing on popular shows such as Survivor's Remorse and Tyler Perry's The Haves and Have Nots. Jones is a philanthropist who enjoys mentoring youth and raising his beautiful daughter.

Allan Jones
Executive Producer
In The Ring with
Tarver & Jones

Being called for a time such as this, Officer Nakia Jones' passionate and heartfelt outcry over the death of Alton Sterling and other young African American males went viral and took the nation by storm. This life altering experience inspired Officer Jones to write her book, The Truth Divided, which was released in April 2018. Officer Jones' fervent plea over the death of Alton Sterling shook the nation. As her words resounded from coast to coast, it became clear that her life would never be the same. She released her book, The Truth Divided and is writing a follow up book as her journey for justice continues. Officer Jones believes, "If you want to change, it starts with the person you look at every day in the mirror. If you want to change you must be that change." Officer Jones is also a well-known gospel playwright in Cleveland. She believes that with a little compassion and unselfishness we all can make a difference and can change the world.

Nakia Jones
Author
Nakia Jones Productions

Maple Heights' very own fashion designer Diane Linston, steps out as one of the most talented fashion designers in the state of Ohio. Linston has participated in New York Fashion Week and 2018 Harlem Fashion Week with the daughters of Malcolm X collection. NGU Collections, Diane's signature line, garnered national attention and caused her to work with local and national celebrities. She also showcased her fashions at the Cincinnati Jazz Festival as an opening act for rapper MC Lyte and DJ Jazzy Jeff. On February 23, 2019, the Mayor of Beachwood, Ohio, Martin S. Horwitz, gave a proclamation to Diane Linston, naming it "Styles of Imagination Boutique Day" in the city. On March 2, 2019, she opened the upscale Styles of Imagination Boutique in the city of Beachwood. Being the only African American female manufacturing company, Styles of Imagination Boutique was honored by the City of Cleveland as the Female Business Enterprise. The award was presented by Mayor Frank Jackson.

Diane Linston
Owner
Styles of Imagination
Women Apparel
Manufacturing

Mike Mathis
Chief Executive Officer
I'm Not Famous.... But I
Made It!

Author Mike Mathis has a book entitled, I'm Not Famous.... But I Made It! : Psalms 23 edition. He is the founder of a self-awareness program which is being utilized in several high schools, elementary schools, and a juvenile center. He is a self awareness speaker, mentor, and a self awareness coach. Mike Mathis has received an Exemplary Award for improving academic performance and behavior in students who are enrolled in his self awareness program. He has been through a series of different trainings and received certificates in leadership tactics, emotional intelligence, and intellectual intelligence. His favorite quote is: "There are so many people who have never been locked up, but may be institutionalized and not even know it!"

Angela Miller
Founder and Director
Furaha Forever
Productions

Angela Miller is the founder and creative director of Furaha Forever Productions, a nonprofit creative arts organization. Its mission is to empower, entertain and educate through the art of creativity. Since 2001, Angela has been bridging her professional career of helping others and her love for the arts to create memorable experiences. She is a licensed social worker and earned her bachelor's degree in Social Work from Cleveland State University. Miller worked for the Division of Children and Family Services for 19 years. Along with her supportive husband, Anthony Miller, they are the loving parents of two daughters and grandparents of three grandchildren. In her spare time, Angela enjoys spending time with her family and friends, creating programs and traveling around the world.

André Morton
Coach and Owner
Rhythm and Stroke
LLC

Coach André Morton is owner of Rhythm and Stroke LLC, an aquatics organization focusing on water safety, swim survival, stroke refinement and aquatic exercise. An aquatics instructor for over ten years, he works with colleges and schools throughout Northeast Ohio. André swam competitively for several years and now enjoys sharing his experience and expertise with others. André teaches swimming to all ages, from infants to seasoned seniors. He also teaches navy recruits and certifies aspiring/current lifeguards. He was awarded "Best Coach" for his ability to break barriers and fight the high statistics of black people who cannot swim. André is WSI and LGI certified, has a master's degree in Communications from Bowling Green State University, a Bachelor of Arts in Speech Communications from Miami of Ohio, and a Bachelor of Science in Water Resource Management from Central State University. He and his queen, Kimberly Morton, work together to push their "Swim Like Me" initiative. It is their mission to help others inhale confidence & exhale fear in the water!

Nakeshia Nickerson is an author, community activist and entrepreneur who writes sympathetic stories that help school-age children learn positive coping, growth mindset, and problem solving using real life scenarios. She has published articles on Thrive Global, a health and wellness site created by Arianna Huffington's behavior change media site for well-being and has been elected as the executive and county central committee member of CCD for the Village of Woodmere. She also served as a board member for companies that benefit growth and development of children. Nakeshia launches The Family Narrative podcast in June 2019 which discusses family and children topics of all kinds. She works facilitating children workshops locally and around the county which have been featured by Kirkus Review, Publishers Weekly, Jack and Jill of America, and various schools and libraries. Nakeshia is also owner of Stratégie: The Business Solutions Company, an interdisciplinary design studio offering designs for mobile apps, visual and printed publications, digital presentation templates, websites, proposal management and writing, creative business strategies and broadcasting.

Nakeisha Nickerson
Author and
Entrepreneur
Tulvia Lane & Stratégie

Nicole Nickerson is the owner of Salon Nicole LLC, a salon for the busy woman, the mom, entrepreneur, businesswoman and the socialite who appreciate great service and care. Nicole's many years of experience in both the corporate field and salon industry allows her the unique ability to recognize the needs of today's modern women. Recently nominated for stylist of the year by her peers, Nicole utilizes the success she has attained as an opportunity to train new members in the industry, sharing with them the importance of professionalism, business skills, extensive hair care knowledge and customer wellness. Her philanthropy in the community with children and families has inspired many. She sponsors complimentary quarterly family events called #familymatters to promote support, bonding and quality time. Nicole also mentors youth in the community who experience depression and self-esteem issues, providing support skills they might not otherwise receive. With a commitment to caring for others, and a driving force for health, style and wellness, Nicole is dedicated to the community living beautifully.

Nicole Nickerson
Owner
Salon Nicole LLC

Pecola "Ms. P" Pointer is that ray of sunshine you seek in the world. She shines that light as the owner and founder of On Point Hair and Nail Salon in Cleveland's historic Halle Building. In 2011, armed with unwavering faith, she followed her passion, opening her first salon on St. Clair Avenue in downtown Cleveland. There she treated celebrities from near and far. She is grounded in faith and has an insatiable love for people. That love and star treatment is what keeps her clients coming back. It is also the fuel behind her creation of the relaxing and refreshing line of On Point Bath Products, she developed in 2017. Ms. P's love has no boundaries. She regularly gives blankets, socks, and snacks to the city's homeless. She is the loving mother of Lanesha and Marvin, and grandmother of Terren, Tia and Tyla. Pointer is a faithful member of New Direction C.O.G.I.C. She serves on the Pastor's Aide, Nurse's Board, Usher Board, and Hospitality ministries.

Pecola Pointer
Owner & Hair Stylist
On Point Hair and
Nail Salon

Seti Richardson
Founder
Circle for Re-entry
Ohio

Seti Richardson has been employed for the past 24 years at Cleveland Urban Minority Alcoholism and Drug Abuse Outreach Program (UMADAOP) as well as director and founder of the Circle for Re-entry Program, a re-entry initiative to provide relapse prevention services for ex-offenders and their families who have been incarcerated for drugs and other related offenses. Seti has received numerous awards locally, statewide and nationally for his ongoing commitment to community service and the uplifting of those in need. Seti provides services to thousands of men and women on parole, probation, treatment, unemployed and those in need of relapse prevention, working in conjunction with the Adult Parole and Probation Department. He is certified as a relapse prevention and quality mental health specialist, recovery and life coach, founder of Re-Entry Alumni Association and is one of ten master trainers statewide certified by The Council on Prevention and Education to train and facilitate passion, honesty, dedication, commitment, sincerity and devotion.

Dominicque Smith
Co-Owner
LOVETIES, LLC

Dominicque Smith is a registered nurse director of case management and a Spoken Word Performing Arts Poet. She obtained an associate degree of Applied Science in Nursing from Bryant and Stratton College and a Bachelor of Science in Nursing from the University of Akron. In 2017, Smith was nominated for a Nursing Excellence and Nursing Alliance Award by the Cleveland Clinic.

Smith performs creative expression of language through poetry performances with a focus on relationship ministry, empowerment and self-growth. Smith is co-owner of LOVETIES LLC and one half of LOVETIES: The Art of Mr. and Mrs. Smith. She opened a show for internationally known jazz artist Najee and performed for The National Urban League, The Ohio Realtist Association, Cleveland Rape Crisis Center, The Northeast Ohio Black Health Coalition and the House of Blues. Smith featured on multiple music projects of local artists, radio shows, short films, plays, fashion shows and written novels. Smith and her husband were recently awarded Poet of the Year at the 2019 Legend Awards.

You can follow Domincque at https://loveties.wixsite.com/artofmrandmrssmith

Jamile Smith
Co-Owner
LOVETIES, LLC

Jamille Smith is a Spoken Word Performing Arts Poet. Prior to meeting his wife and becoming co-owner of LOVETIES LLC one half of LOVETIES: The Art of Mr. and Mrs. Smith, Jamille had been writing poetry since high school. He performs creative expression of language through poetry performances both locally and abroad. Mr. Smith opened a show for internationally known jazz artist Najee and was a keynote speaker for the 2017 Martin Luther King Jr. Day Observance Program for the City of Cleveland; as well as opened for nationally known poet Saul Williams. Jamille was welcomed as a guest performer at Ursuline College for the Department of Diversity and Inclusion, The National Urban League and The House of Blues. Jamille's been featured on multiple music projects of local artists, radio shows, plays, fashion shows and written novels. Jamille and his wife were recent recipients of the Poet of the Year Award for the 2019 Legend Awards. Jamille is also a mentor to teens, young male adults and up and coming poets

Follow Jamille Smith at https://loveties.wixsite.com/artofmrandmrssmith

Getting Our Babies to College 101 (GOBTC) is a consulting firm that conducts interactive workshops with families helping them prepare for the post-secondary education process starting in middle school. Founder, Jowan Smith is a parent that experienced the education process and saw there was a huge need for parents to be empowered. The mother of two loves traveling, sports, and cooking. Jowan graduated from CMSD, attended college and obtained a degree in Business Administration. She worked as a case worker for Cuyahoga County and saw firsthand how lack of post-secondary options impacts the community. GOBTC has assisted over 200 students choose a post-secondary option that were not on track. Jowan started the "1,000 Ties" event this year which teaches young men skills she felt were lost. This year she gave 125 young men ties and taught them how to tie them. Featured speaking engagements include WGBH Ed Forum, National Family & Community Engagement Conference, City of Cleveland Mayor's Youth Summit, President's Council Youth Summit, and CSU Teen Summit.

Jowan Smith
Post-Secondary
Education Consultant
Getting Our Babies to
College 101

Dru Thompson is a recognized leader in the region's fashion industry serving as a public speaker, educator, mentor, and a model for small business success. Dru discovered her love for sewing and fashion at age 13. Later, she gained her own custom clientele and her designs were sold in boutiques throughout Cleveland. Dru continued her passion by pursuing a degree in fashion merchandising from the University of Akron. In 2012, she opened her fashion design studio and boutique, Dru Christine Fabrics and Design and has continued to develop a diverse clientele both locally and nationally. She shares her expertise by hosting fashion, style, and sewing workshops in her studio, as well as serving as a fashion instructor at The Cleveland School of Arts. Dru is also a contributing arts and fashion writer for Cool Cleveland. She continues to improve by offering designs for the bold and eclectic; preserving a studio that fosters creativity, ingenuity, and inspiration; and sharing her experiences with aspiring fashion designers and entrepreneurs.

Dru Thompson
Owner & Fashion
Designer
Dru Christine Fabrics
and Design

Delanie West is noted for helping people and organizations execute creative vision for ideas, projects, products, and brands. She is a hands-on creative with experience leading award-winning product development, design, packaging and global sourcing teams. Delanie formerly led the creative teams for AW Faber-Castell/Creativity for Kids, known for leading premium brands in the adult, children and student art and craft segments. She served on the Faber-Castell U.S. Executive Committee and represented the company in capacity of buyer at international trade shows. Skilled at international manufacturer relations, she has cultivated strong supplier vendor relationships. Delanie has been influential in mentoring designers and developers new to their careers. Delanie has spearheaded innovation and development of many major craft and art categories. Well-known categories such as dimensional stickers, epoxy and rhinestone adhesive embellishments are mainstays but were new-to-the world innovations which West introduced to the art and craft segments.

Delanie West
Founding Creative
Director
BeSuperCreative

Peter Whitt
Owner
Enlightenment Consulting Group, LLC

Peter Whitt founded Enlightenment Consultant Group, LLC (ECG). ECG uses comprehensive community engagement, organizational development, coaching and facilitation as key strategies to build sustainable change in communities, organizations and leaders. A core function of Peter's work centers on leadership development. ECG work supports both youth and adult leaders. He completed two training programs at the Gestalt Institute of Cleveland earning certifications in coaching and effective intervening in organizations (organizational development). In 2005, Peter was selected as a W. Kellogg Emerging Leader in Public Health Fellow at the University of North Carolina's School of Public Health and Kenan-Flagler Business School. During that same year, he was selected as an American Memorial Marshall Fellow. In 2006, he was recognized by Kaleidoscope Magazine's "40 under 40 Club". Peter holds a MSW from the University of Pittsburgh. He is a member of Alpha Phi Alpha Fraternity Inc. He holds the title of Maha Guru (Senior Teacher) in the art of Kun Tao & Silat Willem Reeders-Author Sikes Lineage. He has several awards in martial arts.

Alexis Williams
Founder and Chief
Executive Officer
#CLEgivesback

Alexis Williams is a 19-year old who created businesses for the people and community. She is a Euclid High School alumna and currently attends Lakeland Community College where she studies business management. She became a community activist at the age of 16 when she started #CLEgivesback, which then only served the homeless community. However, Alexis and her team started a monthly mentor program that helps girls between the ages of 12-17 to teach them the importance of self-love and self-worth through ice breakers, guest speakers, field trips and more. Not only does her team help young girls and the homeless, but they also host community events throughout the year. Alexis wanted another way to garner attention even more, so she started a clothing line called Compassion The Brand-A, a brand created for those who can express their regular acts of kindness through street wear fashion.

Stacy Yarbrough
Chief Executive
Officer and Founder
Stiletto Boss Women's
Group

Stacy "PurPose" Yarbrough is the founder and chief executive officer of Stiletto Boss Women's Group. With many ties to both the entertainment and entrepreneurial sides of Cleveland, she is building a strong community of sisterhood and support through empowerment. Her passion for seeing others reach high levels of success as well as walking in their purpose, has been proven through many of her events, Biz Boot Camp, Stiletto Boss awards as well as the addition of her partnership with Lynn Chaney in Hope & Humanity. Hope & Humanity benefits the homeless in Cleveland by collecting and distributing essential items that most take for granted. "PurPose", as she is so affectionately and appropriately called, remains a staple in the community and a beacon of purpose for youth.

"It always SEEMS IMPOSSIBLE until it's done."
- Nelson Mandela